D1642378

SCHOOL OF ORIENTAL AND AFRICAN STUDIES

SCHOOL OF ORIENTAL AND AFRICAN STUDIES
University of London

THREE-DAY LOAN COLLECTION

SATISFYING AFRICA'S FOOD NEEDS

SATISFYING AFRICA'S FOOD NEEDS

Food Production and Commercialization in African Agriculture

edited by Ronald Cohen

Lynne Rienner Publishers • Boulder/London

Published in the United States of America in 1988 by
Lynne Rienner Publishers, Inc.
948 North Street, Boulder, Colorado 80302

and in the United Kingdom by
Lynne Rienner Publishers, Inc.
3 Henrietta Street, Covent Garden, London WC2E 8LU

Library of Congress Cataloging-in-Publication Data

Satisfying Africa's food needs.

    (Carter studies on Africa ; v. 1)
    Bibliography: p.
    Includes index.
    1. Agriculture—Africa.   2. Food crops—Africa.
3. Food supply—Africa.   4. Food industry and trade—
Africa.   I. Cohen, Ronald.   II. Series.
S472.A35S28 1988   338.1'096   88-3164
ISBN 1-55587-083-X (lib. bdg.)

British Library Cataloguing in Publication Data
A Cataloguing in Publication record for this book
is available from the British Library.

Printed and bound in the United States of America

The paper used in this publication meets the requirements
of the American National Standard for Permanence of Paper
for Printed Library Materials Z39.48-1984.

Contents

Preface

This book marks the first in a series being presented by the Center for African Studies at the University of Florida under the general title of *Carter Studies on Africa.* The primary purpose of these books, and the lectures out of which they have grown, is to honor one of our most distinguished and respected colleagues, Gwendolen M. Carter. Her early and enduring research and publications on the politics of race and inequality in southern Africa were a major catalyst in the development of American-based African studies. It was only natural that she be elected president of the African Studies Association once it was formed. At Smith College, then later at Northwestern University, as director of the oldest and best-known of the African Studies programs, Professor Carter led the way in the founding and establishment of African Studies on U.S. campuses. Later, after retirement, she continued these efforts at Indiana. And now in her second postretirement position she is associated with the University of Florida's Center for African Studies, giving to the Center the advantage of her experience and judgment.

A further idea underlying the Carter Studies is a tradition fostered by Professor Carter and exemplified in her own work as scholar and administrator. This is the belief that African Studies expands understanding through its comparative and global approach to knowledge seeking. If the goal of scholarship, whether it be in the humanities, the social, or the natural sciences, is to seek and disseminate new knowledge, then it is fitting that scholars be obligated to test their claims across national and cultural borders, in Africa as well as in the rest of the non-Western world. In this regard all foreign-area studies provide constant threats to our parochialism.

More positively, these new environments create opportunities for all scholars, Africans and non-Africans alike, to develop new conceptions and theories about the human experience and our adaptation as a species to its limitations and potentialities.

In addition to these clearly scholarly purposes, Professor Carter has always emphasized and stood for the development of African Studies as a practical contribution to our own society's need for understanding, and above all to the needs of the African continent and its peoples' search for a better life. The Carter Studies, accordingly, are dedicated to examining African problems that Americans should be more aware of—indeed must be made more aware of and concerned with—if we are to appreciate this shared and shrinking world. Even though many Americans have their roots in Africa, Africa's problems, its long and involved history, and its great variety of cultures, are still poorly known and appreciated. We plan to help in this educational goal, as Carter has done with her life's work, by choosing topics of broad interest to both academics and to other concerned audiences. Presentation will be made by experts on topics chosen for inclusion in the Carter Studies series. The series is therefore dedicated to advancing scholarly understanding while contributing as well to a vast global social movement—that of promoting the cause of development on the continent of Africa. This is a thread that runs through all of Professor Carter's contributions and one we hope to carry on in the series.

This first volume is devoted to the problem of satisfying Africa's food needs. The problem is dramatic, and one that the University of Florida is particularly focused on with its highly developed resources in tropical agriculture. Nevertheless, the papers do not all form one piece. The problem is extraordinarily complex, often involving contradictory viewpoints. None are completely valid, and some are quite wrongheaded. We have tried to see our way through the fads and fashions, and the easy generalizations, to directions of research that give promise of increased food supplies in the context of African realities. The book falls into three parts: a general section on continent-wide issues and then more focused materials on Kenya and on Nigeria. Each of these countries has advanced quite far along the road to the development of a commercial agriculture, one (Nigeria) from the vantage point of relatively ample land, the other (Kenya) with land scarcities permeating the entire food production sector. As editor, I have added two papers by younger scholars to fill in details of the Kenya experience. One deals with the issue of rural differentiation too often overlooked in past work, and the other analyzes an indigenous cash crop that has developed without the aid of government or outside "experts." The overall purpose is clear. The problem of famine in Africa is real and awesome. But the underlying need is to find ingredients whose interactions and operations predict ways and means of avoiding famines, rather than just coping with them as they occur.

Future volumes will deal with the special problems of southern Africa (Professor Carter's own research concern), with problems of human rights in the newly independent states of the continent, and with medical issues, especially that of AIDS. Our desire is to tackle problems at the cutting edge, and to do so in the spirit that Professor Carter established as her own style—that is to say, with a dedicated desire to know, and to help.

Finally, we wish to express our special appreciation to the many private donors whose gifts and pledges have helped to make this project a reality. In addition, the Ford Foundation and the Center for African Studies at the University of Florida have made substantial contributions both to the lecture series and to our capacity to bring the materials into published form. This includes special thanks to Cody Watson of the Center who prepared the final versions of the tables and index. We are grateful to all of these sources, but, of course, only the authors themselves are responsible for the views expressed in this book.

Ronald Cohen
Center for African Studies
University of Florida

Contributors

Robert H. Bates (Ph.D. MIT) is Luce Professor of Political Economy at Duke University. In addition to his doctoral work in political science he trained in social anthropology at the University of London and Manchester University. He has studied local politics in Zambia, and later turned his attention to problems of rural development in Africa in general, and more recently to Kenya in particular. His major works include, *Unions, Parties, and Political Development: A Study of Mineworkers in Zambia* 1971, *Rural Responses to Industrialization: A Study of Village Zambia* 1976, *Agricultural Development in Africa* 1980; *States and Markets in Tropical Africa* 1981, *Essays on the Political Economy of Tropical Africa* 1983, and *Beyond the Miracle of the Market* forthcoming.

Ronald Cohen (Ph.D. Wisconsin) is professor of anthropology, University of Florida, and Chair of the Carter Lectures at the Center for African Studies in the same university. He has worked in Nigeria and the Canadian arctic on problems of social change, state formation, and rural development. Major works are, *The Kanuri of Borno* 1967 (reissued 1987), *Dominance and Defiance* 1971, *From Tribe to Nation* (edited with John Middleton) 1971, *Handbook of Method in Cultural Anthropology* (edited with Raoul Narroll) 1971 (reissued 1973), *Origins of the State* (edited with E.R. Service) 1978, *Hierarchy and Society* (edited with G. Britan) 1981, and *Legitimacy and State Formation* (edited with J. Toland) 1988.

Christopher L. Delgado (Ph.D. Cornell) is the co-coordinator for Africa at the International Research Institute in Washington, D.C. and a part-time faculty member at The Johns Hopkins University School of Advanced International Studies. He has worked on economic problems of rural development in Africa and their effects on the development of agricultural policy and the implementation of policy for specific areas and for the continent as a whole. His published works include *Livestock versus Foodgrain Production in Southeast Upper Volta: A Resource Allocation Analysis* 1979, *The Political Economy of Ivory Coast* (coeditor) 1984, *Accelerating Agricultural Growth in Sub-Saharan Africa* (coeditor) 1987, and numerous articles.

Paul Goldsmith is a Ph.D. candidate in anthropology and african studies at the University of Florida. He has worked previously for ten years in Kenya with various non-governmental groups as a special instructor. He is presently carrying out doctoral research on the influence of agrarian capitalism on the development of marginal lands in Kenya.

Angelique Haugerud (Ph.D. Northwestern) is assistant professor of anthropology at Yale University. She has worked on macro and micro influences on rural household economy in Kenya, and later as a Rockefeller Post-Doctoral Fellow on agrarian change and economic strategies of farm households in Rwanda, Burundi, and Kenya. Her publications include "An Anthropologist in an African Research Institute: An Informal Essay," *Development Anthropology Network* 1986, "Land Tenure and Agrarian Change in Kenya," *Africa* 1988, and "Anthropology and Interdisciplinary Research," in Brokensha and Little (eds.) *The Anthropology of Development and Change in Eastern Africa* forthcoming.

Goran Hyden (Ph.D. Lund) is professor of political science at the University of Florida and senior member of the Center for African Studies. He has spent two decades living and working in East Africa on problems of development theory and practice with special emphasis on problems of rural transformation, administration, and governance, as these apply to Africa. His major works (in English) include *Tanu Yajenja Nchi: Political Development in Rural Tanzania* 1968, *Development Administration: The Kenya Experience* 1970, *Efficiency versus Distribution in East African Cooperatives* 1973, *Developing Research on African Administration: Some Key Issues* 1975, *Beyond Ujaama: Underdevelopment and the Uncaptured Peasantry* 1980, and *No Shortcuts to Progress* 1983.

Michael F. Lofchie (Ph.D. University of California, Berkeley) is professor of political science and director of the African Studies Center at the University of California, Los Angeles. In his early work he focused on the role of political parties in African development. More recently he has turned his attention to issues of food and hunger on the continent. His most important publications include *Zanzibar: Background to Revolution* 1965, *Agricultural Development in Africa: Issues of Public Policy* (edited with Robert H. Bates) 1980, and *Africa's Agrarian Crisis: The Roots of Famine* (edited with Stephen Cummins and Rhys Payne) 1985.

Akinlawon L. Mabogunje (Ph.D. University of London, honorary doctorates, Stockholm, and Michigan State University) is a partner in the Ibadan-based (Nigeria) consultancy firm of PAI-Associates. He was faculty member and dean at Ibadan University for many years and has been president of the International Geographical Union, and member of the Board of The Population Council. Dr. Mabogunje is also the recipient of Nigeria's highest civilian honor, The National Merit Award, for his scholarly contribution on the rural and urban development problems of his country and Africa in general. His major works include *Urbanisation in Nigeria* 1968, *Regional Planning and National Development in Africa* (edited with A. Faniran) 1977, and *The Development Process: A Spatial Perspective* 1980.

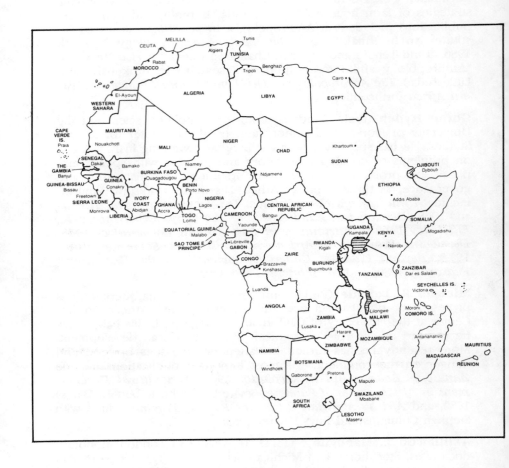

CHAPTER 1

Introduction: Guidance and Misguidance in Africa's Food Production

RONALD COHEN[1]

The Issues

Africa's food shortages have become so much a part of the world view of the peoples of the developed countries that the place and the condition are almost synonymous in popular culture. Television, newspapers, and magazines have depicted famine conditions to such an extent that starvation is now a widely known and discussed feature of life in the newly independent states. But in Africa itself, where actual famine is the exception, widespread concern over growing food deficits has moved the issue into a position of top priority. Population growth, droughts, crop shortfalls, accelerating food import costs along with foreign exchange problems, and the rising debt crisis have exacerbated the problem. And outside, especially in the Western capitalist nations, the dramatic newsworthiness of starving and disabled peoples has stimulated increased aid from both public and private °sources. Suffering sells, but the more ubiquitous, more mundane problem of developing food self-sufficiency is the truly pressing issue.

With significant exceptions, the good rains of the mid-1980s have provided some respite, but as Delgado (in Chapter 2 of this book) points out, long-term vulnerability remains. And here, so far, solutions still elude us. Indeed as Lofchie argues (in Chapter 4), the prolonged lack of an answer may even produce "donor fatigue" on the part of outside agencies and a consequent turning from the issue to other less intractable ones of third world development. In my view, part of the insolubility lies in the overconfidence of the intellectuals and "experts" whose pet theories were often tried out among the hard and poorly understood realities of African contexts.

Much of what has been offered so far in the way of solutions has been logical, well-intentioned, often persuasive, and for the most part insufficient to the task of getting African agriculture moving. Possibly this is the result of the great faith Westerners place in technology. Given a straightforward transfer of scientific knowledge and advanced methods of production, African farmers should be able to grow enough food for themselves and their countrymen. Unfortunately, technology is only one factor, albeit a major one, among many others that facilitate and constrain adequate and increased food supply on the continent. But theories about how such factors operate, which ones to give most attention to, or how best to implement the required changes, have not always been, and are still not, agreed upon.

Not, of course, that this has deterred outsiders from giving advice, offering panaceas, or in extreme instances threatening doom and bloody revolution just 'round the corner unless their own particular guidelines were made the basis for rural development policies. Nevertheless, except (and only temporarily) for a few ideologically led systems, most of the policies emerged from a combination of local conditions and the waxing and waning of particular theories of development that dominated the policies of outside donors. It is these latter notions that have given a kind of periodicity to policies and practices of rural development on the continent, or what Hyden calls "monocultural" approaches. Each of these approaches was wrong about many things, and right about a few. For both these reasons they have furthered our understanding of food insufficiency as the policies were put into practice and/or discussed and then shown to fall short of coping with the massive problems contained in the notion of "rural development."

Reviews of these approaches are now widely read and discussed (see, for example, Lofchie and Cummins 1984, and Staatz and Eicher 1986). They include an early "urban bias" or neglect of the rural areas, a period of emancipatory dependency theory that stressed equitable rural welfare, and the more recent concern with production as deficits forced attention to the supply side of food in the national economies of African countries. Along the way there has been a growing concern for the environment and its deterioration and, most recently, an interest in the social and economic organization of agriculture, especially as this organization affects the requirements of commercialization. Let me go over some of these approaches briefly before discussing the contemporary issues in more detail.

It is widely accepted that one of the most important reasons for Africa's declining per capita food production is the colonial and postcolonial emphasis on urban as opposed to, and often at the expense of, rural development. And there is little doubt that much of this argument is valid. Most revenues from the government-controlled marketing of cash export crops were used by both colonial regimes and their successors to pay for government itself. The bulk of the remainder was then siphoned into hoped-for growth of a "modern" industrialized sector. Indeed, much of the literature of the 1950s used the term "pre-industrial" (implying a solution) to refer to these societies. In Africa, the attractiveness of urban amenities and incomes, the wide appeal of Western-style education that brought school leavers into the migrant stream, and the misguided notion that rural people were "underemployed" soon accelerated urban migration. Theorists suggested that this would provide cheap labor for the initial takeoff to import substitution. On the other hand, food supplies were judged to be adequate and would continue to be so well into the future (World Bank 1972). Added to this, the postwar period saw a dramatic rise in prices for African export crops. This rise provided cash for farmers and revenues for governments that used marketing boards to "mobilize" the increased revenues, depriving the farmers of much of the gain. Parenthetically, one often loses sight of the fact that the late 1950s were among the wettest rainfall periods of the century. Just as independence loomed on the horizon for many of the colonial states, both food supplies and cash-crop exports were booming. That more than any other single factor was the reason for Africa's "false start."

It is sometimes suggested that this early urban bias suppressed food production or its necessary expansion. Certainly the lack of attention given to food crops, and the colonial as well as postcolonial pressures placed on farmers to grow for export to finance urban development, inhibited the intensification of agriculture. In some places exports did indeed replace food, or at least did so for some sections of the farm population (Matlon 1981). In others it simply stimulated farmers to expand the amount of land under cultivation (Tiffen 1976). And even though the absolute production figures for Africa have climbed steadily in most parts of the continent, per capita production began to decline by the 1960s and has continued to do so ever since (World Bank 1981). Add to this the severe droughts of the early 1970s and 1980s and a rising urban taste for imported wheat and rice, along with cheap maize when needed, and the ground work for the food problem was laid. Although this is a somewhat oversimplified view of a more complex period (see Staatz and Eicher 1986:44-50), it summarizes what turned out to be insufficient attention to, and development of, the rural areas.

With the wisdom of hindsight it is easy to look back on this period and see the mistakes. Population growth was underestimated or not even considered seriously, and rapid urbanization was believed to be a means of stimulating the productivity of the "underemployed" farm sector. At the same time, this was calculated to increase the incomes of those remaining in the rural areas (through decreased numbers in agriculture, technology transfers, and expanded urban markets), which would feed back to create a rural market for the newly developed African manufactures. Unfortunately, this logical sequence of linkages was anemic and overgeneralized with regard to the actual facts of rural life. Labor was, and still is, not in oversupply in the rural areas of Africa. Farmers are, often as not, engaged in nonfarm as well as farm occupations, especially in those regions of short rainy seasons, and labor is always a scarce resource. Furthermore, the lack of a tradition of a fully commercialized agriculture meant that serious inattention was given over to the process of establishing and expanding a stable agricultural supply system for both urban and rural demand. Instead, food grain staples were judged to be adequate while in the real world a stagnated peasant agriculture was being called upon to satisfy an accelerating demand. And this oversight was occurring within societies whose economic, political, and social integration, especially that between rural and urban sectors, was, at the very least, problematic.

Emancipatory Ideas

In the 1960s and 1970s the idea of development came progressively under the sway of what, for want of a better word, I have called "emancipatory" theory (Bernstein 1978; Lewy 1982, Cohen 1987b). By this I mean a belief (1) that development is determined primarily by power differences, which support systems of inequality in wealth and access to the means by which wealth is created; (2) that the benefits of economy and society are finite, with the result that differential rewards signal the presence of winners and losers in a zero sum game of resource utilization, nationally and internationally; (3) that consequently the structure of power must be transformed to enable the less powerful to benefit; and (4) that the development process must be regulated, otherwise inequities already present will be exacerbated because of the differential power of the actors in the game. Albeit attenuated, these ideas are the basic propositions offered as an alternative to the earlier neoclassical conception of development inherent in the urban bias. In effect, just as the capitalist theory of development was coming into conflict with the lack of empirical understanding of African rural economies and the harsh realities of political independence, these alternative (and compensatory) theories were gaining currency in Latin America, and soon after in Africa (see Amin 1974; Rodney 1972).

In the most general terms, these notions stimulated an emphasis on welfare and a concentrated attention on the equitable distribution of benefits as the basic criterion for assessing the success or failure of development policy (Seers 1970). It seems both logical and humane to assume that if the vast bulk of the population are left out of the growth of a country's prosperity, then little or nothing has occurred that can or should be called development, at least in the widely accepted welfare sense that Seer's (1970) definition implied. According to this logic, the key questions should focus on how and why such disparities arise, and what can be done to distribute wealth and benefits more equitably. As a consequence, development study and the attempt to guide policies shift to distribution, stratification, and the structures of power that enable and encourage inequities to persist.

In the agricultural sector, this explanation implies that getting agriculture moving has little to do with incentives. Incentives are assumed to exist in sufficient degree but require emancipation if farmers are to benefit from, and contribute their share to, the overall development process. The farmer is constrained by chains of power vastly beyond his reach that bind him to low levels of production and productivity. Development therefore means not just growth but the unfettering of the peasant from political and economic relations that presently give the benefits of production to the few at the cost of the many in a national and international system of exploitative relations developed over many generations. As pointed out by Lofchie and Cummins (1984:4-6) this purports to explain why the export sector has been favored historically over food production in terms of inputs, technology, research, extension, credit, and transportation, leaving peasant food production underdeveloped both in terms of achieving its growth potential and getting the food to the urban markets. The neglect of peasant production is caused (theoretically) by the structure of power and economic relations. This structure forces the African economies to work for the benefit of the "core" capitalist nations, with the cooperation of local elites whose own power derives from their capacity to maintain the exploitative relations of the global system.

The overgeneralized nature of the theory that treats vastly different countries and situations as examples of its sweeping propositions is now widely acknowledged. Furthermore, there is little if any possibility of turning off or withdrawing from what the adherents of this theory refer to as "capitalist penetration." African, indeed all Third World, countries cannot exit the system of international trade and other vital forms of relationships without paying a heavy price. Technology, finance, education, and hosts of imported goods, from medicines to textbooks, are now part and parcel of the national cultures of all the world's peoples. Undoubtedly, some of the inequities can be alleviated and the penetration curtailed, but the withdrawal implied in the theory is a cure calculated to harm the patients rather than to free them from poverty and the dynamics sustaining their underdevelopment (Lofchie and Cummins 1984:6-7). And the actual data on foreign involvement in Third World development strongly supports the opposite conclusion. The greater the level of foreign investment, the higher the level of local prosperity (Lal 1985).

Another macrolevel criticism important for this discussion is the role of the state in combating underdevelopment and mobilizing resources for the benefit of the masses. I shall treat this vector more fully in a later discussion but at this point it is sufficient to note that the earlier belief in the capacity of African governments and specific regimes to combat forces of national and international exploitation has foundered badly on the rocks of real world experience. Whether they are dedicated to such goals or not, these governments have until now faced such extraordinary, powerful forces generating inefficiency and the incapacity to carry out programs that many observers see this "softness" as a major problem. Thus the implied policy directive in emancipatory theory that points to a greater role for the state in allocating resources (in order to ensure greater equity and therefore more development) has, in fact, turned into one of Africa's major constraints. As several of the authors in this book (Hyden, Bates, and Mabogunje) point out, given the lack of internal social, political, and economic integration, the links to the state are those primarily of interest groups that use it as an arena to compete for jobs and favored access to resources. The resulting conflicts sustain the low level of integration and act as a deterrent to rational planning and successful implementation. This does not mean that the state should not play a major role in agricultural development (see Mabogunje's Chapter). It does imply, however, that its most useful contribution is unclear.

At the micro level the image of the African peasant farmer as a helpless cipher caught within the moil of forces beyond his control, made to produce cheap exports in order to obtain cash for taxes and the imports that have impoverished him, is another overgeneralization that has fallen victim to the facts. What has emerged after several decades of intensive research is a picture of extraordinary complexity in which a highly differentiated rural population behaves quite rationally to maximize subsistence needs and to obtain cash, both through on-farm as well as off-farm activities of farm household members. Even more importantly, the degree to which this population is integrated into a national system of food production and distribution is also quite various and in no sense assured (Hyden 1980), or even fully understood. That is to say, whether the market involvement of farmers is more widely a U-curve or a rising curve (when crop sales are plotted against farm incomes) is still a debated point, i.e., farmers are rational except for the poorest who have very little freedom and must (or must not?) sell farm products to obtain necessities. What is clear, however, is that there is no unified, single category of African peasant who as a "class" is forced to act against its own interests because of domination by forces beyond its own control (Hill 1986).

As much as we would have it otherwise, human understanding advances primarily by trial and error even when the process is made more systematic through research. The errors now apparent in the urban bias and emancipatory theories have interacted with events in the real world—the rising food deficits and the droughts of the 1970s and 1980s—to shift the focus of attention towards systems of interrelations and policies that can, hopefully, enhance food production. Not that previous ideas have been totally abandoned. Both the importance of urban markets as well as the concern for rural social welfare and more equitable income distribution are now engrained into development goals and theories to a greater or lesser degree. Residues remain, emphases change.

Satisfying Africa's Food Needs

As the focus has shifted to increasing food supplies through the intensification of farm production, two polar opposite positions have emerged. Although this is admittedly a somewhat distorted view of a more complex situation, still the lack of agreement between them highlights research frontiers and the weight to be given to differing assumptions and policies claimed as solutions to the problem. Both emphasize improved production. And once this set of goals is deemed primary, then the set of factors determining improved crop yields per farm and per farmer takes precedence over others, and theories of development shift accordingly. More concretely, research

has revealed that a number of general (formal theory) factors—
technology, labor, land, marketing, credit, etc.—interact with
contextual determinants such as household composition, inheritance
patterns, local kinship and ritual obligations, and community and
political relations. In other words, both formal and substantive
ingredients are widely recognized as significant pieces of the puzzle.
On the other hand, how best to increase yields, what factors to give
most weight to, and how to implement policy at micro- and
macrolevels, for particular contexts, are all still unclear.

Amidst this lack of any specific or locally applicable
understanding, theory and discussion tilt towards one of two polar
positions. In their most extreme forms one is the unimodal model of
development, the other a multimodal one. Both deal directly with
the problem of increasing food production; both claim a capacity to
predict progress and improvements in rural development; and each
contradicts the other on crucial assumptions and relationships.

The unimodal model rests squarely on the fact that the bulk of
Africa's food comes from smallholder production. Assuming little or
no difference in productivity, the model suggests that a very small
percentage increase in production from the many millions of small
farmers will enhance the food supply significantly. By contrast, for
the proportionately few large farms, which constitute only 10 to 30
percent of the land, to make a dent in the food supply requires very
large increases per farm unit if supply is to come anywhere near
meeting demand (Delgado, Chapter 2).

Based on this logic, the model constructs a series of
propositions (Johnston 1985). Small farmers are said to be more
productive than those on larger farms because they work the land
more intensively. At the same time their numbers are growing in
absolute terms even though their proportion of the work force is
falling. Thus, according to the model, directing scarce resources
solely at this group will provide African countries with the largest
possible production increases. By helping smallholders, the largest
single sector of all African populations, to produce more food the
model predicts reduced malnutrition and higher employment rates.
The model also asserts that African farmland is becoming
increasingly scarce. Arguably then, as larger, less productive farms
expand, the more productive smallholders will be squeezed onto a
diminishing proportion of the land. This hastens urban migration,
increases unemployment (because only a small proportion of
migrants can find jobs or any form of nonfarm work), and it lowers
production below its potential because of the lower productivity of
the larger farms. On the other hand, investing in rural amenities—

schools, roads, rural electrification—slows down migration to the cities, which along with farm development programs and better producer prices helps the most productive farmers to expand the food supply. The answer then is to aim development efforts solely at smallholders. Not to do so automatically diverts scarce resources to the more unproductive farms taking it away from the only subsector that can solve the problem.

This is the bare-boned logic of the model. It is sensible, it builds on comparable experiences in Asia and Latin America (especially the notion that crop yields vary inversely with farm size), and much of it is widely accepted by those contributing their talents to this issue. It is also attractively humane and decent in its belief that satisfying Africa's food needs can be accomplished only by the equitable distribution of resources to the poorest elements in the population—the smallholder farmers. As with the earlier emancipatory theories it equates rural welfare and increased production. And it also requires active government involvement. Thus one writer (Simon n.d.) notes that centralized government control of land and development inputs distributed equitably to rural smallholders can turn the food shortage problem around. Although the argument is directed at Namibia, the general tone of the writing suggests that the author derives a solution for this one place from a widely applicable model. And if this is a valid argument then the solution to Africa's rural development crisis is close at hand. All that is required is to convince African governments of the effectiveness of the model, provide them with the wherewithal in technical and material resources, and wait out the results.

In the unyielding world of policy making, implementation, and the rising tide of empirical research, things are somewhat different. There are great risks in depending on advice that argues for single solutions to multilevel, mercurial problems whose determinants are often context-determined, that shift over time, and that are not clearly understood even for past and present conditions let alone future ones. Under these conditions it seems to many African scholars, as well as others, that the only sure knowledge of the interactions among determinants and outcomes is that shown by experience itself. Or as one African scholar notes (Ijere 1983:304), there are both costs and benefits to all known forms of farm organization and development, and it is simply not safe or wise for Africans to accept guidance that asserts that one solution is more likely than another to solve the food deficit problem, only if all others are abjured. For example, it takes only a very small increase in productivity for African smallholders to upgrade production enormously. However, investments in terms of public facilities such as roads, storage facilities, and the vast increase in agricultural services necessary to implement the model at a mass level are, to say the least, daunting. On the other hand, the reverse is true if the job involves servicing a relatively small number of larger commercialized farm units (see Delgado, Chapter 2). Under such conditions is it wise or even practical to opt for a single solution, even if on the surface it seems more emancipatory and humane?

Advice is cheap, but it is Africans who must thrive or suffer with the consequences. It is better then, say proponents of the multimodal approach, to experiment, to try out a number of possible solutions, and from the outcomes to learn what does and does not work in specific contexts. Nyrere's unimodal *ujaama* policy is the classic type-case. Its failures are by now widely known and discussed, sometimes rationalized (with quite sensible excuses), sometimes not. But enthusiasm for unimodal, government–regulated, bureaucratically implemented policies are being questioned by African intellectuals and policymakers alike. With so many unknowns, and the questionable nature of many of the assumptions of the unimodal model, it is simply less risky to vary development strategies and allow real world outcomes to influence future options.

This brings us to the opposite approach, that of the multimodal or experimental model. Proponents assert that generalized solutions are neither efficient nor rational in a world of both invariant (situationally neutral) relationships as well as variant (context–dependent) ones. In such a world, models have both constant and variable relations, some of which describe universal features while others try to picture those qualities that help determine outcomes under the influence of local conditions. The essence of the unimodal model is its belief in the invariant applicability of its conditions and relationships—land scarcity, higher productivity of smallholders, and the derived set of logical relations that should ipso facto create marketable surpluses if resources are directed solely and equitably at this subsector.

The problem with all this is the variation among actual contexts. Empirical research has tended to make us back away from the constancies of the model and tilt instead towards quite different starting conditions. And these are based as much (or more) on variant relationships as on invariant ones, which means that specific policies cannot be gauged easily (because of unknown or previously unknown context determinants) until they are actually observed and measured over time. Realistically then, the conditions of rural development in Africa require that solutions be applied in real-world places so that relations between invariant and variant relations are exposed and made available as influences on policy formation, implementation, and change.

At present there are (at least) two deeply important constants that affect rural development efforts and four domains whose variant relationships require locally applicable solutions. These factors are expressed in a general proposition that synthesizes present research findings. It is not written in stone. The essence of this kind of eclecticism[2] is a built-in capacity to have its picture of the world shift as our understanding grows, and/or as conditions change. However, as an introduction to this kind of thinking, and to the problems presented in this book, it is useful to pick out those conditions that clearly facilitate and restrain the rapid growth of homegrown food supplies on the continent. Then each domain can be broken down into a set of separate propositions out of which specific and testable hypotheses can be derived. The general proposition states that:

> African food production is significantly conditioned by two constant (i.e., *presently* invariant) features, population dynamics, and "soft" government, along with a number of variant determinants, including land scarcity, productivity, differentiation, and commercialization.

Let me summarize each of these factors briefly to show how and why they hang together to form the ingredients of a multimodal approach supported by both logic and specific research findings.

Population Dynamics

Both the unimodal and the multimodal approaches assume that population growth rates in Africa will continue to be among the world's highest for at least the next several decades. This means that the majority of Africa's peoples will continue to live in rural areas for the foreseeable future, even though their proportion is a falling one. The unimodal model suggests that using resources to aid only this group enhances food supply and slows down urban migration. But contrary to the model's logic, urban migration is tied closely to *more* rather than less rural development. Even the worst urban incomes are better on average than those of the rural areas, and this is part of modern African understanding about the relations of the two sectors (Cohen 1987a; Cohen and Paden 1979). So far, research has shown that the greater the investment in rural amenities, especially schools, the greater the migration to cities (Lipton

1977:252-263). Nothing that has happened, even very recently, has reversed these findings. In other words (and though it is intrinsically desirable), those arguing for more investments and a higher quality of life for the rural areas, hoping in this way to stem urban migration, are supporting the very opposite outcome, thereby accelerating the declining proportion of food producers in the population as a whole.

What is most often left out of this discussion is the attitudes of farmers themselves. Hardly any of the vast literature on African peasants discusses the relative status of rural smallholder farmers to other forms of income generation. When asked, Africans consistently place the smallholder farmer role close to the bottom of desirable sources of income (Cohen and Paden 1979; Spain 1969). The recent emphasis by governments on agricultural development does not seem to have changed these deeply ingrained folk evaluations. In a 1985 survey that I conduced in Nigeria, 47 percent of the household heads questioned reported that they do not want their sons to become farmers (Cohen 1988). This is, not surprisingly, correlated with whether or not the sons are attending school. Thus, aiding peasant farmers and investing in better living conditions in the rural areas means abetting the forces making for fewer farmers.

Macrodata for Africa support this conclusion in another way. As with other parts of the world, the wealthier an African country is in per capita terms, the fewer the farmers. Thus, in those countries with the poorest incomes (GNP under $250 per capita) agricultural workers made up 36 percent of the entire population (at the end of the 1970s), while the figure was 25 percent for countries with GNP over $500 per capita for the same time period (Paulino 1987:26). At the same time, and alarmingly, there is no indication that productivity per worker increases to fill the gap as the proportion of agricultural workers falls (Paulino 1987:26).

The latter point has an historical parallel. In Europe between A.D. 1650 and 1750 population rose rapidly. However, agricultural transformation was not correlated with rising population pressures per se (pace Boserup 1965) but with urbanization and improved transportation. These factors led in turn to the acceptance of technological innovations in the more urbanized regions (e.g., Holland and England) but not in the less urbanizing ones (e.g., France) (see Grigg 1982). Historically and logically, therefore, urbanization should stimulate agricultural growth and development. The fact that this has not happened yet in Africa means that the transition is in its beginning phases, not that it should be artificially delayed by slowing down urbanization (Hyden 1982). The "urban bias" is not completely wrongheaded; it simply ignores the obvious conclusion that agricultural shortfalls caused by the process have to be counteracted.

In sum, African population growth rates are high and most of the people live in rural areas; but the long-term trend forces ever greater proportions of the work force to move into non-agricultural activities is inexorable. The farm sector must therefore produce an accelerating surplus if homegrown supplies are to satisfy demand.

"Soft" Government

Perhaps the most underdeveloped notion in development theory is the idea that Third World governments can live up to the expectations of what Lal (1985) calls *dirigisme,* or what I have referred to as emancipatory ideas. Although Lal's term stresses means, while the latter refers to goals, both involve the assumption that centralized governmental agencies can set policies for the equitable distribution of scarce resources, plan and build the infrastructures, and then carry out the vast allocations necessary to turn unimodal theories into concrete achievements.

Unfortunately, the record in the real world is a sorry one. Waste, corruption, inefficiency, and bad planning are deeply ingrained leitmotifs of resource allocations and development efforts when government takes the lead and carries projects to actual ground-level completion (Hyden 1983). To say that it is solely the fault of specific regimes (see Lofchie, Chapter 4), or of an elite class who serve outside global interests, misses the point (see Mabognje, Chapter 8). The very nature of state-run distribution and bureaucratic capacities in Africa leads inevitably to the conclusion that allocations are consistently distorted by market forces that impinge on government agencies. Under real world conditions of regulation and resource allocation, corruption can be defined as the transformation of regulated distributions into practices based on the profit return to those in charge of administering programs. African state agencies contain almost uncontrollable tendencies for those in charge of allocative decisions to use their discretionary powers to place personal and group membership goals ahead of generalized national policies. If we add the low level of accountability, sparse monitoring, and the notion of government as an arena in which ethnic and regional interest groups compete through bureaucratic representatives for scarce resources, then the difficulty African

governments experience in trying to implement policy, run state
farms, or distribute resources equitably is understandable.

In sum, it is the fate of "soft" governments (i.e., less efficient
ones) to live with implementation constraints that include the
routinized practice of having regulated distributions (e.g., agricultural
inputs, credits, extension services) distorted by affective and/or
profitable links between allocators and the publics they serve. Under
such conditions the interposition of the state to combat forces of
(real or imagined) national and international exploitation
introduces new, or maintains former, sources of inequity, even when
equitable allocations and results are clearly declared goals.

Land

Unlike many other places (see Lofchie, Chapter 4), land in Africa is
not uniformly scarce. Assuming the unavailability of land to be a
constant and increasingly widespread problem eliminates one of the
most viable options for expanding food supplies—that of
augmenting the amount of land under cultivation as rapidly as
possible. There are large areas where up to one half of the arable
land is unused. (There are, to be sure, pockets of very high density
and, indeed, of overuse.) Recent research puts the supply of land at
approximately three to four times the area cultivated—800 million
hectares, compared to 185 million in use, (FAO 1986; McMillan
1986:2). Other figures, based on different assumptions, are lower, but
even conservative estimates (Hyden 1986:16) conclude that the
amount of arable land in Africa is at least three times that now under
cultivation.

Overall, there is little doubt that Africa contains enough land to
feed its present population and more, if rural areas were properly
developed so that the land would grow the food, and if the food
could be distributed to the people who need it. Projections
comparing land use and population growth support the conclusion
that the continent's unused land is sufficient to feed one and a half
times the estimated population of the continent for the year 2000
with relatively low levels of inputs. And this assumes that the present
high rate of growth will remain the same to the end of this century
(FAO 1986; McMillan 1986:2). On the other hand, the country-by-
country figures show an uneven distribution. Land-scarce places like
Lesotho, Kenya, Burundi, Rwanda, Mauritania, and Somalia may be
forced into policies that must rely heavily on increased yields per
hectare. Conversely, in countries with large amounts of arable land

available, such as Congo, Zambia, Sudan, Ghana, Mozambique, Benin, Tanzania, Liberia, Angola, Zaire, Gabon, Ivory Coast, Cameroon, Guinea–Bissau, and Nigeria, both increased yields and expansion of land under cultivation are possible.

Technology and resettlement are important factors. Many fertile riverbottom areas (such as the area north of the Benue River in Nigeria) are so disease-ridden that human settlements are either impossible or are already depopulated by river blindness. Cleaning up such areas as the Niger riverine plains in Burkina Faso has allowed for resettlement, and has resulted as well in sudden increases in arable land, agricultural production, and significant jumps in grain stores for the resettled farmers (McMillan 1986). One of the reasons for variance in estimates for the amount of arable land on the continent is the inclusion or exclusion of these depopulated areas that often contain fertile soil and water resources.

Basing theories and policies on increasing land scarcity in Africa overlooks the great variety of situations and the vast size of the continent. Granted, there are scarcity problems in crucial areas. But policies and theories that rest on the assumption of *either* a land-rich or a land-poor continent distort the facts of specific contexts-real places where policies must be implemented.

Productivity

It has been part of the record for decades that with better research and extension, African farms can produce much more than they do at present (Norman et al., 1981). Given some form of water management and control, along with scientifically proven inputs competently administered, it is clear the risks and instability associated with African food production can be lowered enormously, quite independently of land scarcities. Although there are shortages of capital, of trained personnel, and of more empirical research on diverse contexts, such issues are understandable and agreed upon.

On the other hand, transferring and creating more productive technology is not just a matter of capital, research, and good intentions. The most important constraint on successful outcomes is the dependency of technology on the organizational relationships that are utilized to implement technological innovation in real-world settings. And these are matters of tradition, of choice, and of social theories concerned with which kinds of relations of production have the most payoff in terms both of yields and of distributive justice. This is not nearly so easy a matter to agree upon, because underlying and influencing the assessments of organizations are ideological issues and contradictory research results that are not easily settled.

Possibly the most controversial facet of this problem is the widely used generalization that productivity is inversely related to farm size. If true, then small farms in Africa are better on grounds of yield alone (Johnston 1985; World Bank 1981:52).

There are, however real-world problems. When programs are aimed specifically at smallholders, most newly available inputs— fertilizers and other chemical treatments, as well as HYVs and visits by extension workers—are distributed in greater proportion to the larger, better-off peasant farms. Given this oft-replicated observation, it is predictable that the larger peasant farm units will continue to receive an unequal share of new technologies aimed at increased productivity. Why this group should be *less* efficient, while using *more* scientific inputs and extension advice, is not easy to understand. And even without such advantages in technology, the larger, better-off farmers "are better able to meet the expenses associated with efficient crop production" (Hill 1986:72; see also Rudra, A. and Sen, A. 1980).

Small-farm efficiency assumes that labor resources are spread more thinly in the larger units. But research indicates that African farm size is correlated with increased use of hired labor and with larger households. As Polly Hill notes:

> It is not true as is so commonly assumed that [small farms] are apt to benefit from having more family members per acre on which to call. . . . It is the rich [peasant] farmers who benefit from the efficiency of the large groups of farm workers, both family and hired (1986:73).

Small farms have fewer resources to use for inputs, and they obtain less energy returns per unit of effort than do larger ones (Longhurst 1984). Larger farms have significantly larger households and employ more farm labor more often than do smaller farm units (Norman et al. 1982; Hill 1986). Even more important is the belief (deduced from the theoretically inverse relation of farm size and productivity) that the use of household members is cheaper than hired labor so that small farmers who hire less labor can produce more cheaply. However, most African farmers, especially in high-risk, low-rainfall areas, have nonfarm occupations. Thus, using household labor may be more, not less, expensive when off-farm work is more lucrative than the cost of hired labor (Haugerud 1984). In Botswana almost all of the rural households have at least one wage-employed member during the annual cycle of work, and two-thirds of rural farm families receive over 40 percent of their farm incomes from nonfarming activities (Peters 1986:135).

Unfortunately, there are few direct tests of the size/productivity relation. In land-scarce Kenya, the inverse relation holds (World Bank 1981:52). In land-rich Nigeria measurements of maize productivity indicate an average of 50 kilograms of increased yields for every increase of one hectare of farm size (Balcet and Candler 1982:152). In Africa, at least, it may very well be that the hallowed inverse relation between size and productivity is applicable to land-scarce, but not to land-rich areas. And even that more limited generalization could in the end prove to have significant variations.

There is little doubt that other forms of technology, such as small- and large-scale irrigation, larger farm machines, modern storage facilities, and better transportation capabilities will become steadily more available. It is impossible to think of African agriculture not moving to many times the irrigation works now used. Nigeria, with relatively more capital to invest (but for that reason a bellwether), has gone from 2,000 hectares under irrigation in 1961 to 22,000 in 1970, to 760,000 in 1980; Nigeria is now irrigating over a million nectares (FAO 1986). Although this is still a very small portion of the 30.4 million hectares of arable land in the country, the pace of growth is breathtaking. As Bates notes in Chapter 5, we are beginning to understand irrigation constraints. Problems emerge over administration, capital, scale, and equity concerns. Large-scale irrigation, and even many small-scale efforts (Bernal 1985), can founder on the shoals of poor administration and local conditions. Very expensive projects such as those in Nigeria or Kenya are clearly not cost-effective. They do, however, provide experience and point the way to further developments involving more demanding and more complex technologies. At the same time, these installations create a periurban environment in the rural areas: industrial wage labor, electrification, health facilities, schools, a well-educated elite permanently living in the rural setting, and affluent and highly productive medium- to small-scale farmers (see Cohen, Chapter 9). Very few African countries have as yet used such installations to experiment with rural manufacturing and the long-term comparative advantage of cheap labor already in place in rural China (Lofchie, Chapter 4).

Differentiation

Although it is customary to pay lip service to the facts of rural differentiation, there is a contrary presumption that somehow "smallholder farmers" form a category at whom programs can be directed so that both welfare and production increases are uniformly enhanced. African smallholder farmers differ in household size, wealth, use of hired labor, farm size, off-farm occupation for one or more household members, use of fertilizers, mechanization, and farm credits, to name only the most obvious. And these factors are positively correlated (Cohen 1988). At the extreme lower end the poorest farmers live farthest from roads, know less about prices, and tend to live away from market centers (Usoro 1976).

The possibility that smallholders are similar enough so that equitable distribution and across-the-board benefits result from smallholder programs is at variance with the facts. No matter how well-intentioned special programs, such as spreading fertilizer distribution as widely as possible may be, differences among smallholders are increased once efforts aimed specifically at them are put into effect. Thus, after only a few years of smallholder integrated rural development, observers generally report increased differentiation, with some farmers becoming larger and more successful, others changing very little, and all shades of growth in between (D'Silva and Raza 1980; Cohen 1988). Researchers are now suggesting that factor variations (land, labor, and capital) among peasant households are significant enough to warrant distinctly different packages of input aid if results are to be more generally successful among smallholders (Low 1986:84-86). However, this is at present only a suggestion. The reality is one in which mass programs of farm development, even when they can reach large numbers, do so in uniform ways and means that attract some households, almost ubiquitously the more successful ones, while the more needy ones are left out. In West Africa, researchers report that as programs reach out to the smallholders, the lower 40 percent (in income) are steadily decreasing their share of arable land, while the top 10 per cent (of farm income groups) have been steadily increasing their share (Mellor et al. 1987:280). These same results show no indication of lowered farm sizes for the poorer farmers, suggesting that the increased differentiation results primarily from increased lands under cultivation. And in this book, both Cohen and Haugerud document how differentiation is exacerbated in both East and West Africa by smallholder programs, whatever the policy goals, or lack of them, were to begin with.

In the most general terms, it is possible to postulate that increased farm production in Africa and productivity per farm unit is a function of increased farm size and of organizational *variation* among existing farms. Differentiation presents problems in rural social welfare and the distribution of benefits, possibly even of impoverishment, especially in land-scarce areas. But these results are the inexorable accompaniment of development and growth. China's agricultural transformation makes it clear that successful increases in food production involve a correlated tolerance of inequities resulting from smallholder differentiation. Programs devised to counteract such trends must hearken to history and social dynamics, which predict that the consequence of rural development is enhanced variation among farm units, with the larger farms absorbing the bulk of the development resources. Attempts to intervene can provide some assistance, but ultimate relief lies in the creation of nonagricultural jobs to absorb those who benefit the least by accelerated rural development. There are no other choices.

Commercialization

If Africa is to satisfy its own food needs, urbanization and rural differentiation require the expansion of indigenous African food sales. The unimodal model argues for an emancipatory and egalitarian solution in which Africa's smallhold farmers can be transformed as a class or category into surplus producers. As already noted, the peasant small farmer is not a single homogeneous category. Not only are farmers different in terms of land and labor, but they vary enormously in food self-sufficiency and crop sales. As might be expected from the previous discussion, it is the larger farms from which most of the food sales originate. Surveys from almost all sections of the continent indicate that approximately 70 to 80 percent of smallholder food sales come from the largest quarter to one third of the peasant farms. On the other hand, it is customary for the small- and medium-size smallholders to keep food crops for home consumption and prestations. Thus in Nigeria, both after a drought and later after good rains, very little grain (zero to two bags) was sold by the smallest farm units, while almost all of the large farm units engaged in surplus food sales (Cohen 1988). In Zambia the large majority of smallholders retain staple food crops for home consumption. In Eastern Province 93 percent of all maize sales (1981-82) came from the small minority of larger farms (over seven hectares). Almost all of the smallholders with 2.5 tons of maize crop or less sold no crop (Kumar 1987:43). In effect, the larger farms possess an elasticity of supply for marketed surplus relative to production greater than unity. The smaller farms, i.e., the majority of smallholders, do not.

Even when smallholders accept innovations that result in increased yields, there is no assurance that they will decide to produce surplus foods for the market. In areas where there is a well-established tradition of commercialized agriculture, most smallholders are involved in the buying and selling of foodstuffs, although even in these cases (e.g., Kenya; see Bates, Chapter 5) the large farm minority sell at least half the food on the market. Elsewhere, because much of smallholder agriculture in Africa is woven into a household economy diversified to include higher status nonfarm work, increased yields often reduce the time spent on agriculture and shift efforts to off-farm activities. By doing so, "they undermine government efforts to raise agricultural production" (Hyden 1986:23, referring to Low 1986:288-311). Similar results have been observed in Mali where a government polder project increased rich production and fertilizer use, but actual crop sales *decreased* (Bingen 1985:85-86). And McMillan (1986) reports that although resettlement in Burkina Faso to well-watered farming areas increased crop yields per household significantly, crop sales were disappointingly low. In effect, this means that even with better rainfall, or water resource management, or in response to other *effective* government programs to raise smallholder production, there is no assurance that the small, less-commercialized farmers will commit themselves to food marketing and the needs of the national economy, given the unsatisfied demand of local economies.

There are two counterarguments to these propositions. The first is the U-curve findings and their implications. If the poorest and the larger, more successful smallholders do most of the selling off of food crops, then raising production for the poorest should enhance market supplies, assuming this lowest-income group continues to sell off food crops. Even if the U-curve results are replicable (which so far is problematic), it is just as logical to argue that with better incomes they will join the slightly better-off farmers *at the bottom of the curve* and grow food first and foremost for subsistence rather than the market. The U-curve argument is an outgrowth of emancipatory and dependency ideas. The very poor are pictured as caught in a web of cash needs because of the encroachment into their lives of outside commodities, taxes, school fees, and other consumer expenditures. These blandishments force them to sell off food, thereby impoverishing them still further. Even if this is a valid picture, or valid in some instances, it points to the need for programs that help the rural poor raise their standard of living. On the other hand, whether the use of resources for essential social welfare concerns will increase the commercialization of agriculture is, at the very least, doubtful.

The other counterargument is that of price. Certainly "getting the prices right" (Lal 1985) does increase the incentive to grow surplus food. There is evidence from many parts of Africa that once food prices go higher compared to export crops, surplus producers switch to food-crop marketing. On the other hand, shortages in other factors of production, (i.e., in land, labor, or inputs) tend to suppress this effect (Mackintosh 1985:80). Price increases have also stimulated urban interest in setting up farms, acquiring land, and quickening the pace of rural differentiation. The same is true of increased rural credit and of protectionism. As both Cohen and Mabogunje point out in this book, where these rearrangements are taking place, food is becoming more available; but evidence again points to the larger, more successful farms obtaining the bulk of the market. In addition, very large mechanized modern farms are appearing that could in the longer run transform the rural areas. In sum, better prices and the package of policies that government can implement to increase farm incomes serve to differentiate farming even further. Where there are strongly supported government moves to help smallholders become more commercialized, as in Zimbabwe, it is clear that the newly distributed farms are much larger than the average. But this smallholder sector forms the basis for a successful farm group, which still excludes the majority of the rural population. Better producer prices help to stimulate production increases. They also accelerate rural differentiation, increase the rural labor market, and may even threaten landlessness in areas where land was scarce to begin with.

For those who support a more experimental or multimodal approach, prices are simply one factor that can help increase food production. In many parts of Africa, governments intervene to both set prices and control food-crop buying through government agencies. As Bates points out in Chapter 5, this can lead to serious imbalances because of shortages of storage and/or capital resources that get tied up in food stocks. And as Lofchie in Chapter 4 shows, government intervention can lead to lower incentives as well. For those who advocate such interventions for the purpose of spreading price benefits more widely (and more equitably) in a unimodal manner, regulation is a central concern. Once governments, and theories that support such interventions, embrace price controls and buying boards, the free or parallel market emerges as a problem that must somehow be kept from undermining the moral, and theoretically desirable, goals of equitable development (Mackintosh 1985). Even more disturbing, as Bates shows in Chapter 5, government boards that should be expected to store foodstuffs for periods of shortage, tend to sell off food just when the rains fail! Unfortunately there is no way to completely regulate smallholder farmers or even large ones who wish to sell products outside a controlled system. The traditional distribution systems in Africa are alive and well, and new ones emerge easily in response to need (Goldsmith, Chapter 6). The evasion of controlled prices on a continent with insufficient administrative resources is a fact of life. Again, as Bates points out, it is both inefficient and even dangerous to the nutrition of the population to try and overcome such obstacles through monopoly buying of basic food grains by the state.

A knotty and sensitive issue is that of land commercialization. In China, the transformation of agriculture has witnessed a move from communal to household ownership of land and, even more recently, to the capacity to buy and sell "use rights." This latter development is correlated with a long-term policy of paring down the agricultural work force as it shifts into industry and workers sell land to a growing cadre of specialist farmers (*New York Times*, 27 October 1987). In Africa, the capacity to obtain credit, to mechanize, to consolidate dispersed and fragmented fields, and to care for the land as a resource may demand a response similar to that in China. Certainly the economic changes described by Mabogunje in Chapter 8, along with developments in ownership that have emerged since the 1978 Land Act, make it possible to obtain credit on land if the owner has a "certificate of occupancy," that is, private ownership rights. On the other hand, and especially in land-scarce areas, such change could lead to the fate that so many warn of—the development of a landless peasantry impoverished by the move to private profit-oriented farming that leaves the poor and defenseless to the mercies of the better-off and more powerful. Again this calls for experimentation. In areas of land scarcity, it is probably wise to protect (with state power) the rights of the smallholders to their land. In land-rich areas where production is partially dependent upon expanded acreages under cultivation, private property and a growing land market can stimulate increased production from larger commercial farms whose land assets help capitalize modern farm enterprises.

In the long run, satisfying Africa's food needs depends on the development of a specialized, commercial agriculture (Hart 1982; Hill 1986). Exactly how this is to come about is still somewhat unclear. What is now widely understood is the need for experimentation. Unimodal solutions are based on a hoped-for increase in the food supply through regulated distribution of benefits to the widest numbers of smallholder farmers. But the realities of soft government make regulation a problem rather than a part of the solution. Specialization means a differentiated farm population. Large numbers of African farmers will remain subsistence oriented, often part-time, into the foreseeable future. Others from differing backgrounds—from small farms and large farms—or townsmen looking to diversify their investments through farming, will continue to take advantage of development programs and economic conditions by moving into specialized commercial food production. What is clearly needed is an approach that appreciates and deals directly with these variations in particular contexts. Only in this way can we hope to increase food supply sufficiently on the one hand, and on the other hand raise the standard of living of those who cannot or will not find a way to be included in these changes.

Conclusion

The last few decades have seen the rise and fall of logical, but often contradictory, prescriptions for a better life in newly independent African states. It is easy to condemn policies with the intelligence of hindsight, but we must also realize that our own efforts to understand and to isolate the conditions of agricultural growth in Africa will seem quite puny a few decades hence. Nevertheless, concern for African well-being and a continuing need to know more in order to derive better policies by both governments and by donor agencies create a consistent demand for new and better theories. Under such conditions, and even with the best intentions in the world, guidance and misguidance overlap and even merge.

African rural development is no exception. But what I have tried to show is that as time and events have sifted and winnowed our ideas, residues have survived and been reshaped to answer new questions. Thus the urban bias approach of the 1960s, with its emphasis on a "dual" economy (traditional and modern), has returned in the form of the "exit option" and the "uncaptured" peasant to help explain why peasant farmers, when they find it necessary, reject attempts to be incorporated into a national food marketing system. Instead of seeing this as a means of "modernizing" the urban sector, we now see it as a problem in economic integration, with costs (inequities and dependencies) and benefits (enhanced capacities for food self-sufficiency). Those who take the opposite position of the unimodal approach have retained the priority of social welfare and distributive justice of the earlier emancipatory approaches but do so by placing increased production into question.

By using the materials from the studies in this book, I have tried to show that a multimodal or experimental approach can produce an understanding of the conditions affecting African food production. For the foreseeable future the lack of capacity among governmental agencies to administer and mobilize the rural economies within their jurisdictions is a real-world constraint on the success of any program. To try to override or ignore this constraint turns administration into a free market of resource allocations, which in turn deepens the inequalities it is designed to arrest. Population increases and the gradual but inexorable increase of the nonfarm sector means that food production must accelerate to stand still, and that urban and other nonfarm jobs must expand. It was wrongheaded to bias resource allocations into the urban sector, but the direction of agricultural specialization and the low status of smallholder farming means that urbanization will continue to outstrip population growth. And no matter how much effort is expended in a unimodal direction, increased resource allocations to the rural sector will foster changes towards the production of more food from fewer farms.

These ubiquitous relations are in turn conditioned by a series of interrelated variables concerning land, productivity, differentiation, and the commercialization of food crops that set these general features into specific contexts. Increased food production and availability are associated with increased differentiation and commercialization. Policies that foster this process enhance inequities already present in the rural areas. The positive fallout for the system as a whole is the enhanced integration of the economy that stems from the commercialization of food production. By allowing a society to create the multitudes of relationships across regions, ethnic groups, and incomes necessary to make a private-sector distribution system work, government fosters the creation of efficient and self-policing social formations that are necessary to the successful workings of the society. By not doing so, by decreeing and trying to administer how commercialized products will be produced, bought, and sold, a society drives these naturally selected outcomes underground.

For those who see African development problems from a multimodal or experimental perspective, real development leads to problems of rural social welfare. The intensification of food production is, under these assumptions, bound to leave out many rural households that will remain on the periphery of change as they continue to farm for subsistence and cash, and carry on nonfarm activities including rural (part-time) farm labor on larger farms. The degree to which the benefits of rural developments can be extended to these less well-off households through special mass-oriented IRD-type programs will depend on the general level of prosperity in the countryside and on government commitment to redistributional policies. Although soft government and the differentiation fostered by such programs are a matter of record, it is also true that the number of people who benefit from these smallholder programs increases over time. Given better producer prices, feeder roads, and a commitment to as wide a distribution of inputs as possible, inequalities produced by the success of developments can be assuaged.

The opposite view that stresses equitable distribution and social welfare as the primary goal requires greater "guidance" or *dirigisme* (the Tanzanian term) (Lal 1985) or in Kenneth Kaunda's phrasing, an increased "trusteeship" by government on behalf of the (Zambian) peasants and their interests. The problem is that production increases may not be the automatic results of policies inspired primarily by goals of social justice. And where this is so the danger exists that a set of selective factors have set up a trajectory of development, one of whose outcomes is the need to increase coercive implementation to achieve preset goals by the state. This includes the problem of policing the marketing of foodstuff to state-controlled buying boards at controlled prices, which in turn creates the problem of the so-called parallel markets. In addition, to create sufficient infrastructure capable of making a mass smallholder program work either efficiently or equitably is beyond the scope of most African states.

In the end, neither polar opposite position is completely satisfactory. There must be a strong commitment to social justice on the part of systems oriented primarily to production goals through the toleration, or even the fostering, of rural differentiation. This means expending resources on programs designed primarily to achieve income redistribution as adjuncts to the growth of production. This will provide avenues of advancement for the less fortunate and spread the benefits of development to those left out of the initial phases of the process. On their part, those advocating unimodal models must accept the facts of differentiation and the weakness of African governments to counter evasions of policy in the rural areas. Finally, the state has a role. African agricultural products must receive protection from cheaper or more popular food imports until production on the continent is more efficient. State policy must also provide income protection to farmers through price floors, farm credit policies, as well as research, and vast increases in extension, road building, and storage facilities. At the same time, governments must experiment with programs across differences of scale and technological complexity in order to discover what works in specific contexts. As the studies in this book make clear, there are no simple answers; those who offer widely applicable solutions misguide even with the best of intentions. In the end, and possibly despite the advice of the experts, Africa will satisfy its food needs because it has to. The ingredients to do so are there, and African governments, despite their softness, are alerted and attentive. Meanwhile, this book represents part of our attempt to understand—and possibly to help.

Notes

1. This introduction has benefited from the comments of colleagues whose readings and discussions have contributed greatly to its clarification and, in a number of places, to its amendment. In particular, I must mention H. R. Bernard, R. Hunt Davis, Christina Gladwin, Angelique Haugerud, Goran Hyden, and Marvin Harris. I am indebted to all of these people, as well as to the several cadres of graduate students whose reactions to these ideas in a number of seminars have challenged me to rethink or to recast many of the notions contained herein. I am in the final analysis responsible for having taken or not taken their advice, but above all I am grateful that they gave it.

2. By *Eclecticism* I mean an epistemic creed whose foundation is a stubborn commitment to realism, relevance, and testable validity. This I contrast to the ardor that accompanies beliefs dependent upon a single paradigm. Paradigms explain and interpret reality within the scope of a set of stipulated and unstipulated assumptions whose logic creates a metaphorical depiction of real–world events and their underlying relations. As systems of thought, paradigms produce questions amidst sets of readied answers. These programmed solutions to puzzles cannot be disconfirmed because falsification is absorbed within the interpretive capacity of logics contained within the paradigm. Therefore, errors of omission and distortion in the metaphor (theory, if you like) remain as constraints on the adequacy of the explanation in its application as a guide for the conduct of human affairs. In science these constraints become more apparent over time if and when the disparity between the metaphor and the unfolding of events widens the gap between image and reality—the so-called Kuhnian revolt. Paradigms therefore have their own marginal utility; as beliefs they rise and fall in popularity as the questions they pose move on and off the stage of intellectual curiosity. Policy issues, the need for adaptation and for guidance in human affairs, endure. Eclecticism ("unfettered by narrow system in matters of opinion or practice," OED 1987:831) places the onus on researchers to depict reality, its causal nexi, and the changing weights given to specific factors in its most empirically valid, inclusive, and relevant format. The criterion for choosing questions and seeking answers is therefore not

commitment to a paradigm, but rather policy testing and guidance, i.e., the relevance of the explanation in its applicability to the solution of real-world problems. Paradigmatic thought emphasizes a favored or debatable metaphor whose comprehensive explanation makes the buzzing confusion of observation understandable. Eclecticism favors accuracy, heeds disconfirmation as an unforgiving command to reject previous explanations, and is driven by the policy relevance of questions rather than by the polemics derived from scholastic beliefs whose assumptions are beyond question until they fall from favor. Paradigmatic epistemology follows natural science models. Adherents believe that theory advances through time becoming more useful for application as it develops, independently, in relation to competing paradigms; but it develops away from the hurly-burly of real-world problems, whose solutions are implied and are logical outgrowths of the paradigm. Eclecticism in social science suggests that knowledge grows out of the constant association of improving methods and the call of issues that must be faced and understood by research. The questions come from our human predicament, the theory from our commitment to, and our immersion in, their solution. (For a different view see Harris [1979] in which eclecticism is seen as a set of unrelated and contradictory theories that deter the orderly search for regularity among sociocultural phenomena.)

3. It is impossible within the scope of present knowledge to assess the claim that in Zimbabwe small-scale peasant farmers operating in traditional communal lands have increased their sales of maize from 10 percent to 40 percent of the entire crop (purchased by the government) in the period 1980-1985 (see *African Economic Digest*, April 1985). It is not known if this is a valid measure of increased production and productivity per farm worker, or simply a response to price rises, or to the increased use of women extension workers (most farm workers in the communal areas are women); or if it represents reestablishment of previous levels of production along with the inception of rural peace and stability; or if it is some combination of all of these in varying degrees within specific contexts. Furthermore, the effect on production statistics of white farmer emigration and the consistent move of white farmers out of maize production is also unknown (see *Africa Confidential*, 19 August 1987). Research to investigate this problem is on the drawing board at the Center for African Studies, University of Florida.

References

Amin, S. 1974. *Accumulation on a World Scale*. New York: Monthly Review Press.

Balcet, T. C. and W. Candler. 1982. *Farm Technology Adoption in Northern Nigeria*. Vol. 1. Ithaca, N.Y.: Cornell Department of Agricultural Economics.

Bernal, V. 1985. Household Agricultural Production and Off-Farm Work in a Blue Nile Village, Sudan. Ph.D. diss., Northwestern University.

Bernstein, R. J. 1978. *The Restructuring of Social and Political Theory*. Philadelphia: University of Pennsylvania Press.

Bingen, James R. 1985. *Food Production and Rural Development in the Sahel*. Boulder, Colo.: Westview Press.

Boserup, Ester. 1965. *The Conditions of Agricultural Growth*. London: Allen and Unwin.

Cohen, R. 1987a. *The Kanuri of Borno*. Prospect Heights, Ill.: Wakefield.

———. 1987b. Policy and Social Theory in Anthropology. In *Applied Anthropology in America*. E. Eddy and W. L. Partridge, eds. New York: Columbia University Press.

———, 1988. The Unimodal Model: Solution or Cul de Sac. In Papers Presented at the 1987 Society for Economic Anthropology Meetings, Riverside, California. C. Gladwin, ed.

Cohen, R. and J. Paden. 1979. *Capital Cities of Nigeria*. Report for Planning Team, Nigeria's New Capital City. (Unpublished.)

D'Silva, B. and M. Raza. 1980. Integrated Rural Development in Nigeria—The Funtua Project. *Food Policy* 5:282-297.

FAO (Food and Agriculture Organization of the United Nations). 1986. Country Tables: Basic Data on the Agricultural Sector. Rome: Economic and Social Policy Division.

Grigg, D. 1982. *The Dynamics of Agricultural Change*. New York: St. Martin's Press.

Harris, Marvin. 1979. *Cultural Materialism*. New York: Random House.

Hart, Keith. 1982. *The Political Economy of West African Agriculture*. New York: Cambridge University Press.

Haugerud, A. 1984. Household Dynamics and Rural Political Economy Among Smallholders in the Kenya Highlands. Ph.D. diss., Northwestern University. Ann Arbor: University Microfilms International.

Hill, P. 1986. *Development Economics on Trial*. New York: Cambridge University Press.

Hyden, G. 1980. *Beyond Ujamaa in Tanzania: Underdevelopment and an Uncaptured Peasantry*. Berkeley: University of California Press.

———. 1982. Urban Growth and Development. In *African Independence: The First Twenty Years*. G. M. Carter and Patrick O'Meara, eds. Bloomington: Indiana University Press.

———. 1983. *No Shortcuts to Progress*. Berkeley: University of California Press.

———. 1986. The Invisible Economy of Smallholder Agriculture in Africa. In *Understanding Africa's Rural Households and Farming Systems*. J. L. Mook, ed. Boulder, Colo.: Westview Press.

Ijere, M. O. 1983. The Socio-economic Aspects of Food and Nutrition Policy for Nigeria. In *Nutrition and Food Policy in Nigeria*. T. Atinmo and L. Akinyele, eds. Jos (Nigeria): National Institute for Policy and Strategic Studies.

Johnston, B. F. 1985. Agricultural Development in Tropical Africa: The Search for Viable Strategies. Unpublished paper prepared for The Council on Foreign Relations, and the Overseas Development Council.

Kumar, S. K. 1984. The Design, Income Distribution and Consumption Effects of Maize Pricing Policies in Zambia. Paper presented at the IFPRI Workshop, Chiang Mai, Thailand.

———. 1987. The Nutrition Situation and its Food Policy Links. In *Accelerating Food Production in Sub-Saharan Africa*. Mellor, J. W., C. Delgado, and M. Blackie, eds. Baltimore: The Johns Hopkins University Press.

Lal, D. 1985. *The Poverty of "Development Economics."* Cambridge: Harvard University Press.

Lewy, G. 1982. *False Consciousness: An Essay on Mystification.* New Brunswick, N. J.: Transaction Press.

Lipton, Michael. *Why Poor People Stay Poor.* London: Maurice Temple Smith.

Lofchie, Michael F. and Stephen K. Cummins. 1984. Food Deficits and Agricultural policies in Sub-Saharan Africa. *The Hunger Project Papers,* Number 2, September. (Reprinted from *Journal of Modern Africa* 20:1, 1982.)

Longhurst, R. 1984. The Energy Trap: Work, Nutrition, and Child Malnutrition in Northern Nigeria. Cornell University: Programs in International Nutrition, No. 14.

Low, A. 1986. On-Farm Research and Household Economics. In *Understanding Africa's Rural Households and Farming Systems.* J. L. Mook, ed. Boulder, Colo.: Westview Press.

Matlon, P. 1981. The Structure of Production and Rural Incomes in Northern Nigeria: Results from Three Village Studies. In *The Political Economy of Income Distribution in Nigeria.* H. Beinen and V. P. Diejomaoh, eds. New York: Holmes and Meier.

Mackintosh, M. 1985. Economic Tactics: Commercial Policy and the Socialization of African Agriculture. *World Development* 13:1:77-95.

McMillan, Della E. 1986. Agricultural Development and New Lands Settlement in Sub-Saharan Africa. Paper presented at the American Anthropological Association Meetings, Washington D.C., November 30.

Mellor, J. W., C. Delgado, and M. Blackie, eds. 1987. *Accelerating Food Production in Sub-Saharan Africa.* Baltimore: The Johns Hopkins University Press.

Norman, David W., et al. 1982. *Farming Systems in the Nigerian Savannah.* Boulder, Colo.: Westview Press.

OED (Oxford English Dictionary). 1987. London: Oxford University Press. (Compact edition of 1971 printing.)

Peters, P. E. 1986. Household Management in Botswana: Cattle, Crops, and Wage Labor. In *Understanding Africa's Rural Households and Farming Systems.* J. L. Mook, ed. Boulder, Colo.: Westview Press.

Rodney, W. 1972. *How Europe Underdeveloped Africa.* London: Bogle-L'Ouverture.

Rurdra, A. and A. Sen. 1980. Farm Size and Labour Use. *Economic and Political Weekly.* Annual number.

Seers, D. 1970. *The Meaning of Development.* Agricultural Development Council Reprint. New York: Agricultural Development Council.

Simon, D. 1986. *Small Scale Agriculture in Namibia.* Paper presented to the Commonwealth Geographic Bureau Workshop on Small Scale Agriculture, Australian National University, December 1986.

Spain, David. 1969. Achievement, Motivation and Modernization in Bornu, Nigeria. Ph.D. Diss., Northwestern University. Ann Arbor: University Microfilms International.

Staatz, John M. and Carl K. Eicher. 1986. Agricultural Development Ideas in Historical Perspective. In *Food in Sub-Saharan Africa.* Art Hansen and Della E. McMillan, eds. Boulder, Colo.: Lynne Rienner.

Tiffen, M. 1976. *The Enterprising Peasant.* London: H. M. Stationery Office.

Usoro, E. T. 1976. Observed Disparity in Nigerian Rural Poverty. In *Poverty in Nigeria.* O. Teriba, ed. Ibadan: University of Ibadan Press, for the Nigerian Economic Society.

World Bank. 1972. *Nigeria: Options for Long-Term Development*. Baltimore: The Johns Hopkins University Press.

————. 1981. *Accelerated Development in Sub-Saharan African: An Agenda for Action*. Baltimore: The Johns Hopkins University Press.

CHAPTER 2

Setting Priorities for Promoting African Food Production

CHRISTOPHER L. DELGADO[1]

Only two years ago it was possible to characterize policy debates about short-run growth in food production in Africa as an emerging issue where all means were acceptable to increase the aggregate supply of food, provided that it was done quickly. Policy debates about long-run issues at the time concerned the relative merits of strategies based on "getting prices right" versus greater emphasis on increased government expenditure in agriculture (Delgado 1984; Delgado and Mellor 1984). Fortunately, better rains and policy changes have substantially alleviated the aggregate food supply situation in most of Africa since then. On the analytical side, the "prices right" faction has come to recognize the importance of also cutting agricultural production costs as a necessary part of improving incentives to farmers.[2] African farmers have been and continue to be faced with rapidly escalating costs, especially the opportunity cost of farm labor in terms of off-farm work (Delgado and Mellor 1984). Furthermore, much of the heat has been taken out of the "prices right" position by the fact not only that food prices have risen substantially in Africa in the past few years, but also that national governments' ability to control food prices has been largely eroded.[3]

In sum, the emergency situation has abated in most, if not all, areas of the continent. This has led to greater consideration of short-term initiatives in terms of long-run objectives, and vice versa. There is also a greater willingness among analysts to consider the key role that providing public goods plays in cutting agricultural costs. Examples would be roads, agricultural research, extension, input supply systems, and so forth.

Much of this support for public investment in agriculture is based on the recognition that in sparsely populated areas, or areas

31

with a relatively low value of agricultural output, the private sector around the Third World has tended to be slow to provide supplies and services, such as fertilizer and other inputs—at least in the initial stages of development (Mellor, Delgado and Blackie 1987: pt. 3). The private sector may have to wait even longer before it becomes economically viable to recoup expenditures on research and extension. Some vital goods in especially short supply in Africa, such as rural roads, may remain in the province of government forever.

Another point to consider is that the present willingness of policymakers who count to devote significant resources to food production is perhaps greater now than at anytime since the early 1960s.[4] Past experience suggests that this favorable consideration of the problems of agriculture will pass unless some solid successes can be demonstrated in a reasonable period of time.[5]

The evolution of a consensus on strategy for promoting food production through greater use of market forces for pricing and increased public investment leads to three crucial sets of questions for food production policy: what to do, when to do it (particularly how to sequence myriad interventions); and, how to evolve a policy advice structure that enables interventions to be continuously monitored, evaluated, and changed to take account of rising knowledge and changing constraints. The evolution of policymaking structures themselves is a larger political question that goes beyond the scope of the discussion here; the salient point is that better policy cannot be made if it cannot be understood in a dynamic world. The most responsive political structure still requires analyses of the economic ramifications of decisions to favor one set of interventions over another, if only because the second round of political outputs is likely to come from the first round of economic impacts. Policymakers need to know the consequences of promoting one region or crop over another, beyond the input of the immediate interest groups concerned.

Because there is so much to do in African agriculture, because in a sense it must all be done at once, and because, relatively speaking, there is so little to do it with, a very tight set of priorities is required. While we can draw upon existing knowledge to speculate about these priorities, it is especially important to draw upon what is known about how efficient priorities are determined and set to boost food production, and then how they are maintained. It is not just a question of having a set of priorities; it is having both the "right" set and having them in the areas that count. In terms of ensuring sustained growth in aggregate food production, the former is largely determined by increasing the knowledge base about the latter and ensuring that the output is constantly funneled into the policy process.

If individual countries are serious about accelerating their food production, they must decide upon the type of farmers that they wish to provide incentives to, set regional and commodity priorities, and concentrate resources along functional lines to ensure success at a few key things. As resources expand from success, the list of things to do can be enlarged. The alternative to a few well-informed priorities is to dissipate a small amount of resources among a very large number of different areas, commodities, and tasks, in an environment for agriculture that is especially difficult. Piecemeal solutions are likely to be overwhelmed by the magnitude of the physical problems faced, the rapid growth of nonagriculture as Africa comes into the mainstream of world affairs, and the lack of knowledge about what to do (Delgado and Mellor 1984; Mellor, Delgado, and Blackie 1987).

Critical Choices in Getting Food Production Moving

Smallholder versus Large Farms

It is unlikely that more than 5 percent of current African food production comes from large farms (Mellor, Delgado, and Blackie, 1987: chap. 28). In that sense, a 3 percent growth of productivity of smallholders is equal to a 60 percent growth of productivity on large farms. Conversely, production strategies that maintain large farm output through subsidies would require twenty times more resources if applied to smallholders. Since the proportion of smallholders to large public or private farms varies by country, so will the arithmetic. But the main point remains that an agricultural development strategy that is serious about having an overall impact must be addressed to smallholders and it must be able, in a reasonable period of time, to pay for itself.

Many governments, particularly in eastern and southern Africa where production bimodalism is more pronounced, have tended to regard support to large farms as a production policy and support to smallholders as an income distribution policy. In reality, it should be seen the other way around if a real impact on production is desired. Recent experience in Zimbabwe suggests that this change in view is occurring. At independence in 1980, a small, highly efficient and well-serviced large farm sector supplied 95 percent of the marketed surplus of maize, the country's major food crop. When smallholders were given access to infrastructure, seeds, and fertilizer, it took just three years for them to capture half of the maize market, despite the fact that the large farm sector continued to receive the same support from the government as before.

Given significant government support in terms of items that cut production costs—such as roads, research, extension, cheap labor, input supply, and marketing assistance—smallholders in Mali, Ivory Coast, and Kenya have also rapidly increased the value of farm output. This is fully consistent with experience in the Asian Green Revolution (Mellor, Delgado, and Blackie 1987, chap. 28).

Not only can smallholders increase production when given the incentives previously reserved for large farmers, they can often do so at lesser cost (Johnston 1986). Furthermore, growth in smallholder incomes provides a market for locally produced goods and services that the large farm sector cannot provide. Finally, given that poverty is frequently a rural phenomenon in Africa despite relatively easy access to land, a vigorous smallholder sector will have widespread positive effects on net welfare.

Regional and Commodity Priorities

Rapid growth in smallholder food production, whether in Asia, Africa, or the U.S. cornbelt, has largely been an increased response to already favorable conditions. In India, production in the Punjab took off while Maharashtra stagnated. The smallholder success stories in Africa alluded to above all occurred on good land with reliable rainfall. Such areas tend to be well populated, cutting the overhead cost per capita of investment; the technical constraints that must be overcome by research to raise yields are also less.

Concentrating resources regionally has the advantage that it helps ensure some success somewhere, an important factor at the present time when agriculture—especially the smallholder kind—is on trial. By so doing, it also increases the aggregate supply of food, which is of clear advantage to the nonfood-producing poor.

To a large extent, agricultural development is collinear with increasing commercialization of rural areas. Market outlets provide a vent for surplus, enable farmers to capture the benefits of specialization, and provide a stimulus for local nonagricultural employment. A key operating hypothesis, consistent with evidence from Asia, is that success is more likely in moving one small region at a time intensively than in disbursing investment over a larger region extensively all at once.

On the other hand, the political ramifications of favoring one section of a country over another are especially severe in Africa, given the political importance of ethnic boundaries. The choice may be one of uneven development among regions versus no growth at all.

Regional and commodity priorities are not independent. The same arguments in favor of concentration of resources for success apply to limiting the number of commodities promoted by policy. Agricultural research and extension in Asia have tended to be interdisciplinary, but coordinated along commodity lines. In Africa, research and extension tend to be organized along problem areas, such as pests, soil fertility, and water conservation. The latter may be a reflection of the generally more difficult technical problems posed by crop production in many areas of Africa.

Yet, precisely because of the complexity of moving African farming systems, it is especially important that an interdisciplinary research effort covering all the problem areas be mounted and that the effort be funded over a long period of time at levels consistent with a reasonable hope of success. As a practical matter, it may only be possible to support effectively coordinated work at this level for a very small number of commodities and regions.

It is particularly striking that the international research system, the Consultative Group on International Agricultural Research (CGIAR), which includes only 16 percent of all agricultural research on the continent, is working on twelve commodities in sub-Saharan Africa. CGIAR breakthroughs in Asia involved only two commodities, and that came with substantial investment over time, and help from national research services.

In speculating about ways to concentrate resources by commodity in order to have a chance to do an adequate job, it is instructive to examine past trends in food production by commodity and region. Five commodities—millet, sorghum, maize, cassava, and rice—together accounted for 69 percent of all major food crops produced in the late 1970s, and 71 percent of increases in food production over the 1961–1980 period. Table 2.1 shows that the relative importance of specific commodities varies greatly by major region. Millet and sorghum are aggregated as one commodity because of the difficulty of separating them the way that statistics are typically reported to FAO.[6]

Table 2.1 also shows the share of total increments to production of major staple food crops represented by the major commodities.

Table 2.1. Distribution of Production and Sources of Growth of Priority Food Crops in Sub-Saharan Africa 1961-1980

	Share of All Major Food Crop Production 1961/65	Share of All Major Food Crop Production 1976/80	Regional share of 1976/80 Production of Each Crop	Share of total increase of all major Foodcrops 1961/80	Annual Growth Rates 1961-1980[b] Yield	Annual Growth Rates Harvested Area
Sub-Saharan Africa						
Maize	18	20	100	29	1.0	1.7
Cassava	17[a]	19	100	21[a]	-0.5	2.5
Millet/Sorghum	27	23	100	9	-0.2	0.9
Rice (husked)	5	7	100	12	0.8	2.8
(Four crops total)	(67)	(69)	(100)	(71)	(0.2)	(1.9)
By sub-region and crop						
West Africa						
Maize	8	9	19	14	0.4	0.9
Cassava	13[a]	15	35	16[a]	0.1	1.5
Millet/Sorghum	40	37	64	16	-0.7	1.1
Rice (husked)	4	7	50	27	1.2	2.7
(Four crops total)	(65)	(68)	(38)	(73)	(0.2)	(1.4)
Central Africa						
Maize	14	13	11	11	-0.9	3.4
Cassava	43[a]	44	39	46[a]	-0.4	2.2
Millet/Sorghum	11	8	6	2	0.1	0.9
Rice (husked)	1	2	6	4	0.0	7.2
(Four crops total)	(69)	(67)	(18)	(63)	(-0.4)	(1.8)
Eastern and Southern Africa						
Maize	33	37	70	45	1.4	1.7
Cassava	12[a]	13	26	12[a]	-0.8	3.6
Millet/Sorghum	16	14	30	9	1.5	0.0
Rice (husked)	7	7	44	9	0.8	2.3
(Four crops total)	(68)	(71)	(44)	(75)	(0.9)	(1.9)

Sources:
Paulino (1986) and other FAO data compiled by IFPRI's Food Data Evaluation Program.

Notes:
[a]Estimated by multiplying the share of all roots and tubers by the share of cassava in 1976/80 root and tuber production in each sub-region.

[b]Growth rates for four crops are weighted by shares in 1976/80 production.

In West Africa, although the overall share of rice in food production was low in the 1976-1980 period (7 percent), it accounted for the largest single share in increments to production (27 percent). However, the share of millet and sorghums (37 percent) gradually declined after the early 1960s despite the fact that they still constituted the single most important source of food in the 1976–

1980 period. In both central and eastern and southern Africa, however, the respective share of the preponderant staple in 1976–1980 was high and increasing: cassava in central Africa (44 percent) and maize in the east and south (37 percent).

These results suggest that a minimal research program to cover sub-Saharan Africa would have to at least include millet and sorghum, cassava, and maize. Presumably the focus of activities in semi-arid areas should be on sorghum, for which a number of exciting breakthroughs are in progress, as in Hageen Dura in Sudan (Axtell). The table also suggests that the small yield growth that has occurred has primarily been in sorghum and maize.[7] On the other hand, cassava cultivation area has expanded rapidly continent-wide. In sum, sorghum and maize have shown the best overall record on yield and production increase, while cassava is increasing in importance due to area expansion, primarily into forest areas.

Yet, it would be shortsighted to omit rice from the list of priority crops. Rice's contribution to the increments to output over the 1961–1980 period (12 percent) is considerably larger than its share of output (7 percent) at the end of the period. This relationship is especially evident in West Africa, where rice output grew at 3.6 percent per annum over the twenty-year period. Despite this production growth, rice imports still grew at 11 percent per annum in West Africa over the same period.

Rice consumption is beginning to grow at the expense of millet and sorghum in West African diets, and this trend is expected to continue with income growth and further urbanization (Delgado and Mellor 1984).

Functional Priorities

The emphasis on concentrating resources on higher potential regions should not be confused with integrated rural development of the type embodied by large comprehensive projects on small land areas. Rather, the goal of policy should be to alleviate a few key constraints in areas where little else is holding back agricultural production. Thus, while regional priorities must be chosen, only a few key interventions should be emphasized within regions, at least until new constraints on production growth become evident and the resources are forthcoming from growth to alleviate them. It is precisely because public investment should be a catalyst and not a substitute for private investment that it should not attempt to alleviate all constraints at once.

The prioritization of public investment on economic grounds

should start with areas where a single element is holding back sustained growth. This situation might exist because of the noncapturability of benefits, as in the case of public goods such as roads. It could come about because of moral hazard and the high covariance across farms within a given region of yield risks, as in the case of rural credit schemes. It could stem from the diseconomies of small-scale operations in remote areas, as in the case of input supply systems. Or it could be the reflection of poor policy in the past, as in the case of both input and output marketing controls. In the latter case, one or several of the other types of problems are also likely to obtain. It then becomes imperative to make the complementary public investments, such as transportation infrastructure, to allow policy reform through market liberalization to work.

In much of sub-Saharan Africa, it is likely that the main element holding back food production is lack of viable technical packages ready for application outside irrigated areas (Vallaeys et al. 1987). A very notable exception is maize production in highland areas, where the complex of factors determining actual fertilizer use is probably a more critical problem. Where fertilizer is a constraint, policymakers are in the unusual position of being able to rapidly increase food production through reform and public investment. Given the need to maintain the attention of key policymakers, considerable emphasis should be put on understanding why fertilizer use in sub-Saharan Africa is so low relative to other developing areas.

Fertilizer. Sub-Saharan Africa accounted for only 2.5 percent of inorganic fertilizer use by developing countries in the early 1980s (Desai 1986), despite having roughly 11 percent of the agricultural population and 16 percent of the agricultural land of all developing countries (FAO). A first priority is to invest in national institutions that can effectively monitor fertilizer use in areas of good technical potential, and make informed judgments as to why use is not expanding as rapidly as elsewhere in the Third World. Second, fertilizer of the right sort must be available to farmers at the right time, along with complementary inputs such as credit. Asian experience suggests that the private sector is slow to provide fertilizers when activity levels are low (Desai 1986), but rapidly expands operations when agricultural growth occurs, accompanied by government provision of good roads (Wanmali 1983; 1985).

Agricultural Research. Many authors, rightly so, have emphasized the importance of agricultural research in Africa. Research on food crops expanded rapidly in the 1970s, in no small part due to a reorientation of foreign assistance support in that direction. Yet, at the same time, national research systems became more fragmented geographically and functionally. Although expenditures on research over the decade rose to the point that many nations approached the standard target of devoting 1 percent of agricultural GDP to research, much of the latter was fragmented among production projects and microstations. As has been well documented elsewhere, individual researchers frequently were assigned to work on a broad spectrum of commodities over a multi-year period; poor work conditions and low incentives led to gaps in the most scientifically productive middle ranks of researchers (Idachaba 1980; Eicher 1986; Jha 1986).

Another problem that accompanied growth of support for agricultural research over the 1970s was the guiding view that research in Africa should be adaptive, that it should use the technologies and varieties available elsewhere. In practice, this has not always worked well, especially because of pests and diseases, as Spencer demonstrated convincingly for rice in West Africa. The West African Rice Development Association screened 2,000 Asian high-yielding rice varieties over seven years; only two did as well as local varieties.

A variant of this problem stems from recognizing the particular complexity of African farming systems, especially in the less humid areas. The sharply peaked nature of rainfall, relatively lower water retentiveness of soils, and steeply sloped supply curves for agricultural labor in these areas of Africa, relative to south Asia, for example, lead to the relatively much greater importance of seasonal labor bottlenecks in Africa (Delgado and Ranade 1987). These can have major implications for the overall profitability of innovations, thus encouraging a well-placed concern for the farming systems implications of technologies. However, the basic problem of the noncompetitiveness of low productivity agriculture faced with a rapidly growing nonagriculture can only be solved with technologies that greatly increase *average* returns to labor as well as *marginal* returns. Such increases are only likely to occur as a result of basic breakthroughs on the biological side, of the type normally associated with major increases in yields per hectare. The latter involve substantial attention to basic—strategic—research issues as well as to adaptive research.

The policy response to recognizing some of these problems has been rapid and incomplete: expenditure on agricultural research in West Africa fell from .9 percent of agricultural GDP to roughly .65 percent from 1980 to 1984 (Oram 1986). The external funders of agricultural research have quit doing things that were bad for the long-run strengthening of national systems, but have not reinvested the funds saved in a logical manner. This would be to strengthen national systems along lines already well established in other areas of the world in an earlier time period. This involves support over the long term for stable research teams of an interdisciplinary nature, but organized around a single commodity and coordinated from a single location (Eicher 1986; Mellor, Delgado, and Blackie 1987).

Rural Infrastructure. A strategy to boost agricultural production through improvement of incentives on the cost side needs to give priority attention to the improvement of rural infrastructure. The latter can be understood in both the broad sense of social overhead capital, including service structures and institutions, and the more restricted sense of centrally provided grid infrastructure. Sub-Saharan Africa is short on both, relative to other developing areas.

Given tight resources and the need for priorities, public investment should concentrate on providing the basic grid of roads and communications (and irrigation where costs permit it). Where major infrastructural investment of this type occurs, the private sector can then mobilize a much larger set of private resources to provide most other services (Wanmali: 1983, 1985).

Large countries such as Nigeria and Zaire had from 2 to 3 km. of roads per km^2 of land area and million rural inhabitants in the early 1980s. The comparable figure for Kenya was 6 km./km^2/million rural people, while those for Korea, Malaysia and Chile *at the end of the 1960s* were 31, 45, and 13, respectively.

Ahmed and Rustagi (1985) examined marketing margins from studies in Nigeria, Sudan, Malawi, Kenya, and Tanzania, on the one hand, and India, Bangladesh, Indonesia and the Philippines on the other. They found that marketing margins were on average twice as high in the African cases, and that 40 percent of the difference between the African and Asian examples was due to transportation costs alone.

The point is driven home for the SADCC countries by Koester (1986) who shows the enormous differential between export and import parity prices in that region. Table 2.2 shows that although the share of land transport costs within Africa is highly variable among destinations, they are on average very high. In the case of Zambia, half of the import parity price for maize, the principal food staple, is due to intra-African transport costs. Koester (1986) also makes the point that such high transport costs prevent the world market from providing a stable set of opportunity costs for domestic resources

Table 2.2. Differentials Between Import and Export Parity Prices for Maize in the SADCC Countries Attributable to Intra-African Transport Costs 1983/84

Country and Location		(a) Import Parity Price	(b) Export Parity Price	(c) Amount of Difference between (a) and (b) attributable to intra-African transport costs	(d) (c) as a % of import parity
		----U.S.$/metric ton----			----%----
Botswana	(Gabarone)	244	65	104	43
Lesotho	(Maseru)	227	82	70	31
Malawi	(Blantyre)	213	96	42	20
Mozambique	(Tete)	214	95	44	21
Swaziland	(Manzini)	199	110	14	7
Tanzania	(Arusha)	213	96	42	20
Zambia	(Lusaka)	254	55	124	49
Zimbabwe	(Harare)	214	95	44	21

Source: Calculated from tables 17 and 18 of Koester (1986). The import and export parity prices are for trade with countries outside Africa. The differential between import and export parity prices for maize landed in East African ports in 1983/84 is assume, following Koester, to be US$75/metric ton.

used in cereals production. Domestic cereal prices are thus subject to wide year-to-year fluctuations in the absence of intraregional trade and stocking, leading to considerable risk for both producers and consumers.

Irrigation infrastructure is also much less widespread in sub-Saharan Africa than elsewhere in the developing world, perhaps because of excessively high development costs and relatively lower natural potential. Kenya and Senegal, countries experiencing population pressure and with large agricultural areas subject to severe climatological risk, had only 2.1 and 3.4 percent, respectively, of arable area under irrigation in the early 1980s, compared with 33 percent of arable area in Korea and 9 percent in Malaysia in the mid 1960s (FAO Production Yearbooks).

Given the major outlays involved in providing rural infrastructure, considerable attention must be given to setting priorities within the overall activity. The goal, as elsewhere, should be to alleviate a constraint where the returns to investments in alleviating the constraint are not easily capturable by private investors, yet the other elements in production growth are ready to go and overall social returns are high. The principal consideration is the availability of proven technology to produce for a market served by the proposed infrastructure. A policy of building roads in the desert "to open areas up" where neither technology nor market is available is highly questionable.

Human Capital. Along with agricultural research and transportation infrastructure, priority attention should be focused on the appropriate types and levels of investments in human capital, principally education. African countries of all political leanings have invested heavily in the latter, although results, as measured by school attendance, suggest that further efforts should be made. The percentage of the appropriate age group enrolled in secondary schools in Senegal, Nigeria, Kenya, and Zambia ranged from 10 to 18 percent in 1979. Comparable figures for Malaysia, Korea, Argentina, and Chile at the end of the 1950s were 20 to 30 percent (World Bank 1983).

Furthermore, foreign assistance allocations have not been consistent with the principle that skilled decisionmakers are central to defining and implementing a tight set of priorities. Examination of World Bank Annual Reports, for example, shows that in the 1960s, 50 percent of World Bank lending to Africa went to transportation and 11 percent to education. The comparable figures in the 1980s are 15 percent to transportation and 4 percent to education. In the final analysis, there is some inconsistency in the willingness of major donors to maintain 80,000 expatriate advisers in Africa at US$4 billion per annum, in the context of lack of willingness to make major investments in higher education (Lele 1987).

Promoting the Making of Choices

Perhaps the one commodity scarcer than a decision in many African governments is an informed decision. The political process will always influence choices and indeed should, since it is the same process that should serve to lend legitimacy to decisions made. It is therefore unrealistic to expect that policy decisions will be made in an economic vacuum, divorced from social and political considerations. Nevertheless, policymakers often have some— sometimes even considerable—room to maneuver within political constraints. However, the more important the policy change, the greater the risk of unanticipated political costs. Policy research and analysis, based on solid data, substantially reduces the risk of the unknown.

It is also unrealistic to think that the usefulness of policy advice is independent from who gives it. It is even more unrealistic to think that policy reform is a one-shot deal. Rather, it is an exploratory process involving sequences of actions based upon the results of earlier interventions. Furthermore, the economic (and political) context of policy reform is constantly changing—with changes in world prices, trade flows, weather, and so forth.

Therefore, the greatest priority for national governments and foreign assistance agencies alike should be to strengthen the institutional capability of African nations to continuously generate and use knowledge for policy reform. This involves the creation and staffing of institutions that can constantly identify emerging policy issues, analyze options, and monitor the execution of decisions.

The first requirement for these functions is solid data, a good that must be continuously generated by government, guided by a sense of priorities as to what is to be collected. The second function is policy research, which frequently identifies policy issues before politicians and policymakers are fully aware of them as priority areas of concern. For this reason, policy research must occur outside the day-to-day exigencies of government bureaucracies, given their built-in emphasis on immediate, "useful" results. Finally, policy analysis takes the results of policy research that have become relevant and presents the consequences of different options to policymakers. For the same reasons that policy research should occur outside government, policy analysis units should be housed within it.

In sum, some priority areas for attention by policy researchers, analysts, and decisionmakers have been suggested. These involve a tough set of choices along regional, commodity, and functional lines and within each category. Until national structures have a capacity to deal with such issues, governments and foreign assistance agencies alike should devote priority attention to building such institutions, while dealing as best as they can with the policy issues themselves. The apparatus necessary to improve the intellectual quality of decision making is neither cheap nor easy to build rapidly. It involves substantial outlays of foreign exchange, at least until domestic universities can take up some of the burden. Yet, there is no alternative if the objective is to promote sovereign government in a mode likely to find viable prioritized solutions to the myriad problems posed.

Notes

1. This paper draws heavily on the concluding chapter of a forthcoming book edited by J.W. Mellor, myself, and Malcolm Blackie. The contribution of J.W. Mellor to these conclusions, and the need for a tight set of priorities in particular, is consistent with his first authorship of that chapter. Remaining deficiencies are mine alone.

2. The 1984 World Bank report entitled "Towards Sustained Development in Sub-Saharan Africa: A Joint Program of Actions" was a large step in this direction, relative to the Berg report in 1981, which had defined the terms of the debate (World Bank 1981, 1984).

3. A point made by Elliot Berg in an oral presentation to the House Subcommittee on African Affairs, 30 April 1986, more fully documented for one region at least by a new major study on cereals policy reform in the Sahel performed under his direction (Elliot Berg Associates 1986).

4. This willingness is sensed by many professionals who habitually visit African governments; it has most recently been expressed publically by the assembled heads of state attending the Special Session of the UN General Assembly on the Critical Economic Situation in Africa (27 May to 1 June 1986).

5. Witness the complacency that set in about agricultural matters in the Sahel in the late 1970s, as the memories of the great drought in the first half of the decade wore off. In my view, changes of attitudes on the part of decisionmakers were more a reflection of frustration with the lack of progress than anything else.

6. Even for those countries that report sorghum and millet separately, the split is often arbitrary since the crops are frequently intercropped.

7. Data not shown suggest that yield growth attibutable to "millet/sorghum" in the table is primarily attributable to sorghum.

References

Ahmed, Raisuddin and N. Rustagi. 1985. Agricultural Marketing and Price Incentives: A Comparative Study of African and Asian Countries. Paper prepared for the Food and Agriculture Organization of the United Nations (FAO). Washington, D.C.: International Food Policy Research Institute.

Axtell, John. 1985. Personal communication to the author.

Delgado, Christopher L. 1984. The Role of Science and Policy in Alleviating Long-run Food Production Problems in Africa. Paper presented at the 67th meeting of the Board for International Food and Development (BIFAD), 5 December 1984.

Delgado, Christopher L. and J.W. Mellor. 1984. A Structural View of Policy Issues in African Agricultural Development. *American Journal of Agricultural Economics* 66:665-670.

Delgado, Christopher L. and Chandrashekhar G. Ranade. 1987. Technological Change and Agricultural Labor Use. In *Accelerating Food Production in Sub-Saharan Africa*. J. Mellor, C. Delgado, and M. Blackie, eds.

Baltimore: The Johns Hopkins University Press.
Desai, Gunvant M. 1986. Fertilizer Use in Africa, Notes for a Factual Perspective. Washington, D.C.: International Food Policy Research Institute (IFPRI). Mimeograph.
————. 1987. Commentaries on Marketing Systems. In *Accelerating Food Production in Sub-Saharan Africa*. J. Mellor, C. Delgado, and M. Blackie, eds. Baltimore: the Johns Hopkins University Press.
Eicher, Carl K. 1986. *Transforming African Agriculture*. The Hunger Project Paper Number 4. San Fransisco.
FAO. *Fertilizer Yearbook*. Various Years. Rome: Food and Agriculture Organization of the United Nations.
FAO. *Production Yearbook*. Various Years. Rome: Food and Agriculture Organization of the United Nations.
FAO. *1982 Statistical Yearbook*. New York. United Nations.
Idachaba, Francis S. 1980. *Agricultural Research Policy in Nigeria*. International Food Policy Research Institute Research Report 17. Washington, D.C.: IFPRI.
International Road Federation. 1967. *World Road Statistics*. Washington, D.C.: International Road Federation.
————. 1973. *World Road Statistics*. Washington, D.C.: International Road Federation.
————. 1983. *World Road Statistics*. Washington, D.C.: International Road Federation.
Jha, Dayanatha. 1986. Personal communication. IFPRI.
Johnston, Bruce F. 1986. An Analytical Framework for Assessing the Impacts of AID's Activities in Support of Agricultural and Rural Development. Washington, D.C.: World Bank. Unpublished MS.
Koester, Ulrich. 1986. *Regional Cooperation to Improve Food Security in Southern and Eastern African Countries*. International Food Policy Research Institute Research Report 53. Washington, D.C.: IFPRI.
Lele, Uma. 1987. Growth of Foreign Assistance and Its Impact on Agriculture. In *Accelerating Food Production in Sub-Saharan Africa*. J. Mellor, C. Delgado, and M. Blackie, eds. Baltimore: The Johns Hopkins University Press.
Mellor, J., C. Delgado, and M. Blackie, eds. 1987. *Accelerating Food Production in Sub-Saharan Africa*. Baltimore: The Johns Hopkins University Press.
Oram, Peter A. 1986. Report on National Agricultural Research in West Africa. Washington, D.C.: IFPRI. Mimeograph.
Paulino, Leonardo A. 1986. *Food in the Third World: Past Trends Projections to 2000*. International Food Policy Research Institute Research Report 52. Washington, D.C.: IFPRI.
Spencer, Dunstan S.C. 1987. Commentaries on Price Policy and Equity. In *Accelerating Food Production in Sub-Saharan Africa*. J. Mellor, C. Delgado, and M. Blackie, eds. Baltimore: The Johns Hopkins University Press.
Vallaeys, Guy, P. Silvestre, M. Blackie, and C. Delgado. 1987. Development

and Extension of Agricultural Production Technology. In *Accelerating Food Production in Sub-Saharan Africa.* J. Mellor, C. Delgado, and M. Blackie, eds. Baltimore: The Johns Hopkins University Press.

Wanmali, Sudhir. 1983. *Service Provision and Rural Development in India: A Study of Miryalguda Taluka.* International Food Policy Research Institute Research Report 37. Washington, D.C.: IFPRI.

———. 1985. *Rural Household Use of Services: A Study of Miryalguda Taluka, India.* International Food Policy Research Institute Research Report 48. Washington, D.C.: IFPRI.

World Bank. 1981. *Accelerated Development in Sub-Saharan Africa: An Agenda for Action.* Baltimore: The Johns Hopkins University Press.

———. 1983. *World Tables: The Third Edition.* Baltimore: The Johns Hopkins University Press.

———. 1984. *Toward Sustained Development in Sub-Saharan Africa: A Joint Program of Action.* Baltimore: The Johns Hopkins University Press.

CHAPTER 3

Beyond Hunger in Africa— Breaking the Spell of Mono-Culture

GORAN HYDEN[1]

The crisis in Africa has reached crippling proportions. Although the food situation has temporarily improved after the 1984/85 drought, less food is being produced than twenty-five years ago, and the hunger cloud continues to loom heavy on the horizon. With cash-crop production being no higher than it was in 1961 and manufacturing being generally below 50 percent of installed capacity, export earnings are down. To add insult to injury, many African countries sell their cash crops on the world market only to import food that could have been grown more cheaply by local farmers. Although the foreign debt of countries in sub-Saharan Africa in absolute terms is no larger than that of Brazil, its ratio as a percentage of export earnings of GDP is higher and the debt service burden therefore much heavier.

Although several African governments now accept the need for a more effective mobilization of domestic resources, a prevailing view, both in Africa and in international circles, is that the crisis can only be resolved with a larger dose of foreign assistance. To this end, various measures have been taken in international fora to increase the flow of grants and loans to Africa, the most notable assembly being the Special Session on Africa held at the United Nations in New York in May 1986.

But are more capital and technical skills from outside really the answer to those African governments seeking a way out of the present crisis? The experience with development aid to Africa from the industrialized North—both communist and noncommunist countries—has not been very encouraging. In fact, against the backdrop of that experience, one may suggest that the international donor community is as much a part of the problem as the solution

47

when it comes to tackling the present situation on the African continent.

Thus, Africa cannot satisfy itself with a prescription that argues only for more of the same old medicine. A debate must be initiated whether African governments, by continuing to seek answers and resources from the outside, are not in fact proceeding down a blind alley. Over the last two decades, bilateral and multilateral donor organizations, and the many and diverse interest groups dependent on their largesse, have grown into a corporate community with its own momentum and its own conceptualization of development. As presently constituted, it is not particularly sensitive to the kind of changes in either conceptual or operational terms that are needed if Africa is going to have a future beyond hunger.

Especially disturbing is the tendency within the donor community to overlook the complexity of the development process and to let its own organizational imperatives determine the flow and nature of aid. Donor organizations often have little sense of the historical context within which development is taking place in Africa, limited knowledge and understanding of the physical and cultural realities of the continent, and an excessive desire to shape Africa in forms familiar from other continents.

The official donor position has always been that outside aid can never be anything but a complement to local efforts, but as official aid agencies have come to play an increasingly dominant role in Africa, that view is no longer plausible. Today donors not only provide a growing share of national budgets (both development and recurrent budgets), but they also have a major hand in project design and, above all, in setting the conceptual framework within which development is perceived and pursued. By calling the tune, the donor community has encouraged a trend whereby African leaders not only look outside for solutions to their problems but also give priority to options that reflect the dominant outlook within that community at the time.

This has led to what I call a mono-cultural legacy which expresses itself in many ways throughout Africa—e.g., mono-cropping in agriculture, single fixes in technology, monopoly in the institutional arena, and uniformity in values and behavior. While these phenomena are inherent in the development process in any society, they tend to become particularly detrimental in the African context for reasons that this paper intends to further explore.

The Concept of Mono-Culture

The concept of *mono-culture* as used in the economic sciences implies the emergence of a dominant production strategy or technology at the expense of alternative, competing approaches. The rise of a hegemonic mono-culture is usually proceeded by a situation characterized by a high degree of diversity and experimentation. This is well illustrated by the developments within new industries built around a fundamental innovation such as the automobile, the airplane, or the computer. In the early stages of the industry there are many small firms, each exploring a somewhat different technological approach. Competition tends to be centered on innovations aimed at product and performance rather than price, or even on such qualities as reliability, compatibility with other products of the same genre, or service and maintenance. As competition continues, one particular approach normally emerges as the dominant technology. Competition shifts to incremental improvements in this dominant technology and to small cumulative manufacturing and managerial innovations that bring down production costs and improve reliability and standardization. As the dominant technology emerges, its competitive position benefits more and more from the cost advantages derived from higher volume production than its competitors.

The very snowballing success of the dominant technology, however, tends to steadily narrow the technical basis of competition. The search for cumulative improvements covers a smaller and smaller domain of technical possibilities even as it becomes more intensive within that domain. In the process, many technical possibilities that were deemed very promising in the early stage of experimentation receive declining attention from designers. In particular, options that might have been inherently superior, either in cost or performance or both, but which require more development or depend on more numerous or more problematic ancillary innovations, may simply fall by the wayside because of the growing cost advantage of the dominant technology arising from its headstart in the market.

Commercial success, however, is often a mixed blessing, because it tends to reduce flexibility in a situation of unanticipated change. The automobile industry in this country is a case in point. For several decades it relied on the commercial advance brought about by the rationalization and standardization measured of Henry Ford and Alfred Sloan in the 1920s. The resulting reductions in cost and improvements in reliability of the dominant technology guaranteed that more radical competing innovations could never hope to catch up. The locus of engineering innovation gradually shifted to Europe and subsequently to Japan. It took a series of external shocks to enlarge the technological agenda within the U.S. automobile industry—the political activism of the environmental movement, which chose the car as its first target; competition from increasingly stronger foreign competitors; two successive oil-price shocks; and the worst economic recession since the Great Depression.

Brooks (1986) refers to the emergence of dominant technologies that develop unexpected side effects at a critical scale of application as the problem of "technological mono-cultures." The term derives from the obvious analogy with agricultural or forest mono-cultures which, because of their density, become vulnerable to insect pests, pathogens, environmental stresses, or the absence of ancillary inputs such as water or fertilizer. Like agricultural mono-cultures, technological mono-cultures are highly successful in a stable and predictable environment (or market). Though more "efficient" than alternatives, they are less "robust" and "resilient" when the environment becomes less predictable.

To reduce their own vulnerability, organizations are constantly engaged in strategies aimed at increasing the predictability of the environment. Corporations that have successfully commercialized the dominant technology are particularly well placed to influence the external environment or the market through such measures as more sophisticated marketing techniques or lobbying for protection against environmental regulations or foreign competition. J.K. Galbraith popularized the idea of technology controlling its own political and market environment in his book *The New Industrial State* (Galbraith 1967). It was written at a time when American corporations were at the zenith of their competitive strength and appeared invulnerable to foreign competitors or societal regulation, as typified by the monolithic U.S. auto industry. The decade of the 1970s, however, showed clearly the limitations—both at home and in foreign countries—of the power of U.S. corporations to control their environment in their own interest. In fact, any success in controlling their environment in the short term has often proved inimical to the long-range interests of corporations, because it delays the adaptive measures that they will eventually be forced to take anyway. These corporations have found their environment much more complex and much less predictable than their leaders assumed in the optimistic growth years of the 1960s and advocates of the "dependency" school echoed later (Frank 1969).

The costs of mono-culture are particularly high in agriculture because it is constantly exposed to an unpredictable environment. As the perception of agricultural growth has become increasingly influenced by the principles of rationalization and standardization, exploitation of the land is today nevertheless more and more based on mono-cultural practices that leave both farmer and plant in a more vulnerable position. To be sure, there hasn't yet been a repetition of the dust bowl disaster of the Midwest in the 1930s, but questions are still being raised concerning the ecological soundness of current production methods in U.S. agriculture (Douglass 1984). Are the immediate gains in productivity really worth the loss in resilience that accompanies that trend? By reducing the genetic variety and increasing the demand for scarce water resources, margins for maneuvering, in the case of unanticipated events, are lowered.

The dominant approach to agricultural development in the North borrows from the industrial sector the equilibrium-centered view that emphasizes constancy in behavior over time. It represents a policy world of a benign nature where trials and mistakes of any scale can be made, with recovery assured once the disturbance is removed. Since there are no penalties to size, only benefits to increasing scale, it lead to notions of large and homogeneous development projects or programs that are seen as affecting other biophysical systems but not being affected by them. In this perspective, which reflects the arrogance of our industrial civilization, these interventions are meant to create "domains of stability" by reducing variability within the system and minimizing changes caused by factors external to these domains. Complex management structures are created to sustain and expand these domains and thus enhance control over environmental variables. As suggested above, these systems may prove highly efficient in a predictable environment, but they are very vulnerable to unanticipated events.

An alternative view of nature presupposes that the structure and general patterns of behavior are maintained through the experience of instability. In this perspective, which echoes an arcadian humility, designs assume that there is insufficient knowledge to control all aspects of a system and hence attempt to retain variability while producing economic and social benefits. This approach not only stresses the inherent value of diversity but also of resilience—i.e., the ability of a system, natural or social, to maintain its structure and pattern of behavior in the face of disturbance (Holling 1973).

Returning now to Africa, it is important to ask how far the crisis on the continent can be ascribed to an uncritical application of the notion that nature is benign, that it can be fixed, that it won't "hit back," and that reducing variability in the biological environment is a necessary prerequisite for progress, irrespective of how it happens and who is in charge of that process. Certainly, prevailing project designs in Africa stress efficiency over resilience, homogeneity over diversity. In this perspective, it is not surprising that the conclusion most officials and analysts draw, when examining the crisis, is that not enough has been done within the parameters that they take for granted. Thus, for instance, the debate about what should be done to get Africa out of its present predicament tends to be confined to such issues as economic policy reform, the timeliness of inputs, improvement of public management, or the provision of external funds on more concessionary terms.

But the debate needs to go further. It must question the very assumptions that underlie the approaches to development that prevail today. For instance, does tropical agriculture really lend itself to approaches that stress mono-cropping and standardized input packages? Do Africa's precapitalist social formations respond to interventions whose designs reflect criteria drawn from an industrial world? Can Africa ever become self-reliant if it is dependent on policies that ignore the local initiative and the local resource base?

The crisis in Africa isn't so much the result of its own physical limits as it is the product of our own technological arrogance. Although there is a growing readiness in certain circles to recognize that Africa's emergencies and disasters are man-made (Wijkman and Timberlake 1984), the prevailing view is still that these events are merely "interruptions" of development. Yet they are, in fact, as Mary Anderson (1985) stresses, indicators of the failure of development. Disasters and progress are two sides of the same coin. If the wrong design of development efforts is repeated too often, the inevitable outcome is crisis and eventually disaster. In exploring the thesis that Africa is the victim of a spell of mono-culture, I will be guided by three principal propositions, which are derived from the discussion of the concept above:

1. In their urge for rapid progress, African leaders have confirmed their search for answers and solutions to policy domains determined by the dominant outlook within the international donor community—their chief benefactor—at the expense of other potentially superior, indigenous options that have been deemed, both in economic and political terms, too costly to develop, thus basing their development strategies on premises that have proved feasible only in non-African settings.

2. In their design of development projects and programs,

African leaders have adopted the view prevailing in the industrial world that nature can be transformed at no real cost to mankind, thus stressing only the benefits and not the risks associated with development in a largely unpredictable environment.

3. In their desire to reduce variability and diversity, African leaders and representatives of the international donor community have overlooked the potential fragility that follows from such a process of specialization and standardization, thus underestimating the vigilance and added management capability that is necessary in order to sustain the original goals.

With regard to all three propositions, I intend to discuss further why a mono-cultural outlook has emerged, why it has been perpetuated, and what the implications are for Africa's ability to move beyond hunger.

The Limited Search for Answers

The stage for the emergence of a mono-cultural approach to development in Africa was set several centuries ago when advances in European agriculture, through such innovations as the wheel, the plow, and other "intermediate technology," paved the way for a European hegemony in the pursuit of defining and determining development across the globe (Goody 1971). Africa's failure to acquire technological advances in earlier centuries cannot be explained by the denial of such innovations by other powers, because the African empires and kingdoms of those days compared in wealth with those of other continents. But African emperors and kings sustained their regimes not by advancing agriculture but by appropriating surpluses from long-distance trade, tributes from surrounding state, and forced contributions from slave settlements.

It is not clear why these rulers left agriculture largely unchanged. Was it because they appropriated enough revenue from these other sources and therefore felt no pressure to transform production on the land? Or was it because they, like the peasant producers they ruled, were aware of the physical limitations inherent in the African soils—notably their tendency to become too sandy, lateritic, or eroded if subject to intensified use? Whatever the reason might have been, the fortunes and power of these rulers waned with the decline of the long-distance trade they had controlled, once the European powers began to replace it with their own trade along the African coasts in the sixteenth century. Thus the rural cultivators in precolonial Africa were never effectively captured by an indigenous ruling class with the ambition to alienate land and transform the systems of production. Power relations tended to rest on control of labor within given kinship structures rather than control of land (Meillassoux 1971).

It must be stressed here that this does not mean that precolonial agriculture failed to meet the needs of the population, except at times of natural calamities such as drought or floods. European travelers in eastern Africa in the middle of the last century reported lush vegetation and plenty of food and domestic animals (Kjekshus 1977). There was trade in local grains both in East and West Africa catering to the population in urban areas located along the coast or inland trade routes. All the same, technology was simple, limiting the scope for surplus production.

Physically removed from the scientific traditions that had emerged in Europe and Asia, African systems of agricultural production remained largely prescientific in the period prior to colonization. Their sustainability rested on respect for the physical properties of the soil rather than on maximizing productivity. Derived from an accumulated practical experience, African cultivators developed production strategies that stressed resilience and robustness—i.e., the qualities that stress survival even in unpredictable circumstances. For instance, in many parts of the continent, people learned that fertility was quickly used up and could be replaced only by replenishing humus and soil nutrients. The important trick was to use the soil in such a way that it was not physically destroyed (Timberlake 1985). Two principal strategies become particularly prevalent in dealing with this constraint. The first was shifting cultivation, where an area is cleared, planted, and harvested for a few years, and then left to regenerate while farmers plant elsewhere. A variation of shifting cultivation was rotational fallow cultivation, where people stay in the same village but plant fields in rotation with years of fallow in between to allow for regeneration of fertility. The other strategy was intercropping, whereby different crops with varying qualities are planted together to secure an organic restoration of the qualities of the soil.

To the European colonizers, these forms of agriculture in Africa were regarded as primitive and backward. To be sure, compared to European agriculture at the time, African techniques were less efficient, but they ensured maximum resilience. The latter point, however, was of little importance to the majority of colonial officials, for whom agricultural production in Africa was seen not as a source of food for the local population but as a means to extract wealth. They wanted to introduce new and more efficient systems of production centered on crops that were in demand by the increasingly industrialized and urbanized Europe. Although the introduction of crops like cocoa, cotton, groundnuts, sisal, or tobacco never was quite as devastating to local food producers as popular writers on the hunger issue—e.g., Lappe and Collins (1979)— imply, the enforcement of new crops and techniques did in some instances meet with active opposition from Africans, as illustrated by the Maji Maji War in Tanganyika early this century (Rodney 1972).

Although the early European colonial administrators engaged in a fair amount of experimentation both in the economic and social fields, their own view of agriculture as an increasingly intensified use of land, the reliance on mono-crop regimes, and the development of new technological packages to sustain their efforts soon emerged as the dominant ideology. This mono-culture, however, did not arise as a result of competition on the market among different approaches but out of political domination. Agricultural innovations were introduced by law or administrative fiat from above rather than as a result of a growth process from within, involving the local producers themselves. The search for solutions was confined to a limited set of problems, all determined by the view prevailing in colonial agricultural circles.

This meant that Africans were brought up to become imitators rather than innovators. They were encouraged to discard their own knowledge of agriculture in favor of new insights derived from experiments by people who, despite their scientific training, knew less about African agriculture than the local producers themselves. This arrogance on the part of the colonial regime was a major factor in the anticolonial struggles, as documented in various studies—e.g., Cliffe (1975) on Tanzania.

The colonial authorities were not interested in encouraging competition or diversity, and the mono-cultural outlook was extended to other spheres of activity. To be sure, there was a period in which the concept of "indirect rule"—i.e., the use of indigenous authorities for the purpose of governance—was alive, but it was soon superseded by the notion that African societies could be adequately developed only by replacing or transforming local institutions.

The cooperative society is a case in point. Such societies were imported to Africa modeled on the type prevailing in the respective home country of the colonial government. No only did colonial officials ignore the immense variety of cooperative origins and developments in both Europe and North America, but they also ignored indigenous African forms of cooperation. In 1934, for instance, a British cooperative expert, C. F. Strickland, ruled out the modernization of any traditional institutions in Nigeria, referring to the ubiquitous rotating credit societies among the Yoruba as "fraudulent" and "improvident" (Seibel, n.d.). His report was adopted and subsequently become the blueprint for cooperative departments throughout anglophone Africa.

Although the struggle for political independence to a very large extent was fought against imposition of the dominant ideology of the colonial powers, it did not lead to a reversal of the mono-cultural legacy. A major reason for this continuity was the fact that the battle for independence was fought on European turf. Whether with words or with arms, Africans had to prove their strength in the political or military arena over which the colonial power had vested control. The logical outcome of these battles, therefore, was not a return to indigenous solutions but a search for alternatives within the dominant eurocentric worldview. The relatively liberal nature of the colonial economy was replaced by an increasingly state-controlled economy; limited government involvement in the social sector was replaced by the vision of a "welfare state"; microplanning was replaced by macroplanning; etc. In rejecting colonial capitalism, the new African leaders opted for various forms of socialism. Even in those cases where the leaders recognized that indigenous values and principles were still a valid base for development, such as in the case of Julius Nyerere of Tanzania, the end-state of their political trajectory still resembled a European model of the good society.

It would be an oversimplification to attribute the tendency towards ideological uniformity only to this mono-cultural legacy, but the predominant notions of development in the industrialized world took on special importance to African leaders, who, in the words of Nyerere, tried "to run while others walk." Europe had proved its supremacy; it had the technological means and the human expertise. What was more natural than to borrow these and take a shortcut to progress? Such was the thinking in African government and donor circles in the 1960s. In practice, this meant that the African governments provided a political rationale for the continued dominance of a eurocentric perspective. The search for solutions was led by Western economists and technologists. This became obvious in the preparation of official policy. During the 1960s development plans were prepared virtually everywhere by experts from Europe or North America; individual projects were almost unexceptionally designed by consultants hired by donor agencies.

Particularly detrimental to Africa was the prevailing attitude among the bilateral donors that they should give aid in those fields where their respective country was believed to have a comparative advantage. For instance, in the case of Sweden, aid officials argued in the 1960s that the country should concentrate its assistance efforts in such fields as adult education and cooperative development, where it had unique experiences to tap. While this opinion is understandable in the case of a newcomer to the development arena, it had the effect in Africa of reinforcing the mono-cultural outlook. When Swedish cooperative development workers, joined by their counterparts from other Scandinavian countries, went to Kenya, Tanzania, and Zambia in the late 1960s to assist the governments of these countries to promote rural development, they replaced the cooperative model introduced by the British with their own rather than develop new forms of organizations based on indigenous types of cooperation. In a study of Swedish aid for rural development in these three countries, Birgegard (1975) has shown how specific project proposals were generally adopted on both donor and recipient side without much question and without any explicit comparison, on a cost-benefit basis, of alternative options. I am not suggesting that Swedish aid in this respect is any worse than aid from other countries. The point is rather that what these examples tell is likely to be the rule rather than the exception.

It is a priori an open question as to whether endogenous or exogenous factors are more important for the development of nations (see, for example, Chisholm 1980). Specialization and identification of the comparative advantage within a global division of labor are important in determining a country's progress. Yet in the case of African countries, it must be recognized that specialization in the last hundred years has been driven almost exclusively by external rather than internal forces. The result is that Africa's economies are among the most externally oriented in the world, while having at the same time particularly weak foundations. In aggregate terms, this is manifest in the heavy dependence on the export of single crops. More than half of the export earnings of many African countries (e.g., Ghana, Rwanda, and Uganda) depend on the sale of just one crop.

The notion that Africa's development stage was set from without in a mono-cultural fashion and that solutions to its problems therefore must also come from outside sources has almost become a self-fulfilling prophecy. Against the backdrop of declining agricultural production on the continent, many influential persons, particularly in donor circles, argue that Africa's indigenous forms of agriculture are inadequate. The solution must involve a modernization of production that implies the development of more complex technological packages designed to enhance efficiency rather than resilience.

This is accompanied by the notion that Africa must "export" itself out of the present crisis by giving primary attention to export crops. This argument is best set out in the 1981 World Bank Report *Accelerated Development in Sub-Saharan Africa; An Agenda for Action* (World Bank 1981):

- export crops are the nucleus around which extension, input supply, and marketing services are built; these also benefit food producers;
- food production directly benefits from the after-effects of fertilizer expended on the commercial lead crop;
- the existence of a commercial crop facilitates the propagation of productivity-increasing equipment;
- cash-crop production creates a local market for food-crop producers that is often more secure and stable than distant urban markets.

What World Bank analysts and others seem to have overlooked, however, is the fact that as long as Africa's economies are dependent on the export of single crops and the demand that drives the economy therefore is external rather than internal, it is hard to see that agricultural growth can serve as the engine of development in the way it is assumed to have done in other economies. This has become particularly evident in recent years as cash crops have produced less and less cash on the world market.

There is plenty of evidence to suggest that agricultural policies, when determined by external demand and implemented by government extension services, tend to have little positive impact. Input supply schemes are designed in ways that show little understanding of how farmers behave and decide in rural Africa. Two recent doctoral theses, one focusing on Kenya (Shipton 1985) and the other on Tanzania (Mascarenhas 1986), demonstrate the high opportunity costs that arise as a result of inappropriate design: use of inputs for purposes other than those originally intended, evasion of loan repayment, alienation of farmers, etc. To be sure, there are some positive aspects too, notably the ingenuity with which local farmers adapt input schemes for alternative and sometimes more beneficial uses. It seems, however, that these innovations take place in spite of rather than thanks to the outside assistance, which continues to be designed by planners who view farming families as discrete economic units and not, as the majority of Africa's farmers do, as parts of social networks of kin and neighbors stretching across the countryside. Agricultural project planners have narrow notions of what farmers ought to maximize or optimize: they usually forget that farmers have their own debts to pay, funerals to contribute to, and prestige to be bought, and that many will do so with whatever resources come their way.

Shipton concludes his study of the response of the Luo people to directed development with the following observation:

> Nairobi's plans for land tenure reform, farm credit, and a link between them have been styled on western examples. To the Luo the plans are foreign indeed. The plans come from towering economies with expensive long-distance communication systems, cheap farm chemicals, low inflation rates, elaborate institutions for personal cash savings, and seemingly unlimited industries to absorb farmers who lose their land. They come from cultures that conceive morality more as blind universals than as responsibilities to real kith and kin. They come from societies with universally spoken languages, more or less isolated nuclear families, little respect for elders, and less for ancestors. They come from people with curiously naive beliefs in central governments and fixed prices, and puzzling superstitions about printed paper. (Shipton 1985:319)

By confining the search for solutions to areas and methods that are already familiar as a result of scientific work in other parts of the world, Africa has incurred substantial opportunity costs. One is the loss stemming from neglect of local seed varieties in favor of imported hybrids. This orientation emerged at a time when African leaders and donors were very optimistic about the possibilities of transforming Africa's agriculture through an extension of the Green Revolution. Since then, circumstances have changed considerably. Hybrid seeds tend to perform well only when supported in a reliable fashion by expensive inputs. In situations of drought, local seeds continue to perform better. Africa is a highly drought-prone continent, and as long as the capacity to forecast droughts eludes the scientific community, it seems that reliance on the most versatile and resilient varieties—usually the local seeds—makes the best sense (Glantz and Katz 1985:336). By paying greater attention to local seeds, African countries can reduce their dependence on international sources of supply. As Mooney (1983) argues, there is a tendency among international agencies and multinational corporations to control the production of germ plasm and to centralize the supply of seeds to a few "banks" controlled by themselves.

A second opportunity cost relates to the lowering capacity of Africans to cope with challenges and changes in their own social and technical environment. The limited search for solutions to a policy domain that is completely shaped by the experience of industrialized countries means that there are few, if any, incentives to ordinary Africans to devise methods of improving agriculture—or any other productive activity—derived from local know-how. As Boserup (1965) and Wilkinson (1973) argue, the historical experience of other societies suggests that development is the result of initiatives taken by local people in response to changing circumstances, whether these are growing scarcities of key resources or population growth. Africans have been generally denied this opportunity and have been turned into cripples in their own homeyard. In agriculture, the dominant technology has been developed at research stations by specialists who, despite their technical proficiency, have little sense of the conditions associated with applying the technology on the farm. As always happens when one approach, outlook, or technology becomes dominant, interest in alternatives declines; learning is concentrated on the dominant variety only. So ingrained is this orientation in some instances that officials seem unwilling to change, even when facts and figures suggest otherwise. Art Hansen, for instance, tells of the experience in a farming systems research project in Malawi where agricultural department staff insisted on pushing high-yielding imported varieties, even though they yielded no more than local varieties. These officers had made up their minds in advance that "including local types in trials was a waste of time; it was counterproductive, a step backward into the past, and an insult to the breeders and agronomists" (Hansen 1986:154). Here, as in so many other fields, Africans in government positions turn their backs on their own history and their own resources. Instead of developing a flexible range of technologies appropriate to the objective of self-sustained progress, African government departments have become so committed to certain approaches or technologies that the free and scientific adjustment of means and ends is effectively limited. While this occurs in many other contexts—see, for instance, the Tennessee Valley Authority experience (Selznick 1966)—this mono-cultural spell becomes particularly harmful in Africa because it is so pervasive and there are so few means to challenge it.

A third opportunity cost is the failure to develop indigenous institutions outside government that can participate in and take responsibility for certain public activities. Although it would be a mistake to attribute this shortcoming only to the influence of a mono-cultural legacy, there is no doubt that it has aggravated the tendency for policy making to be stunted in African countries.

Donors certainly cannot escape blame for the top-down and monopolistic nature of public policy making in these places. By being so dominant in both funding and policy design, these agencies preclude the emergence of a more participatory and pluralistic policy environment as long as their clients remain only government departments or government-controlled enterprises and advisers hired with their support being focal points in the evolution of specific policies. The notion that African development is fostered by the provision of technical expertise is oversimplified because it overlooks the opportunity costs associated with the presence of such people in government departments and other public institutions.

Even if these "experts" are successful in transferring new knowledge to African counterparts, these costs are still there. First of all, there is the question of the relevance of the knowledge imparted. Western policy advisers almost always start from the naive assumptions that the environment is predictable and that policy actors can shape it, both of which are highly questionable in Africa. Second, they have a magic belief in written communications and documents, something which African policymakers do not share, the latter preferring to operate on the basis of informal and oral types of communications. Third, their presence tends to justify the neglect of other, nongovernmental actors. Donors are willing to provide such advisers only if there is evidence that they are listened to. African policymakers, wittingly or unwittingly, make this an excuse for limiting the involvement of others, thus enhancing the role of the dominant ideology or approach and confining the search for solutions to the domain identified by the outside expert.

The outcome is a double tragedy for Africa. Not only does it usually get stuck with a set of policy prescriptions that is difficult, sometimes impossible, to put into practice on a sustainable basis, but it is also caught in a situation where confidence in government is lowered and citizens feel alienated from the state.

The Indifference to Nature's Own Limits

A prominent dimension of the mono-cultural legacy in Africa has been the notion of a benign nature that can be exploited without real costs to mankind.

The enforced introduction of new crops in colonial days was accompanied by the import of new techniques derived from the more intensive forms of cultivation practiced in Europe. White settlers in Kenya, for instance, engaged in a practice that was later described as "land mining" (Blom 1985:89), which caused serious soil erosion. According to this practice, the same parcel of land was used as long as it yielded enough harvest, after which it was abandoned in favor of a new parcel. Although this practice had something in common with the indigenous system of long fallow, it had much more adverse effects on the soil because it was pursued with less knowledge of the soil and with heavier equipment.

Agricultural practices introduced during the colonial period have contributed to the decline of Africa's physical environment in a variety of ways, as analysts are now increasingly recognizing. Lofchie (1985), for instance, maintains that this deterioration stems from the introduction of both mono-crop regimes within local farming systems and new methods of cultivation that are directly harmful to Africa's soils. Crops that follow an annual cycle of planting and harvesting have proved to be especially damaging, for their introduction has commonly involved land-clearing, which strips the soil of its original cover, thereby interrupting the natural cycle of organic replenishment. This is visible in various parts of Africa where cotton, groundnuts, and tobacco have been introduced. Those crops make particularly heavy demands on the soil's nutrients, and the loss of fertility is quick, but similar trends can be observed in areas allotted to wheat and corn.

The European agricultural officers who were responsible for bringing new crops and methods of cultivation to Africa were not mindful of the significant ecological differences between temperate and tropical or subtropical forms of agriculture. Temperate agriculture is generally characterized by: (1) a dense and relatively rich soil base; (2) a generally stable climate that includes a relatively long summer growing season followed by a winter frost that reduces substantially the incidence of human, animal, and crop diseases; and (3) moderate—and more importantly, highly predictable—rainfall patterns from one year to the next (Dumont 1966). This unique set of conditions did much to facilitate the emergence of highly productive, large-scale agriculture characterized by the intensive cultivation of wheat, corn, and other cereals.

A particularly dramatic illustration of this "temperate" bias in the direction of Africa's agricultural development during the colonial era is the Groundnut Scheme in Tanganyika. The best European agriculturalists of the day tried to plant peanuts on 1.2 million hectares of land which did not get enough rain for such a crop and which turned cement-hard in the dry season. It took ten years and 35 million pounds sterling before the experts realized their folly, but the failure was so spectacular that it almost led to the downfall of the

British Labour Government. Less visible efforts with harmful implications for sustained agricultural development were carried out all over Africa in the colonial days. In northwestern Tanganyika, for instance, where an ingenious intercropping system helped peasant farmers sustain a prosperous agriculture on otherwise nutrient-deficient laterite soils, the British insisted on the introduction of mono-cropping on the unproven assumption that insects living in the banana stems were harmful for adjacent coffee trees with which they were interplanted (Hyden 1969).

The situation did not change with political independence. The last twenty-five years have, for a variety of reasons, been characterized by a continued disrespect for nature. One reason is that African government leaders were understandably reluctant at independence to acknowledge constraints in the local environment. They rather preferred to concentrate their attention on how agriculture in their countries could be made to grow as fast as possible. The coincidence of the Green Revolution in Asia and Latin America reinforced their belief that Africa's agriculture could grow in leaps and bounds with the importation of improved crop varieties and new methods of cultivation. Little consideration was given to the point that the Green Revolution had proved its technical success in regions where mono-cropping practices had been in use for generations and where there was already in place the economic and physical infrastructure for such a major transformation of the agricultural production system. It is not surprising, therefore, that the strong wish among many African policymakers to take advantage of the international agricultural research centers has produced very little. Much of their work, certainly until more recently, has been based on premises that are not very applicable to African agriculture at this stage. No wonder, therefore, that the director-general of ICRISAT has had to admit that the experience of, for instance, importing improved sorghum and millet varieties from India to the Sahel in the mid-1970s was generally disappointing (Eicher 1986:12).

Two other interrelated reasons for this continued disrespect for nature are that African agricultural officers had been trained by European agriculturalists and that the latter have continued to have a significant influence on agricultural policies since independence. The majority of Africa's agricultural researchers and policymakers have been trained by individuals and in institutions articulating a temperate agriculture bias. They are often more at home with crop varieties and techniques developed by outside experts than with indigenous varieties and methods of cultivation. As suggested in the discussion of the first proposition, it has not been uncommon for government agricultural officers in Africa to look down upon the latter.

Experts from the nations of Europe, America, and Asia that lie between the 35th and 60th parallels have continued to have a significant influence on African agriculture, either directly as experts assigned to governments, or indirectly as representatives of international agencies assisting agricultural development on the continent. Many of them are still among the strongest advocates of the introduction of commercial large-scale farming or the intensification of peasant agriculture through the introduction of mono-crop regimes and a biological simplification.

A case in point is the large-scale wheat project started by the Tanzanian government in 1970 with Canadian assistance. At that time, the Canadian government committed $7 million to a project which, in their view, would help grow most of the wheat needed by Tanzania. By 1983 Canada had spent $44 million on this project—a sum that had been matched by a Tanzanian government desperately short of foreign exchange. Using mechanized equipment purchased from Canada and run on expensive imported fuel, 24,000 hectares were plowed up on the Hanang Plains southwest of Arusha. This project provided only about 250 skilled jobs for Tanzanians and recruited only 100 local men as casual labor at less than $1.00 a day. The Barbaig pastoralists who had used the land for generations were squeezed onto poorer range, which their cattle overgrazed. Although the soil is fertile and able to hold water because of a high clay content, it is very sticky when wet and shrinks and cracks when dry. Severe erosion now threatens to turn the whole wheat-growing area into a dust bowl. Canadian officials admit that there is no possibility of Tanzanians taking over the project in the forseeable future and that it is costing Tanzania some $3.6 million a year in hard currency. But they claim that by producing one-third of the nation's wheat, it saves $11.4 million per year—a figure based on Tanzanian "demand" for wheat, which comes almost entirely from the better-off city dwellers and tourists, while maize and other crops are still the staples for 80 percent of the population (Timberlake 1985:chap. 4). Short-term gains are being purchased at the expense of longer-term sustainability in Hanang as in so many other places on the continent.

This example demonstrates that good intentions are not enough when it comes to promoting agricultural development in the tropics. Designed in the typically temperate mold and approved by a government in a hurry to make progress, it soon turned into yet another illustration of the harm that the mono-cultural legacy does both to the natural resource base and consumer tastes in Africa. It may be unfair to compare it to the Groundnut Scheme, but it is instructive that since both the Canadian and Tanzanian governments have a vested interest in the project and there are no other institutions strong enough to press for a change, it continues in spite of a deterioration of soils in the area and a high cost in scarce foreign exchange to Tanzania.

Indifference to the inherent limits of the natural resource base in Africa is also evident in various policies aimed at bringing people together in village settlements, on the assumption, among others, that peasants, when living and working together, can enhance both their own livelihoods and strengthen the country's economy. As Shao (1985) has convincingly demonstrated, Tanzania's villagization policy, under which several million people were moved into villages between 1973 and 1976, was pursued with little or no respect for nature's own economy and dynamics. The result was that, in several parts of the country, peasant households quickly exhausted scarce soil fertility and ended up unable to sustain their livelihoods in the new setting. In this case, there is no evidence that policymakers took any notice of the failure of similar settlement policies in the colonial days. Although pursued for somewhat different reasons (Kjekshus 1977, McHenry 1976), colonial efforts to concentrate peasants into planned settlements had to be aborted for ecological considerations. Cattle overgrazed the land, and as bush vegetation was allowed to expand, the risks of trypanosomiasis increased. Ten years after the villagization in Tanzania was completed, the country's policymakers have allowed people to move out of settlements where solid degradation is evident. At the same time, however, the Ethiopian government is going ahead with a similar scheme modeled on the Soviet experience of agricultural transformation.

The disregard for nature's own dynamics and the blind pursuit of policies that limit rather than enhance the prospects for a sustainable agriculture on the African continent are evident in many other contexts and countries. An often overlooked dimension of this problem is the continuous narrowing of the genetic base of the world's main crops. This poses a particular threat to Africa, not only because it tends to make them less resistant to the vagaries of climate, but also because it limits the access of soils to biological information that enables them to stay put and remain healthy. In other words, one of the implications of the present mono-cultural spell is the decline in the range of invertebrate and microbial forms. Furthermore, it implies that botanical and hence chemical diversity above ground is also absent, inviting epidemics of pathogens or epidemic grazing by insect populations, because in this situation they can concentrate their respiratory energy on reproducing, eating, and growing. Insects are better controlled if they are forced to spend a good part of their energy buzzing around hunting among many species (Jackson 1984:165). This is an important point, because various types of insects continue to pose a threat to both plants and livestock in many part of Africa; in fact, this threat has increased in recent years, as organizations with a mandate to combat insect invasions have failed to perform their function adequately.

The continuous manipulations of the physical environment that have accompanied the introduction of mono-crop regimes in Africa have also favored the selection of opportunistic and highly competitive weeds. Of the various factors that influence the crop-weed balance in a field, the density of crop plants and weeds plays a major role in the outcome of competition between them. In multiple-cropping systems the nature of the crop mixtures (especially canopy closure) can keep the soil covered throughout the growing season, shade out sensitive weed species, and minimize the need for weed control (Altieri, Letourneau, and Davis 1984:182). Plant diversification also results in increased environmental opportunities for natural enemies and, consequently, improved biological pest control in those areas where insect populations pose a serious problem.

Faced with a considerable deficit in its overall food production, African policymakers may be tempted to continue relying on strategies aimed at conquering the natural environment as quickly as possible. Prescriptions for "modernization" of Africa's agriculture along the lines of the ideology prevailing in the international donor community abound. It must be recognized, however, that maximization of yield without greater attention to how the natural resource base can be stabilized is a very perilous strategy. It is doubtful whether African agriculture can continue to be guided by a paradigm in which nature has been transformed into a reflection of the modern corporate industrial system; in which ecology has little or no influence on economics—which reign supreme. The mono-cultural bias is thus perpetuated.

The division between economics and ecology may have helped the rigorous analysts in both fields, as Jackson (1984:172) suggests, but it has been harmful to the practitioner. By accepting the division between economics and ecology, he treats one part—economics—as a whole. This may be acceptable in a society with a functioning market economy and a pluralistic policy environment, but the cost implications of following such an approach in a context where these features are lacking, or are very weak, can be catastrophic. The present crisis in Africa is only too painful a reminder of this.

The Fragility Stemming from Specialization

A third dimension of the mono-cultural legacy is the notion that Africa's problems can be solved with an improved management capacity. There is a widespread belief, both in African government and donor circles, that institutional capacities can be enhanced by the adoption of management principles and techniques that originated in the industrialized countries. Today this is a questionable proposition. Experience since independence suggests that it is not so much a matter of refining the existing machinery as it is a question of creating a new institutional setup in which the costs associated with past approaches can be reduced and eliminated.

The problem of African agriculture is not that it is being run with what are perceived to be "outdated" techniques and approaches. It is rather that these approaches and techniques have never been the subject of interest and concern. Instead of basing development strategies on what Africa possesses in terms of skills and know-how, the continent has been almost blindly looking only for what, in comparison with other more developed countries, it is missing. The inevitable outcome, as I have tried to demonstrate, has been the erection of a very narrow and largely artificial foundation of progress. Concentration, therefore, on the improvement of management capacity within existing structures is a strategy with only limited payoffs. It is necessary to discuss this point further.

Specialization is an inevitable ingredient of development, with outcomes that are potentially both positive and negative. It encourages creativity and fosters new forms of social behavior and action, but it also alienates people from the means of production and gives rise to one-dimensional approaches to problem solving. These ambiguities have been possible to reconcile reasonably well in societies where the specialization process has grown from within and thus has been guided by its own internal dynamics. This is particularly evident in the First World, where "checks and balances" have emerged even with an accelerated division of labor. To be sure, there are examples of specialization running away from society, creating potential and real hazards to man, the development of a nuclear power industry being one obvious case in point. But even if the vulnerability of industrial societies should not be underestimated, it is a mark of their development that somehow the necessary capacity to cope with the risks of a new technology is created.

In fact, it may be precisely this ability of industrial society to generate the capacity to solve problems that is the greatest threat to humankind. It encourages a technological arrogance and a false sense of always being in charge. This becomes potentially dangerous, particularly in a situation where, as a result of outdoing its competitors, a single technology or approach has emerged dominant. Robert Kates (1985) discusses this point with reference to hazard management. He argues, after a thorough study of a broad range of cases, that confidence in single fixes—technological or behavioral—is usually misplaced. The projected diminution in risk or consequence from the single fix is often overestimated, partly because of the energetic advocacy of its proponents and partly because it overlooks some process in the chain of causation that either increases the releases, exposures, or consequences of the hazard or introduces a new chain of hazard.

Specialization in the colonial context, where the process is driven by external rather than internal forces, is especially problematic. It tends to touch down in the host society like a tornado. It has a narrow focus with a powerful impact, but its overall consequence tends to be negative because there are few, if any, local barriers to controlling its rampage. Society is not equipped to take advantage of the new winds brought by this outside force. Translating the metaphor to the African development context, one can say that the problem to date has been that rather than trying to understand the origin of the tornado or to erect institutional barriers with the capacity to mitigate its effects, policymakers and analysts have been singularly preoccupied with the impossible task of taming it from within. Scarce resources have been devoted primarily to improving management capacity of the institutional sphere that has emerged in the wake of the externally driven process of division of labor. Development management has inevitably turned into a top-down exercise aimed at promoting what is "rational," "optimal," or "feasible" to the outside analyst rather than what matters to the local actor on the ground.

For governments who believe that "they must run while others walk" and for donor agencies whose decisions are shaped by the identification of suitable blueprints, the priority has been to perpetuate the uniformity inherent in the top-down approach rather than to encourage diversity and initiatives from below. In this scenario, bureaucratic action begins with an expert analysis of the problem and proceeds with implementation based on a request for funds from the donor (usually necessitating more expert assistance). It is totally organized and controlled from the center. Economists are the practitioners, and macroeconomics provides the theoretical underpinning. According to this rationale, development derives from capital investment. The resources that are requested from outside are regarded as too critical to be left to local allocation and should be dispensed from the center in accordance with rational criteria (Moris 1981:89-98).

Actors who are preoccupied with this blueprint approach often develop a misplaced sense of importance. Their orientation becomes especially harmful in the context of rural development. Rather than accepting that they represent at best a strong wind that touches the ground only intermittently and often with questionable consequences, they pursue their task as if theirs is the only acceptable approach to progress. A serious flaw with the blueprint approach is that it leaves the designer outside the implementing organization (Korten 1980). Planners request information from the field, process the information into projections, diagnose emerging problems where output is falling below what is needed, and establish projects to rectify the shortfall. The next phase in the design process usually involves the choice of an institutional model and then a paring down of the institutional requirements until they reach a favorable cost-benefit ratio. To turn the proposed action into a strategy, planners borrow guidelines from key policy documents like the five-year development plan, which states macroeconomic goals and sectoral commitments. Thus the planner relies on plan documents as a physical record of commitments among participating public institutions. "Programs" simply become budgetary headings within the plan document, typically constituting all the projects of one type that a particular department is expected to implement. In short, the blueprint approach splits program planning and organization into three disconnected segments: (1) an initial determination of resource requirements, often reached in advance of operational experience; (2) a scheduling in time and space of anticipated implementation activities; and (3) the assignment of operational responsibilities.

In his review of the Masai Range Development Project, Moris (1981: 99-113) demonstrates the many shortcomings associated with the blueprint approach. One is the inability of the project administration to modify activities in such a way that they better fit local capacity among the Masai. Another is the tendency of those in charge to treat the pastoralist dilemma in an "interventionist" fashion rather than as a "systems" problem (e.g., to assume that a single measure is likely to change things greatly, although reality suggests that the problem is subject to the influence of other weaknesses in the total rural system). Yet another shortcoming of the blueprint approach is the policy of tying program resources to projects and not to other operational agencies with greater capacity to sustain activities beyond the life span of an externally funded project.

Although warnings about the problems of adopting a Western planning and management approach to the African situation have been issued for many years (see, e.g., Onyemelukwe 1973; Moris 1977), governments and donors have been slow to change their view because its top-down character suits their own purposes. The crisis on the continent in the last few years may have had the beneficial effect of hammering home the message that to cope more effectively with the uncertainty that characterizes especially rural development programs, donor and governments must relax, and in some instances discard, the formalistic, analytical processes that now govern project choice and accept the reality that these are at best experiments (Rondinelli 1983). There is also reason to be wary of the economists' fallacy that policy reforms can be self-implementing or can be implemented entirely through market mechanisms. Even when market processes are involved, the implementation of most policies and programs requires the creation and strengthening of institutions that grow out of local initiatives and resources and that can therefore serve as countervailing forces to initiatives that come from above.

There is now overwhelming evidence that Africa's own potential and its own resources have remained largely untapped because of excessive attention to the initiatives that have been taken and designed from without. The process of specialization in Africa has led to a situation in which the countries are highly dependent on fragile and fickle linkages with the outside world rather than reliant on their own resource bases. Development management, therefore, cannot be viewed merely as a matter of strengthening existing institutions. It must involve reallocation of responsibilities in such a way that a better institutional balance between public, private, and voluntary sectors is achieved and efforts to cope with the uncertainty that characterizes rural Africa are shared with those individuals and institutions that have ongoing practical experience in dealing with it.

Towards a Future Beyond Hunger

In any situation where a particular technology or approach emerges into a mono-culture, its relevance and effectiveness get challenged as environmental variables change in unanticipated fashions. In a competitive market, the mono-culture cannot survive without adjusting to the new circumstances. Economic forces serve as corrective mechanisms and compel the institutions captured by this dominant technology to engage in a process of "creative destruction"—i.e., a transformation that allows them to cope with a more turbulent and unpredictable environment.

The problem with the mono-cultural legacy in Africa is that it is not directly subject to the corrective influences of a market; it is being sustained by governments and donor agencies whose readiness and capacity to modify their positions are limited. Yet, as this paper has tried to demonstrate, the way governments and donors have gone about the task of developing Africa has been such a disaster that they can hardly escape the grim signals of despair that reality is sending back to them. The predominant ingredients of this mono-cultural legacy—that Africa should be primarily concerned with what it is missing rather than what is possesses, that development is the monopoly of government, that aid is most effective if channeled in large chunks through government treasuries, that reduction of variability is part of progress, that the physical environment is predictable and subject to control by human institutions, and that there is always one approach that in the interest of economy should be pursued—are all evidence of what Thorstein Veblen once referred to as "trained incapacity." This incapacity is particularly ingrained in official donor circles; in fact, the representatives of major donors are usually the most powerful defendants of the mono-cultural legacy that plagues Africa. Thus, while African governments themselves have to accept a major change in their outlook in order to provide a way out of the present crisis, donors cannot be exonerated. A redirection of their work is an equally high priority if Africa is going to have a future beyond hunger.

Fortunately for Africa, the many interventions that have been made in the name of development on the continent both before and after independence have failed to achieve their objectives. Although considerable damage has been done, particularly in the blind pursuit of substituting natural diversity for scientific homogeneity, Africa has rejected or modified these approaches by depending on its own robustness and resilience. To be sure, much indigenous knowledge, insight, and understanding has been lost as a result of the premium attached to the narrow search for solutions that has characterized official policy in most African countries; but ordinary people—men and women, rural and urban—have not given up their own know-how altogether. In fact, in recent years, as official policy has become increasingly ineffectual, these people have actively engaged in generating solutions that build on indigenous knowledge and institutions.

Today there are two Africas: (1) the *robust and resilient*, stemming from the application of its own human and natural resources, and (2) the *fragile and fickle*, reflecting its legacy of dependence on a mono-cultural outlook designed principally by outsiders. Thus, it is not uncommon to find on the continent that environmental degradation takes place, although Africans have for generations known ways of preventing it; that hunger occurs, although both farmers and pastoralists have methods of establishing before its onset that it is coming; that agricultural productivity declines, although it has proved possible to develop local seed varieties and farming practices in the past. Contradictions of this kind abound.

A future beyond hunger for Africa involves breaking the spell of mono-culture and promoting a greater reliance on Africa's own resources and initiatives. A growing body of literature is beginning to advocate exactly that.

The vast majority of Africa's agricultural producers are still small-scale peasants with the interest and capacity to use only limited amounts of outside resources. A future strategy of agricultural development cannot ignore this basic fact. It must also recognize that contemporary agricultural systems in Africa have evolved over a long period of time through adaptation to local environmental circumstances (Kowal and Kassam 1978). Although these systems can be classified and generalized, each production unit is unique in terms of available resources and management skills. Each unit has a significant potential for improved productivity, but technological development must recognize the potential diversity of the recipients. While the individual identity of production units must be recognized, they must not be treated as isolated enterprises. Many of the mistakes in the past stem from the fact that agricultural practices have not been treated as integrated systems of resources which are linked in time, space, and the use of human resources. Management strategies must be sustainable and imply minimum risk to the producer—for instance, by providing for greater continuity with regard to seed and germ plasm, as well as technological practices. New technologies should be chosen or developed in such a way that they do not increase vulnerability or failure under suboptimal conditions. New technologies that offer higher returns in average or better circumstances during the crop year, but threaten greater vulnerability during poorer years, may not be attractive for adoption by the average farmer. No doubt some commercial farmers, those with greater willingness and capacity to take risks, might adopt these technologies. But even in those cases, it is important that short-term gains not be allowed to ruin longer-term prospects for a sustainable agriculture by adopting practices that are ecologically harmful. Although the principle of comparative advantage no doubt will continue to be applied in rural Africa, it is likely to yield sustainable benefits only if diversity is first used as a major strategy to maximize returns to resource use and to minimize risk and uncertainty. Africa needs to strengthen its resource base as a prerequisite to greater specialization and commercialization. As a result of past legacies, the base has narrowed, and there is no way Africa will be able to achieve progress in the long run without pairing the promotion of economic growth with strengthening resilience.

Intercropping has been a particularly common device used by African farmers to successfully minimize risks and maximize return under low levels of technology and resource input. Described as "one of the great glories of African science" by one observer (Richards 1983:17), intercropping occurs throughout the continent, both in major staple enterprises and in household gardens. Igbozurike (1978), for instance, evaluated the economic returns to poly-culture (intercropping) as opposed to mono-culture in a group of eastern Nigerian communities, finding consistently greater economic value from intercropping enterprises. Other research has come to much the same conclusion. Indigenous agroecosystems have, for example, higher productivity per unit of land area; better utilization of soil resources and photosynthetically active radiation; higher resistance to pest attack, disease epidemics, and weed interference; higher biochemical contribution to the local diet; and higher utilization of locally available resources and nonhybrid, openly pollinated, locally adapted seeds. Indigenous agroecosystems also contribute to economic stability, social viability, and direct farmer participation (Harwood 1979; Steiner 1984; Richards 1985; Harrison 1987).

The various dimensions of how to promote a sustainable agriculture are too many and too complex to cover here. Variations will no doubt continue to exist among countries and even within a given country. A general guideline must still be that Africa cannot afford to sit back and wait for a miraculous scientific breakthrough by the international research community (Eicher 1986). Instead, there is reason to examine more systematically how far the diversity of local agricultural skills can be used as a profitable resource for de-

velopment (Office of Technology Assessment 1984; Richards 1985).
At a minimum mono-cropping and other components of the mono-
cultural legacy must be *proven* as an appropriate technological
alternative, rather than assumed as such from Western experience.

This point is equally applicable to other spheres. For instance,
architectural and blueprint models of institutional structures and
behavior derived from Western experience are especially vulnerable
to unknown and unanticipated local preferences, expectations, and
patterns of behavior. This has become evident throughout the
continent in recent years as official institutions set up to serve the
public have failed to adjust to new situations. Peasants have fallen
back on indigenous institutions and local practices that are more
resilient. Trade has become increasingly localized as farmers have
shifted production from export to local food crops (Chazan
1983:200; Hill 1977:26-27). The overwhelming evidence of peasants
exiting from the commodity nexus (e.g., Berry 1984:76-77; Guyer
1981:114; Hyden 1980:121; Williams 1980:33) is one more example of
institutions failing to relate to local societies and failing to allow
adjustment and revision in the original designs, even when outsiders
believed that they had already taken local experience and variation
into account.

Peasant ability to withdraw from the official market and escape
official demands of various kinds has saved Africa from total ruin,
but their inability to gain recognition for their own initiatives and
organizations has also meant that their productive potential has
been left untapped. Such recognition is very important, as Bratton
(1986) shows in the case of Zimbabwe, where organized maize farmers consistently out produce unorganized farmers. Their margin of
superiority increases as rainfall and soil conditions become less favorable, implying that local organizations are particularly appropriate in situations where the environment is least predictable and
controllable.

Conclusions

Africa's crisis is, as this paper has tried to demonstrate, less a matter
of the inability of the peasant producers to feed the continent than
an institutional and policy problem that has to be resolved through
a redirection not only of African governments but also of the official
donor agencies, whether bilateral or multilateral. Analysis of Africa
can no longer proceed within the same paradigm as in the past.
Africa's future beyond hunger depends on the evolution of a new

paradigm that opens the door to a wholly new development cycle in which Africa's own resources, whether human or natural, constitute the base for fresh policy action. In this emerging scenario, it is the local plant, as opposed to the foreign hybrid, that takes on, both in a figurative and a literal sense, the prime significance. What is needed to facilitate and accelerate a development in this direction is not a blueprint approach, but a "greenhouse" approach—i.e., an effort in which government and donor increasingly play a facilitating role by improving the social, economic, and political climate in which local initiatives can grow and become significant for national development.

Ever since Kuhn's work on the structure of scientific revolutions (Kuhn 1962), there has been much debate about how shifts among paradigms occur. Are they, as the classical model suggests, the result of progressive accretion? Or, are they, as Kuhn himself argues, the outcome of "non-cumulative development episodes in which an older paradigm is replaced in whole or in part by an incompatible new one" (Kuhn 1962:91)? Or are they, as some of his critics imply (e.g., Lakatos 1970), the consequence of scholars beginning to ask new questions because the old ones no longer seem valid or relevant?

The last interpretation seems particularly helpful to the social sciences whose key distinguishing feature is that its empirical problems are in large measure constructed, weighted, maintained, changed, and dissolved by social forces external to the research community. This external influence, as Dryzek (1986) has pointed out, is rooted in the fact that the social conditions and problems requiring explanation or understanding change with time. Changes of this kind affect the content of the empirical problems confronting social scientists.

We have argued here that the social and economic conditions in Africa have deteriorated as a result of too blind an application for a long time of scientific solutions that have been developed elsewhere and whose value for Africa, therefore, must be questioned. Sustainable economic development in Africa as well as progress within the social sciences can be achieved only by asking the new questions that enable the rise of a new paradigm. Our inquiry suggests that these questions should reflect the shifts that do take place on the continent, e.g., from giving greater priority to production as opposed to welfare, diversity as opposed to uniformity, and security as opposed to vulnerability.

Note

1. I am grateful for comments on an earlier draft of this paper by Nelson Kasfir, Norman Miller, and Catherine Doles at Dartmouth College and Ronald Cohen at the University of Florida, Gainesville.

References

Altieri, M.A., D.K. Letourneau, and J.R. Davis. 1984. The Requirements of Sustainable Agroecosystems. In *Agricultural Sustainability in a Changing World Order*. G.K. Gouglass, ed. Boulder, Colo. Westview Press.

Anderson, M.B. 1985. A Reconceptualization of the Linkages Between Disasters and Development. *Disasters* (Harvard Supplement) 9.

Berry, S. 1984. The Food Crisis and Agrarian Change in Africa. A Review Essay. *African Studies Review*, 27:2 (June).

Birgegard, L.E. 1975. *The Project Selection Process in Developing Countries*. Stockholm: The Economic Research Institute, Stockholm School of Economics.

Blom, K.O. 1985. Poverty Reconsidered: An Inquiry into the Use of Natural Resources in the Interior of Kenya During the Last Hundred Years. Ph.D. diss., Department of Peace and Human Ecology, University of Gothenburg.

Boserup, H. 1965. *The Conditions of Agricultural Growth: The Economics of Agrarian Change under Population Pressure*. London: Allen and Unwin.

Bratton, M. 1986. Farmer Organizations and Food Production in Zimbabwe. *World Development* 16:2.

Brooks, H. 1986. The Typology of Surprises in Technology, Institutions and Development. In *Sustainable Development in the Biosphere*. W.C. Clark and R.E. Munn, eds. Cambridge: Cambridge University Press.

Chazan, N. 1983. *An Anatomy of Ghanaian Politics: Managing Political Recession*. Boulder, Colo.: Westview Press.

Chisholm, M. 1980. The Wealth of Nations. *Transactions, Institute of British Geographers n.s.* 5:3.

Cliffe, L. 1975. Nationalism and the Reaction to Enforced Agricultural Change in Tanganyika during the Colonial Period. In *Socialism in Tanzania: Politics*. Vol. 1. L. Cliffe and J.S. Saul, eds. Nairobi: East African Publishing House.

Douglass, G.K. 1984. *Agricultural Sustainability in a Changing World Order*. Boulder, Colo.: Westview press.

Dryzek, J.S. 1986. The Progress of Political Science. *The Journal of Politics* 48:2:301-320.

Dumont, R. 1966. *False Start in Africa*. London: Andre Deutsch.

Eicher, C.K. 1986. *Transforming African Agriculture*. The Hunger Project Paper Number 4. San Francisco: The Hunger Project.

Frank, A.G. 1969. *Capitalism and Underdevelopment in Latin America*. Harmondsworth: Penguin Books.

Galbraith, J.K. 1967. *The New Industrial State. New York: Houghton Mifflin*.

Glantz, M.H., and R.W. Katz. 1985. *Drought as a Constraint to Development in Sub-Saharan Africa. Ambio 14:6:334-339*.

Goody, J. 1971. *Technology, Tradition and the State in Africa*. London: Oxford University Press.

Guyer, J.I. 1981. Household and Community in African Studies. *African Studies Review* 24:2-3:87-137.

Hansen, A. 1986. Farming Systems Research in Phalombe, Malawi: The Limited Utility of High Yielding Varieties. In *Social Sciences and Farming Systems Research: Methodological Perspectives on Agriculture and Development*. J.R. Jones and B.J. Wallace, eds. Boulder, Colo.: Westview Press.

Harrison, P. 1986. *The Greening of Africa*. London: International Institute for Environment and Development.

Harwood, R.R. 1979. *Small Farm Development: Understanding and Improving Farming Systems in the Humid Tropics*. Boulder, Colo.: Westview Press.

Hill, F. 1977. Experiments with a Public Sector Peasantry: Agricultural Schemes and Class Formation in Africa. *African Studies Review* 20:3:25-41.

Holling, C.S. 1973. Resilience and Stability of Ecological Systems. *Annual Review of Ecology and Systematics 4:1:1-23*.

Hyden, G. 1969. *Political Development in Rural Tanzania*. Nairobi: East African Publishing House.

————. 1980. *Beyond Ujamaa in Tanzania: Underdevelopment and an Uncaptured Peasantry*. Berkeley: University of California Press.

Igbozurike, U.M. 1978. Polyculture and Monoculture: Contrast and Analysis. *GeoJournal* 2.5:443-450.

Jackson, W. 1984. Toward a Unifying Concept for Agriculture. In *Agricultural Sustainability in a Changing World*. G.K. Douglass, ed. Boulder, Colo.: Westview Press.

Kates, R.W. 1985. Success, Strain, and Surprise. *Issues in Science and Technology* 2:1:46-58.

Kjekshus, H. 1977. *Ecology Control and Economic Development in East African History*. Berkeley: University of California Press.

Korten, D.C. 1980. Community Organization and Rural Development: A Learning Process Approach. *Public Administration Review* 40:5:481-511.

Kowal, J.M. and A.H. Kassam. 1978. *Agricultural Ecology of Savanna*. Oxford: Clarendon Press.

Kuhn, T.S. 1962. *The Structure of Scientific Revolutions*. Chicago: University of Chicago Press.

Lakatos, I. 1970. Falsification and the Methodology of Scientific Research Programmes. *In Criticism and the Growth of Knowledge*. *I*. Lakatos and A. Musgrave, eds. Cambridge: Cambridge University Press.

Lappe, F.M. and J. Collins. 1979. *Food First: Beyond the Myth of Scarcity*. New York: Ballantine Books.

Lofchie, M.F. 1985. Africa: Agrarian Malaise. In *African Independence: The First Twenty-Five Years*. G.M. Carter and P. O'Meara, eds. Bloomington: Indiana University Press.

Mascarenhas, O. 1986. Adaptation or Adoption? Ecological and Socio-Economic Implications of Adopting a New Technology in Agriculture. Ph.D. diss., Graduate School of Geography, Clark University.

McHenry, D., Jr. 1976. Peasant Participation in Communal Farming: The Tanzanian Experience. Paper presented to the 19th Annual Meeting of the African Studies Association.

Meillassoux, C. 1971. *The Development of Indigenous Trade and Markets in West Africa*. London: Oxford University Press.

Mooney, P.R. 1983. The Law of the Seed. *Development Dialogue* 13:1-2.

Moris, J.R. 1977. The Transferability of Western Management Concepts and Programs: An East African Perspective. *Education and Training for Public Sector Management in Developing Countries*. L.D. Stifel, J.S. Colemen and J.E. Black, eds. New York: Rockefeller Foundation.

————. 1981. *Managing Induced Rural Development*. Bloomington, Indiana: International Development Institute, Indiana University.

Office of Technological Assessment. 1984. *Africa Tomorrow: Issues in Technology, Agriculture, and U.S. Foreign Aid*. Washington, D.C.: Congress of the United States.

Onyemelukwe, C. 1973. *Men and Management in Contemporary Africa*. London: Longman.

Richards, P. 1983. Ecological Change and the Politics of African Land Use. *African Studies Review* 26:2:1-72.

————. 1985. *Indigenous Agricultural Revolution*. London: Hutchinson.

Rodney. W. 1972. *How Europe Underdeveloped Africa*. London: Bodle-L'Ouverture Publications.

Rondinelli, D. 1983. *Development Projects as Policy Experiments: An Adaptive Approach to Development Administration*. New York: Methuen.

Seibel, H.D. n.d. Indigenous Self-Help Organizations and Development: The African Case. Department of Sociology, University of Cologne. Unpublished paper.

Selznick, P. 1966. *TVA and the Grassroots: A Study in the Sociology of Formal Organization*. New York: Harper and Row.

Shao, J. 1985. Politics and Food production Crisis in Tanzania. *Issue* 14:1.

Shipton, P.M. 1985. Land, Credit and Crop Transitions in Kenya: The Luo Response to Directed Development IN Nyanza Province. Ph.D. diss., Cambridge University.

Steiner, K.G. 1984. Intercropping in Tropical Smallholder Agriculture, with Special Reference to West Africa. Paper prepared for the Deutsche Gesellschaft fur Technische Zusammenarbeit Gmbh. Eschborn.

Timberlake, L. 1985. *Crisis in Africa*. London: Earthscan Publications.

Wijkman, A. and L. Timberlake. 1984. *Natural Disasters: Acts of God or Acts of Man?* London: Earthscan Publications.

Wilkinson, R. 1973. *Poverty and Progress*. New York: Praeger.

Williams, G. 1980. *The World Bank and the Peasant Problem*. In *Rural Development in Tropical Africa*. J. Heyer, P. Roberts, and G. Williams, eds. New York: St. Martin's Press.

World Bank. 1981. *Accelerated Development in Sub-Saharan Africa: An Agenda for Action*. Baltimore: The Johns Hopkins University Press.

CHAPTER 4

China's Lessons for African Agriculture

MICHAEL F. LOFCHIE[1]

The African Agricultural Crisis

Since the early 1970s, a majority of Africa's independent countries have been undergoing an agricultural crisis of monumental proportions. The most dramatic manifestation of this crisis is the periodic famine conditions that seem to afflict vast regions of the continent with increasing regularity. Episodes of acute food scarcity attract media coverage and thereby focus on the tragedy of insufficient food production. But such episodes are intermittent in character and therefore create a misleading impression, especially during periods when famine conditions abate, that famine is related to drought and that agricultural recovery takes place when rainfall returns. The fact of the matter is that the continent's agricultural problems are of a long-term structural nature; many countries have become chronically dependent upon food imports even during periods of relatively normal climatic conditions.

A series of studies by the World Bank has helped to provide a portrait of Africa's agrarian difficulties. The problem is twofold. First, Africa is the only developing region of the world in which food production per capita has been falling steadily since the early 1970s. In Asian and Latin America, by contrast, food production has been rising steadily during this same period. The magnitude of the problem varies considerably from one African country to another. In the twenty-four countries most seriously affected by drought, the drop in per capita food production has averaged about 2 percent per year for the past fifteen years (World Bank 1984). For the sub-Saharan countries as a group, the average decline has been about 1 percent per year since the early 1960s. As a result, per capita food production in the early 1980s was only about four-fifths of its level some twenty years earlier. This problem may have worsened during the 1980s. It is now estimated that even during periods of unusually rapid agricultural growth, such as 1980–1982, African food production increases only about 2 percent per year. Since population increase is now estimated at about 3.25 percent per year, this means that per capita food production is now falling by more than 1.25 percent per year.

The second dimension of Africa's agricultural crisis is the poor performance of the export sector. An earlier World Bank study provided dramatic evidence that Africa had also failed to keep pace with other developing regions in the promotion of its agricultural exports and that, as a result, its share of the world's agricultural trade fell by almost half during the 1970s and that its share of the developing areas' agricultural trade fell by a like amount (World Bank 1981:19). Even these figures must be read with particular care. The fact is that much of the increase in export volume that has occurred is accounted for by the successful performance of a small number of countries, including Ivory Coast, Kenya, Cameroon, Botswana, and Zimbabwe. Their inclusion in the overall figures improves the picture for the continent's export performance as a whole and thereby obscures how very badly the vast majority of countries have done in this area. The authors of the World Bank concluded that failure to maintain world market share has been a more important source of Africa's foreign exchange difficulties than declining terms of trade.

The ominous feature of Africa's agricultural crisis is that it portends a long-term pattern of economic decline. The trend toward declining per capita food production that has already resulted in increasingly large annual volumes of food imports can no longer be understood as the outcome of transient or episodic events such as droughts, war, or crop blights but must, instead, be analyzed as the consequence of long-term factors that are likely to continue into the future. These include certain fundamental features of the international economic system, including declining terms of trade, and a set of internal factors, including inappropriate agricultural policies on the part of African governments. The long-term character of this agricultural decline has itself begun to complicate the search for workable remedies. On-the-spot observers have begun to report on "donor fatigue" and there is concern that some of the continent's most active donor organizations have grown weary of the effort to develop solutions for seemingly intractable problems.

It is common to date the beginnings of Africa's agricultural decline from the early 1970s, a period that coincides with the first oil crisis (1973) and, more importantly, the first great Sahelian drought. But the fact is that the early warning signs of agricultural decay were visible as early as the immediate post-independence period. Though an agricultural continent, Africa had already become a net food importer as early as the 1960s. But, because the international environment was relatively favorable, food imports did not appear to be a matter of great concern. A study completed by the United State Department of Agriculture in 1981 concluded that Africa's food imports during the 1960s were not a major source of economic stress. Import volumes were relative low; adequate low-cost supplies were readily available from donor countries prepared to make grain shipments on concessional terms; and, perhaps most importantly, foreign exchange reserves were adequate to permit the continued importation of other necessities (USDA 1981:4–5).

In the African political environment of the 1960s, food imports did not give rise to difficult and fundamental questions. This was the era of early post-independence enthusiasm and it can be characterized in retrospect as a period of virtually uncritical optimism about the continent's economic and political future. The emergence of nationalist movements that had propelled the continent toward independence had enjoyed widespread international acclaim, and it was widely assumed that the end of the colonial period would usher in a new era of sociopolitical development and economic growth. If there were problems in the performance of national economies, as evidenced, for example, by the continent's incapacity to feed itself, these could easily be attributed to the neglect or deliberate maladministration of the colonial powers. It seemed certain that independent governments, motivated by a concern to improve the well-being of their peoples, would not repeat the same mistakes. This optimistic perspective was widely shared by Western governments including those of former colonial powers.

By the end of the 1960s, however, such attitudes were no longer tenable. Even before the Sahelian drought of the 1970s, food imports had grown to become a matter of utmost concern, revealing chronic weaknesses in the performance of the agricultural sectors of a large number of countries. Africa's food imports approximately doubled in volume during this decade but, because of increasing prices, the cost of these imports had increased nearly sixfold. More importantly, it was clearly impossible to insulate the effects of poor agricultural performance from other subsectors of fledgling national economies. African economies, unlike those of industrial nations, are utterly dependent upon agriculture to generate the resources for other economic sectors. As a result, poor agricultural performance had become the root cause of a broader and more diffuse economic crisis that deeply affected the vitality of the industrial and commercial sectors as well as the quality of public services.

Faltering agricultural performance has long posed a fundamental constraint on the performance of Africa's urban industries. Since much of Africa's industrial sector is based on import-substitution, it depends upon the hard currency earning of other sectors, principally agriculture, to finance the import of needed inputs. As the earning from export agriculture have stagnated and as diminishing reserves of foreign exchange have been required to finance the acquisition of other necessary imports such as food and energy, Africa's industries have begun to suffer from the lack of replacement capital goods, spare parts, and raw materials. The most visible symptom of these shortages has been a falling rate of capacity utilization, already as low as 25 percent, or lower in some countries. But other symptoms of this problem are to be discerned in such phenomena as high rates of inflation, caused partially by the scarcity of consumer goods; increasing rates of urban unemployment, caused by industrial closures; and a falling real wage rate, caused partially by the fall in labor productivity.

To understand the effects of the agricultural crisis in a comprehensive way, it is critically important to appreciate the absolute indispensability of foreign exchange. A shortage of hard currency, rooted in the stagnation of export-oriented agriculture, will affect virtually every aspect of economic, social, and political life. To operate at all, African countries must be able to obtain an overwhelming proportion of their national needs on world markets. The list of economically essential goods that cannot now be produced domestically is practically endless. It ranges, for the overwhelming majority of countries, from petroleum derivatives to any sort of large-scale equipment. Trucks, buses, automobiles, road-building equipment, and railroad cars and engines will almost certainly need to be imported for the indefinite future as will a whole array of agricultural inputs, including tractors, harvesters, irrigation pumps, and fertilizing machinery. Scarcities of any of these items endow the agricultural crisis with a self-reinforcing quality: stagnation of export levels reduces foreign exchange earnings, and reduced earnings, in turn, lower the availability of infrastructural and transportation inputs to the agricultural sector.

The foreign exchange constraint has also had a profound effect on Africa's educational and medical services. Rare, indeed, is the African university that has not had the quality of its academic program substantially reduced by the difficulty of obtaining up-to-date books and journals, by the sheer impossibility of purchasing laboratory equipment and supplies and, in extreme cases, by the unavailability of basic operating equipment such as typewriters, copy machines, and audiovisual aids. Similarly, many of Africa's major hospitals report a steep deterioration in their inability to import medical equipment and supplies. Other public services, including water and electricity supply, have also been affected as African governments find it increasingly difficult to replace or repair aged equipment. And at least one theory traces Africa's problems of bureaucratic corruption to the decay of the agricultural sector, citing the problem of urban inflation with its attendant scarcities as a source of painful financial pressure on hard-pressed civil servants.

If African governments allow the agricultural crisis to worsen, the result will inevitably be a much heightened immiseration of their populations. Further decline would provoke an increased exodus of rural populations from the countryside to the cities. Because of the shrinkage of economic opportunity, the results of such an exodus would be growing urban unemployment and the creation of more and more periurban slum areas. Newly arrived urban dwellers would be compelled to support themselves through a variety of relatively low-paid economic activities in the informal sector. Thus, the price of agricultural shortfall is far greater than the cost of food imports to make up caloric and nutritional deficits. It involves the quality of life in its broadest social and economic dimensions. In countries where the effects of agricultural recession are most severe, the cost of poor agrarian performance is a generation of lost opportunity.

The costs of agrarian recession are also to be reckoned in political terms. It is to be anticipated that the unemployed and underemployed residents of Africa's major cities will increasingly become a volatile and somewhat unpredictable force. Economically deprived and poorly educated urban populations could easily provide a popular base for ideologically extreme political movements. To control the threat posed by such movements, African governments may employ survival techniques that involve political repression and the curtailment of human rights.

Does China Have Lessons for Africa?

At first glance, the idea that China could have lessons for Africa appears dubious on its face. The political and economic differences between these two world regions seem so vast as to rule out from the very outset the notion that China's modern developmental experiences could have relevance for Africa. It is difficult to avoid an immediate conclusion that China and Africa are so different as to belong to separate analytical universes. But even the vast differences between the two serve an important theoretical purpose. For they call out attention to certain important features of the African continent that, perhaps because they are so very obvious, can be easily overlooked in efforts to grapple with its economic problems. Viewed from the standpoint of an Africanist observer, China demonstrates at least five major characteristics that, because of their striking contrasts with contemporary sub-Saharan Africa, throw a fresh spotlight on some of that region's fundamental economic constraints.

The most striking difference is that China is a single country with a population of almost 1.2 billion. This is nearly three times that of sub-Saharan Africa, which is divided into approximately forty-five separate nation-states. From an economic standpoint, the implication of this difference alone is staggering. As a single nation-state, China features a unitary economic system. It has one currency (and, therefore one exchange rate policy), one tax code, and one system of tariffs and trade regulations. China's economic singularity calls fresh attention to Africa's extreme politico-economic balkanization. Africa features as many separate economic systems as there are independent nations. Despite the fact that some francophone nations utilize the CFA franc, sub-Saharan Africa still operates on the basis of more than thirty separate national currencies. Despite efforts to create regional trading unions, each country still has its own system of tariffs and trade regulations. And each country has its own system of taxes and industrial regulations.

The second broad area of difference, stemming from the first, concerns the level of territorial integration. As one of the world's oldest nation-states, China has developed a high degree of infrastructural integration. It has a well-developed system of roads and railroads and a national airline, CAAC, that effectively incorporates even the most remote regions into a cohesive system of travel and transportation. Although this infrastructure could doubtless sustain considerable improvement, the contrast with sub-Saharan Africa could not be more striking. As a continent of forty-five or more separate countries, Africa is characterized by an equivalent number of physical infrastructures. It has forty-five or more road systems, an almost equal number of railroads and, astonishingly, separate national airlines for all but a tiny handful of its independent countries. Moreover, as has been so often observed, Africa's infrastructures are often not well suited to promote internal trade within individual countries, much less larger-scale patterns of trade across regions.

The third broad area of difference is cultural. China is, to an extraordinary degree, a culturally monistic society. Well over 90 percent or more of the Chinese people are of a single nationality, the Han. There is also a significant degree of linguistic integration. Despite regional differences in dialect that sometimes make oral communication difficult, China has a single written language that is mutually intelligible to all literate persons, thereby facilitating written if not spoken interaction. Moreover, China's minority nationalities are also, to a very large degree, culturally integrated into the society, since they almost invariably speak and understand the Chinese dialect of their region. As a result, China simply does not suffer from the divisive, energy-sapping, and economically costly ethnic conflicts that so plague the African continent. There are no irredentist movements that pose a military challenge to the central government and no civil wars that place a staggering burden on human and financial resources.

Africa, by contrast, is the world's continent par excellence of ethnic heterogeneity, featuring literally innumerable ethnic communities and, by latest count, more than 2,000 separate languages. At least five African countries—Angola, Mozambique, Sudan, Ethiopia, and Chad—are now engaged in civil wars stimulated at least in part by ethnic considerations. In any number of other countries, ethnicity takes a less visible economic toll by diminishing bureaucratic efficiency, by compelling political leaders to allot economic resources in such a way as to promote ethnic balance, and, more directly, by interfering with the internal movement of capital and labor.

A fourth major area of difference stems from the fact that China has been an independent sovereign nation for several thousand years. One of the most conspicuous features of Chinese history has been the development of a national bureaucracy that effectively extends the writ of governance throughout the entire country. Africa, on the other hand, having remained colonized until more recently than any other of the world's developing regions, comprises the world's most newly independent countries. With the possible exception of one or two countries, Africa's tradition of national self-governance extends back for only the length of a single generation, about twenty-five years. Perhaps more importantly, there is serious reason to doubt that its juridical sovereignties are effectively sustained by governments that can truly exercise authority over their national territories. Robert Jackson and Carl Rosberg (1986:1–2) have put this point succinctly:

In Tropical Africa, many so-called states are seriously lacking in the essentials of statehood. They are ramshackle regimes of highly personal rule that are severely deficient in institutional authority and organizational capability. The writ of government often does not extend to all parts of the country, and where it does is observed irregularly and without obligation or fear in many quarters— including even state agencies themselves.

The Jackson-Rosberg analysis has serious implications, for it suggests that sub-Saharan Africa is, in fact, far more subdivided politically than forty-five separate nation-states. For personal rule has subjected the continent to a political process of sub-infeudation. The real units of governance are those where locally powerful individuals have been able to establish and assert their authority. And the total number of these is countlessly larger than the official number of sovereign units suggests.

The fifth difference concerns the existing level of industrialization. China has already become a major industrial society. This may not be commonly recognized among those who have not had the opportunity to visit the country, because domestic needs are so great that few of its industrial products as yet enter the world market. But China manufactures such heavy industrial equipment as railroad locomotives, buses, tractors, earth-moving and road-building equipment, a variety of heavy-duty trucks, and hydroelectric generating equipment. China also produces a wide variety of consumer goods, including television sets, stereophonic equipment, refrigerators, bicycles, automobiles, and motorcycles. China's advanced level of industrialization contrasts fundamentally with the extremely low level of industrial development throughout independent sub-Saharan African where industry is by and large limited to the production of light consumer goods.

The critical question is what these differences add to. Twenty years ago, the economists Reginald H. Gren and Ann Seidman (1968) wrote their classic work, *Unity or Poverty*, to suggest that the "gravest barrier to African economic development" was the continent's lack of economic integration. So long as Africa remained balkanized into small economic units, its prospects of development were minimal:

> No African state is economically large enough to construct a modern economy alone. Africa as a whole has the resources for industrialization, but it is split among more than forty African territories. Africa as a whole could provide markets able to support large-scale efficient industrial complexes; no single African state nor existing sub-regional economic union can do so. (Green and Seidman 1968:22).

For Green and Seidman, the limited size of markets within small nation-states ensured, by deterring industrialization, that Africa would remain economically dependent upon Europe both for markets for its own products and for manufactured goods.

China's Agricultural Revolution

If the need for larger economic units can be discerned from the considerable differences between China and Africa, there is also much to be learned from their similarities. Of these, by far the most important is the fact that, during the 1960s and 1970s, China suffered profoundly from agricultural stagnation. It has been estimated that, between 1957 and 1978, the per capita real income of Chinese peasants rose by only about 0.5 percent per year. The following passage could easily describe Africa during the same period.

> Aside from the adverse effect of this slow income growth on peasant incentives and morale, the stagnation in agricultural production led to a decline in marketing rate, which, in turn, posed growing problems for urban food supplies. . . Along with edible oils, sugar and cotton, grain imports rose throughout the 1970s, and it is estimated that, by the mid-1970s, over one-third of urban grain consumption came from imports (Perry and Wong 1985).

These same authors concluded that since prolonged agricultural stagnation could not be accounted for by natural factors or by a lack of progress in the production of agricultural inputs, it was the product of serious organizational and incentive problems.

The most conspicuous system of China's agricultural crisis was its mounting grain imports. During the mid-1970s, China's need for imported grains had begun to skyrocket. Its grain imports rose from only about 4 million tons in 1976/77 to almost 12 million tons only two years later, in 1978/79. By the early 1980s, China's grain imports were averaging between 14 and 16 million tons per year (USDA 1985:19). Although grain imports did enable China to avoid massive famines and, indeed, to prevent widespread caloric deficits, there were serious nutritional deficiencies in the Chinese diet. Moreover, the cost of grain imports represented a serious drain of resources away from the country's efforts to develop its industrial sector. There were critical shortages of industrial and capital goods and major scarcities in other areas, especially housing.

Between 1979 and 1984, China engineered an agricultural revolution of monumental proportions. Some of the broad outlines

of this revolution can be discerned from the figures in Table 4.1.[2]
Within a brief period, China moved from being a food-deficit
country to one beginning to produce prodigious agricultural
surpluses for export. Between 1978 and 1984, total agricultural output
increased by 40 percent or approximately thirty-nine per capita. The
increase in grain production was particularly dramatic. During the
five-year period from 1979 to 1984, grain production increased by
about 23 percent, more than 4.5 percent per year. Rice production
increased 24 percent, wheat production 40 percent, and corn
production 21 percent.

One of the remarkable aspects of these production increases is
that they were achieved entirely by an increase in yields. The total
acreage allotted to these crops decreased by about 5 percent for all
grains during this period. To achieve a 22.6 percent increase in total

Table 4.1. Agricultural Production Changes in China 1979-1984

Commodity	1979	1983	1984	Total % Change 1979-84	Annual Growth Rate
TOTAL GRAIN PRODUCTION					
Volume (million metric tons)	332.1	387.3	407.1	22.6%	4.5%
Sown Area (mil. hectares)	119.3	114.0	113.4	-4.9%	-1.0%
Volume per Hectare	2.8	3.4	3.6	29.0%	5.8%
RICE PRODUCTION					
Volume (million metric tons)	143.8	168.9	178.0	23.8%	4.8%
Sown Area (mil. hectares)	33.9	33.1	32.3	-4.7%	-0.9%
Volume per Hectare	4.2	5.1	5.5	29.9%	6.0%
WHEAT PRODUCTION					
Volume (million metric tons)	62.7	81.4	87.7	39.9%	8.0%
Sown Area (mil. hectares)	29.4	29.1	29.4	-0.2%	0.0%
Volume per Hectare	2.1	2.8	3.0	40.1%	8.0%
CORN PRODUCTION					
Volume (million metric tons)	60.0	68.2	72.3	20.5%	4.1%
Sown Area (mil. hectares)	20.1	18.8	18.5	-8.0%	-1.6%
Volume per Hectare	3.0	3.6	3.9	30.9%	6.2%
CLOSED PRODUCTION[a]					
Volume (million metric tons)	6.4	10.6	11.9	85.9%	17.2%
Sown Area (mil. hectares)	7.1	8.4	8.4	18.3%	3.7%
Volume per Hectare	0.9	1.3	1.4	57.2%	11.4%
COTTON PRODUCTION					
Volume (million metric tons)	2.2	4.6	6.0	172.7%	34.5%
Sown Area (mil. hectares)	4.5	6.1	6.8	51.1%	10.2%
Volume per Hectare	0.5	0.8	0.9	80.5%	16.1%

Note: [a]Does not include soybeans and cottonseed.

grain production while reducing the number of hectares assigned to grains by almost 5 percent, China had to increase production per hectare, on a national basis, by almost 5 percent. The culmination of China's agricultural revolution occurred in 1984 when total grain production reached an all-time record of approximately 407 million tons. Total grain production that year was nearly 35 percent higher than it had been only seven year earlier. The agricultural revolution was by no means confined to the major grains but extended to a wide variety of other crops as well. Oilseed production, for example, increased a staggering 86 percent, rendering China self-sufficient in edible oils. Cotton production nearly tripled during this period, increasing from about 2.2 million metric tons in 1979 to 6 million metric tons in 1984.

The economic benefits of the agricultural revolution have been considerable. Within five years, China moved from being a heavy net importer of agricultural products to a position as a major exporter of agricultural goods. As late as 1980, China's deficit on agricultural trade was about $1.25 billion. Only four years later, in 1984, China's trade surplus in agricultural commodities was well over $2.2 billion. Indeed, it has now become a major world exporter of cotton, corn, and soybeans, commodities that only a few years ago it imported in significant volume.

Inevitably, a production revolution of this magnitude has had profound ramifications for the quality of life in Chinese society. One of the most significant changes is the improvement of rural incomes. The World Bank's report on Chinese agriculture, cited earlier, estimated that rural incomes increased in real terms by about 70 percent, or about 14 percent per year, between 1979 and 1983. This has facilitated a striking qualitative improvement in the diet of China's rural population. Rural per capita consumption of red meat increased more than 50 percent; of fish, over 125 percent; and of poultry, over 150 percent. Increases in income have also made it possible for China's rural population to avail itself of a wide variety of consumer goods, and the Chinese Government has estimated that the number of sewing machines, bicycles, and radios per capita roughly tripled during this period of time. Today, even the most casual visitors to the Chinese countryside are struck by an atmosphere of growing material comfort and heightened prosperity.

There are reasons to believe that the agricultural revolution may have helped bring about a greater degree of social equality in Chinese society. One is that it has helped to narrow the traditionally wide gap between rural and urban incomes. Between 1979 and 1984, rural per capita incomes in China increased at a rate of about 15 percent per year while urban incomes grew at a rate of only about 8 percent. A second factor is that the benefits of the revolution were concentrated, at least initially, in the poorer regions of the country and among grain-producing farm families who were traditionally among the poorest rural families. The socially equalizing impact of the agricultural revolution may be somewhat ironic, since it is beginning to appear that social equality is no longer a major objective of Chinese leadership. In numerous interviews with this observer, officials of the Chinese government state that "it is permissible for some persons to become wealthy first," indicating that the growing affluence of a few might, in some sense, be acceptable as a precondition for broader economic growth. This attitude appears especially strong in the countryside where credit for the massive production increases is officially assigned to improved economic incentives for individual producers.[3]

The initial phase of China's agricultural revolution came to an end in 1984 because by then the agricultural revolution had achieved its major political and economic objectives. It enabled China to become self-sufficient in staple foodstuffs, thereby ending its long-term dependence on external suppliers, most notably the United States. It also enabled the country to become self-sufficient in important industrial crops such as cotton and, in this way, to provide on its own the raw material requirements of one of its major urban industries. The agricultural revolution also enabled China to become a new exporter of agricultural commodities, not only ending the perennial drain of agricultural imports on foreign exchange reserves but improving the country's foreign exchange position. And, though opinions differ, prosperity in the countryside appears to have generated a ground swell of rural support for a regime that is intent on introducing fundamental and far-reaching changes in other areas of Chinese life.

All these important objectives having been attained, the pace of agrarian change can be expected to slow somewhat in the future. If this should occur, it will be the result of deliberate economic planning, not a failure of agricultural policy. Chinese economic planners do not feel that China's overall process of economic growth will be abetted by continuing to place a major emphasis on agricultural transformation. Since China's domestic agricultural needs have now, for all practical purposes, been satisfied through increased production, further increases in agricultural output could only be handled as exports onto the world market. China's record in producing high volumes of agricultural commodities for export indicates that it could continue to be successful in this area. But the critical question is whether this would generate a high rate of economic growth.

To answer this question, Chinese policymakers have turned to the classic economic principle of comparative advantage. In their view, it would be a serious mistake for China to enter the world trading system as a seller of primary agricultural commodities, because the severe glut of these commodities on the world market is likely to suppress the prices of these products for the foreseeable future. This means that the rate of return on resources invested in the agricultural sector is likely to be low. There is a very strong conviction that if the level of agricultural exports continues to rise dramatically, this will reflect a serious misallocation of resources. The official judgment of some of China's high-ranking policy planners is that China's comparative advantage lies in its large supply of extremely low-cost industrial labor. It is their judgment that resources invested in the industrial sector are, therefore, likely to produce a much higher rate of return than resources invested in agriculture. In this respect, China's conception of its long-term economic future conforms closely to that of other large-scale newly industrializing countries such as Brazil and India. All three of these countries share the view that agricultural exports are likely to sustain a continuing high rate of economic growth.

China's Agricultural Relevance

China's agricultural revolution has direct relevance for contemporary Africa. One basic lesson becomes immediately clear: the performance of the agricultural sector is absolutely fundamental. Before anything else can happen, the agricultural sector must be performing well. China may now be in position to enter a different phase of a longer-term process of rapid economic growth. But before it could do so, it had to formulate and implement a program of massive reform of its agricultural policies and practices.

The Chinese believe that their recent agricultural success has considerable relevance for contemporary Africa. In their view, there is a fundamental socioeconomic similarity between these two world regions. In China, as in most of independent Africa, more than 80 percent of the total population are agriculturists and continue to depend upon farming as their basic means of economic livelihood. Chinese academics and policy planners insist that China's recent experiences demonstrate that it is possible, on the basis of agricultural development alone, to provide a major and rapid improvement in the material conditions of peasant smallholders who constitute an overwhelming percentage of the total population. They also insist that there is no mystery to what is involved in triggering agricultural growth. The one absolutely vital and indispensable ingredient in bringing about improved agricultural performance is the introduction of a system of economic incentives that reward individual producers for increased production.

The Responsibility System

The basic building block of China's agricultural revolution was a new system of producer incentives generally called "the responsibility system" that was introduced experimentally in 1978 and given widespread official implementation in 1979.[4] The term is, in fact, a shorthand designation for a longer expression that translates roughly as "contracted responsibility for household production *with remuneration linked to output*" (author's emphasis). In an agricultural society as variegated as China, it is to be taken for granted that the implementation of the responsibility system differs considerably from one region of the country to another, indeed, from district to district or even from farm to farm. But the essential feature of the new system, wherever applied, was to change the basic unit of production from the large-scale collective farm, where individuals were treated as wage laborers on a state enterprise, to the family household in possession of its own land and producing for itself.

The contracted responsibility system works in roughly the following way. The collective farm, or commune (now renamed township) is subdivided into a number of small farm units that will eventually be assigned, generally on a long-term leasehold basis, to individual households. A subunit of the township, the production team, then allocates these farms to the households on a contractual basis, generally stipulating a certain minimal level of production that must be sold to the production team, or township, at a fixed price. The flexible feature of the responsibility system is that it allows the households to sell their produce on the open market once the contracted quota has been satisfied. As a result, there is a direct connection between labor input, level of production, and household earnings.

The Chinese today are vocal in criticizing the disincentive effects of the agricultural system that was in place until the responsibility system was introduced. Under the old system, the state was a monopolistic buyer and seller for all basic agricultural commodities.

There was a highly centralized system of production quotas established by the national Ministry of Agriculture and passed downward through the administrative hierarchy by subagencies of the central and provincial governments. At the collective farm level, this translated into a rigid pattern of fixed production quotas that, by decree, had to be delivered to designated state agencies at a fixed price. This system provided no incentives whatsoever for the efficient use of agricultural inputs, for changes in the crop mix so as to maximize the value of farm output, or, most importantly, for individual farmers to maximize production. Indeed, Chinese academics and civil servants now speak with contempt of the "iron rice bowl" characteristic of the old system, the fact that every worker on the collective farm was given a basic minimum wage regardless of the quality of his or her contribution and regardless of the aggregate level of farm output.

The Role of the State

The Chinese agricultural system appears to have been far more rigid and state-directed than anything attempted by African governments, though it did provide a rough working model for the socialist village programs in Tanzania and, later, Mozambique. No African country, for example, sets production quotas by region or district. And in few, if any, have peasants been converted into wage workers on state farms. Indeed, in most African countries, state farms, though often justified for their research and demonstration effects, have failed to assume significant economic proportions. Nor, aside from the tendency to restrict the sale of basic commodities to state agencies, have African governments significantly interfered with the economic freedoms of the peasant household. African farmers, for example, have generally had a high degree of freedom in their selection of crops and have enjoyed wide latitude to supplement agricultural income with income from other sources such as animal husbandry or wage labor.

Despite these considerable differences, there are distinct similarities between statist agriculture in China and some of the policies that have been adopted by African governments. The most important of these, by far, has to do with the establishment of state monopolies over the pricing, purchasing, processing, and marketing of agricultural commodities. The vast majority of African governments, even those that reject identification with socialist agriculture, have sought to create effective state control over the pricing, procurement, and marketing of major commodities. These monopolies have generally been exercised through parastatal corporations rather than through the formal state apparatus. But the underlying motivation has been identical, namely, the downward suppression of agricultural prices.[5] There has been a long-standing and all-pervasive reluctance to allow for the play of market forces that might increase price levels either for basic food staples or for important export crops. Like statist agriculture in China, this set of policies has had significant disincentive effects on agricultural production.

Although the Chinese and African systems of agricultural control exhibited marked organizational and administrative differences, the goals of state regulation of the agricultural sector were remarkably similar. In each case, the basic idea of regulation seems to have been to (1) ensure an adequate supply of cheap food for the major cities so as to reduce the possibility of urban political discontent; (2) to minimize urban inflation, and objective that is also connected to the maintenance of political order; and, (3) to extract from agriculture an economic surplus that could be used to finance the development of the industrial sector. This was most conspicuously evident in China during the 1950s when the agricultural surplus was used to finance the "great leap forward," an ill-fated attempt to industrialize that, because of the suppression of the agricultural sector it involved, is now estimated to have possibly caused the deaths of millions because of hunger and hunger-related diseases. The corresponding policy in Africa has been the effort to industrialize through import-substitution, a policy that has also involved serious capital depletion of the countryside.

Price and Rural Welfare

It would be a mistake to interpret China's new agricultural policies as a wholesale embrace of free-market practices, particularly with regard to commodity pricing. China has not moved any further toward free-market agricultural pricing than other highly successful agricultural exporters such as the United States or the countries of the European Economic Community (EEC). Indeed, under the conditions that prevail in the contemporary international marketplace, where world market prices for a wide variety of agricultural commodities reflect high levels of subsidies by some of the most active exporters, the very notion of free-market prices for any goods that are traded internationally, makes little sense whatsoever. In China, as in virtually every country that has sought to use the pricing mechanism as a stimulus for heightened levels of agricultural production, state intervention in the setting of producer prices has had an extremely important role (Lardy 1983).

This point may be of extreme importance to African governments that continue to be mistrustful of the free market and continue to believe in the need for some degree of state involvement in the agricultural sector. The new Chinese pricing model is not a free-market model; rather, it is a model that combines state-set producer prices with free-market prices in various complex combinations. It would be pointless here to attempt to describe in detail China's current system of producer pricing. Not only is this system subject to enormous variation by region and crop, but it is being continuously subjected to modification with a view toward both simplification and a greater role for the free market. Suffice it to say that, during the period of the agricultural revolution, China had essentially a four-tier system of producer prices that operated roughly as follows.

1. A state quota price: each farmer was required to sell a fixed amount of his or her production to the state at a state-set price. State purchases at the quota price level amounted to approximately 48 percent of agricultural production by value.
2. Above-quota price: each farmer was required to sell an additional amount to the state, generally at a price level between 25 percent and 50 percent higher than the quota prices. These purchases amounted to approximately 28 percent of agricultural production by value.
3. Sales negotiated with the state at the free-market price: these amounted to about 13 percent of agricultural production by value.
4. Free-market sales.

Since 1984, the Chinese government has sought to simplify this somewhat cumbersome system, principally by moving toward a single state price that would be a weighted average of quota and above-quota prices.

The purpose of describing the Chinese system of producer pricing is not to suggest its relevance for Africa. It would probably be administratively impossible for most African governments to attempt to replicate this highly complicated system of producer pricing. And, in any case, it is doubtful that the system would achieve the same purpose in Africa it has in China. The relevance of Chinese pricing practices for Africa is that Chinese farmers have been able to sell a larger and larger proportion of their production on the free market without the need to deal with monopolistic state agencies as intermediaries.

The critical distinction being suggested here is not between regulated and unregulated prices. It is, rather, between price levels that reflect realistic market considerations, and therefore act as incentives to agricultural producers, and those that do not. It may be just as important, then, that the Chinese government has increasingly tended to take its clues for quota prices from the free market and to set these quota prices at levels that are a reasonably high proportion of those prevailing there. The lesson being conveyed about producer prices in so many African countries is that those prices are often so out of touch with those that would prevail if a free market operated as to have become powerful disincentives for producers.[6]

The critical question for Africa is not how to replicate the structure of the Chinese model but how to combine state involvement in producer pricing with a more pronounced role for market forces. Since governmental intervention in the agricultural marketplace in Africa tends to take place through the modality of parastatal corporations, this becomes a question about the appropriate role of this kind of quasi-governmental agency. In an effort to reduce the role of government and increase the role of the private sector in agricultural marketing, World Bank economists and representatives of other aid agencies have suggested that African parastatals become "buyers and sellers of last resort." The idea here is that the parastatal would declare a minimum or floor price at which it would be prepared to purchase and a maximum or ceiling price at which it would be prepared to sell. In this way, it would establish outer parameters within which private traders would be forced to operate. This idea is valid as far as it goes, since it assumes that floor and ceiling prices would bear some correspondence to market realities. But it would be useful to make that assumption more explicit as an integral component of the floor and ceiling system of official pricing.

The Chinese approach to rural taxation is a derivative in spirit of its approach to producer pricing, in that great care is taken to see that taxes are not so burdensome as to reduce the incentive to increase personal income through increased production for the market. Chinese peasants are subject to a variety of taxes and public obligations. The principal taxes are to the central and provincial governments, but peasants are also expected to make a financial contribution to the welfare fund of their township and to make labor time available for collective tasks such as the maintenance of physical infrastructure and irrigation systems and the repair of public buildings. Although this may appear burdensome, the tax load on peasant producers is extremely light, amounting to only about 3 percent, in aggregate, of agricultural incomes. Indeed, the tax burden on agricultural producers is so light that the World Bank regards it as a major constraint on governmental revenues (World Bank 1985).

Government officials explain this policy by reference to China's modern history and stress repeatedly that one of the most deeply embedded memories in the contemporary Chinese political consciousness concerns their country's long tradition of exploitive landlordism. Much of the legitimizing imagery of the Chinese revolution depicts the appalling conditions under which peasants lived before the communist movement came to power in the late 1940s. And there is constant iteration of the view that one of the principal motivations for the communist revolution was the determination to eliminate a system of taxation that immiserated the peasantry to create state revenues or income for a feudal nobility. Thus, the Chinese government's unwillingness to impose heavy taxes on the countryside may be an important legacy, in the area of agricultural policy, of its revolutionary tradition. One reflection of this tradition is that Chinese observers of socialist countries in Africa, such as Ethiopia and Tanzania, are sometimes privately appalled at the level of taxation imposed directly or indirectly on rural producers. In their view, the purpose of a socialist revolution is to lower the tax burden on the peasantry, not increase it.

China's commitment to improving rural incomes is evident in a variety of other policy areas as well. One of the more important of these is industrial policy. The government has committed itself to a program of establishing large numbers of small-scale industries in the rural townships. Typical examples include factories for the manufacture of parts for automobiles, trucks, and tractors, but the list of rurally manufactured goods also includes small machines, textiles, and a wide variety of consumer durables. The program of ruralizing industry serves a variety of purposes. Since the labor needs of the agricultural sector are highly cyclical, with labor requirements peaking during planting and harvesting seasons, the new factories provide secondary employment opportunities for rural dwellers during periods when the need for agricultural labor is relatively low. By providing additional sources of income in the countryside, the rural factories have also helped to slow the process of urban migration. Since these factories can take advantage of low rural wages, industrial decentralization is also an important means of implementing the government's commitment to the principle that its international comparative advantage lies in the availability of a large supply of low-wage industrial labor.

African governments, by contrast, have done little to improve rural incomes by locating manufacturing industries in the country side. Such rural industries as do exist are largely in the catch-all category of informal sector and function principally to provide services or cheap goods for the agricultural sector. As such, they receive practically nothing in the way of official governmental support. Indeed, those informal industries in the rural areas that do seek to develop a manufacturing capability are often politically harassed as a means of providing economic protection for urban industries that receive governmental support.

The results are frequently anomalous. It is by now fairly well established that one of the causes of Africa's crisis of stagnating agricultural production is the labor constraint, caused by the fact that persons in the economically vigorous age categories leave the rural areas to seek urban employment. Because of the high cost of living in the cities, industrial wages must also be relatively high. Not only does the high wage pattern contribute to the ongoing influx of rural migrants to the cities, but it has made it difficult for Africa's industries to enter international markets, even on a regional basis. This, in turn, has reinforced the tendency of Africa's industries to function only in the area of import substitution, which means that they tend to be a net drain on national foreign exchange reserves rather than a source of hard currency. There is little doubt that African governments could take an important step toward solving a variety of economic problems by taking steps to emulate China's policy of rural industrialization.

Conclusion

China does not provide a precise model whose recapitulation in Africa would be a key to triggering economic growth in the agricultural sector. Not only are there immense differences in national scale, political organization, and bureaucratic capacity, but many of the factors that operated as constraints on agricultural growth in China until the late 1970s do not exist in Africa. China during the cultural revolution from 1966 to 1978 suffered from a degree of ideological rigidity, enforced central planning, and coercive state control that cannot be found in any contemporary African state. But there are enough similarities to make the comparison worthwhile. Among the causes of agricultural stagnation common to both are the attempt to implement official systems of commodity pricing and the establishment of commodity prices that have posed severe economic disincentives for rural producers. In both China and Africa, agricultural policy during the 1960s and 1970s can be said to have reflected pronounced tendencies toward urban bias: the inclination to treat agriculture as a source of cheap food for the cities and as an economic surplus with which to finance the cost of urban industries.

Even a superficial examination of China's agricultural revolution, then, can be helpful in establishing guidelines for an agricultural recovery in Africa. The first and most basic lesson is the need to revise agricultural prices upward in such a way that the prices of basic agricultural commodities provide an economic incentive for their producers. For those governments that consider state control of commodity prices essential to their political survival, this need not be a matter of price decontrol. It could as easily take the form of upward revision of state-set prices. The notion of price incentives, by itself, may be somewhat misleading, because an integral part of China's agricultural revolution has been an unprecedented boom in the availability of consumer goods. For increased commodity prices to be effective as stimulants of heightened levels of production, it is essential that peasant producers be able to use their increased income to buy the goods and services that they value.

China's agricultural revolution also serves to re-legitimate the enduring value of the classical economic principle of comparative advantage. For China, this principle has involved a determination that, because the country's principal advantage lies in the availability of low-cost labor, it is appropriate to begin gradually to redirect economic resources away from agriculture toward the industrial sector. China's economic planners today have no doubts about the necessity to participation in the international marketplace as a condition for economic growth. The only critical question was whether this participation would take the form of agricultural or industrial exports.

Sub-Saharan Africa today is in a different position. Since the agricultural revolution has yet to begin, decisions about the allocation of resources to industry are premature. But the principle of comparative advantage may nevertheless offer instructive lessons. A great many African countries are adopting an opposite principle as their guiding agricultural strategy, namely, the principle of food self-sufficiency. This goal, for all its apparent humanitarian appeal, is simply the principle of import-substitution applied to the agricultural sector. The goal of food self-sufficiency appeals to those who feel that specialization for export is a colonial legacy and one that has resulted in a hemorrhage of economic resources from the continent. Those who hold this view tend to believe that African countries are better-off when they identify opportunities to withdraw from the international marketplace.

For countries interested in maximizing their economic growth, a diversion of economic resources away from export crops to food production has little to recommend it. The goal of food self-sufficiency in Africa is partially sustained and spread by the unstated assumption that, when the crops being grown are food staples for local consumption, the foreign exchange costs are minimal. The opposite is often the case, however. For a number of reasons, the cultivation and marketing of food crops in Africa are often far more import-intensive than the production of export crops for the world market. Among other factors, food staples such as maize and rice, whose local price is now between $150 and $200 per ton, often have very low value-to-weight rations. As a result, transportation costs, made up principally of foreign exchange expenditures on vehicles, parts, and fuel, are extremely high per unit when compared to high value-to-weight commodities such as coffee or tea, whose world market prices are now more than $2,000 per ton, or cocoa, whose world market price is well over $4,000 per ton. An agricultural strategy of food self-sufficiency raises a host of difficult and as yet unanswered questions about foreign exchange availability, not to mention the opportunity costs involved when scarce economic resources are deliberately invested in the production of commodities whose net return to investment is low.

The Chinese example suggests unambiguously that African countries should rethink their commitment to the principle of food self-sufficiency and concentrate instead on the production of high-value exports such as coffee, tea, cocoa, and other tropical commodities in high demand in the industrial world. The most common response to this proposition has to do with the commodities crisis and with the fact that the glut of commodities on the market tends to push prices downward. The Chinese economic experience, however, offers an interesting perspective on this issue. By its emphasis on industrial development, China has, in effect, announced its intention not to compete intensively in the world market as an exporter of agricultural commodities. There is reason to believe that other large countries that are now heavy agricultural exporters may be in the midst of a similar decision. Brazil and India, for example, seem also to be taking cues from the Chinese and to be dramatically realigning internal resources toward the production of industrial goods for export. If so, there will be major niches in the international market for tropical agricultural goods. In this scenario, it is not difficult to anticipate the day when Africa will export tea to China, now the world's largest producer.

Notes

1. The author wishes to express his deepest thanks to the Institute of West Asian and African Studies of the Chinese Academy of Social Sciences and to the Chinese Association for International Understanding for the opportunity to visit China on consecutive occasions in the fall of 1984 and, again in the fall of 1985. I am profoundly grateful to the many Chinese academics and government officials who shared their time and reflections for this study.

2. The figures in this table have been compiled from The World Bank (1985), Table 1.4 and the United States Department of Agriculture (1985: 35-36), Tables 8 and 9. The percentage figures for annual growth rates are not compounded. The author wishes to thank Mark Catlett of the Graduate School of Architecture and Urban Planning, University of Florida, Gainesville, for his assistance in compiling this table.

3. The agricultural revolution does appear to have been accompanied by growing income inequality in the countryside, especially after 1981. See David Sunding, "Rural Income Distribution in China, 1978-1984" (Department of Agricultural Economics, University of California, Berkeley, 1986, unpublished MS).

4. For a full discussion, see Hartford (1985).

5. For a full treatment of this policy and its consequences for agricultural production, see de Wilde (1984).

6. This, after all, is the central thesis of Robert Bates's now-classic volume, *Markets and States in Tropical Africa* (1981).

References

Bates, R. 1981. *Markets and States In Tropical Africa: The Political Basis of Agricultural Policies*. Berkeley and Los Angeles: University of California Press.

DeWilde, J.C. 1984. *Agriculture, Marketing and Pricing in Sub-Saharan Africa*. Los Angeles: African Studies Center and African Studies Association.

Green, R.H. and A. Seidman. 1968. *Unity or Poverty: The Economics of Pan-Africanism*. Baltimore: Penguin Books.

Hartford, K. 1985. Socialist Agriculture is Dead; Long Live Socialist Agriculture! In *The Political Economy of Reform in PostMao China*. Elizabeth J. Perry and Christine Wong, eds. Cambridge, Mass.: Council on East African Studies, Harvard University.

Jackson, R.H. and Carl G. Rosberg. 1986. Sovereignty and Underdevelopment: Juridical Statehood in the African Crisis. *Journal of Modern African Studies* 24:1:1-2.

102   MICHAEL F. LOFCHIE

Lardy, N.R. 1983. *Agricultural Prices in China.* Baltimore: The Johns Hopkins University Press.
Perry, E.J. and C. Wong, eds. 1985. *The Political Economy of Reform in Post-Mao China.* Cambridge, Mass.: Council on East African Studies, Harvard University.
Sunding, D. 1986. Rural Income Distribution in China, 1978-1984. Berkeley: University of California, Department of Agricultural Economics. Unpublished MS.
USDA (United States Department of Agriculture). 1981. *Food Problems and Prospects in Sub-Saharan Africa: The Decade of the 1980s.* Washington, D.C.: Government Printing Office.
————. 1985. *China: Outlook and Situation Report.* Economic Research Service. Washington, D.C.: Government Printing Office.
World Bank. 1981. *Accelerated Development in Sub-Saharan Africa: An Agenda for Action.* Baltimore: The Johns Hopkins University Press.
————. 1984. *Toward Sustained Development in Sub-Saharan Africa.* Baltimore: The Johns Hopkins University Press.
————. 1985. *China: Long-Term Development Issues and Options.* Baltimore: The Johns Hopkins University Press.

CHAPTER 5

From Drought to Famine in Kenya

ROBERT H. BATES[1]

A drought can be defined as a failure of the rains so great that crops also fail. A famine can be defined as hunger and/or starvation resulting from a lack of food. This paper studies the relationship between droughts and famines in Kenya.

Not all droughts in Kenya have become famines. A relatively unsystematic reading of the evidence suggests the occurrence of major droughts in 1889, 1894, 1898, 1914–1919, 1928, 1931–1934, 1939/40, 1943/44, 1948, 1954, 1960/61, 1964/65, 1970/71, 1973/74, 1979/80 and 1984.[2] Some, but far from all, of these droughts have led to famines.

Three sets of factors appear to influence the likelihood of drought resulting in famine. Only one set is in the short run under human control. This paper focuses on the behavior and impact of the "controllables": the public policies and political institutions that affect the relationship between rainfall and food supply.

Determinants of the Transition

The Magnitude of the Drought

A major factor affecting the likelihood of drought resulting in famine is the magnitude of the drought. An appropriate measure is the number of plantings by farmers that fail to result in harvests. One determinant of magnitude is duration. Most rural families store enough food to survive the loss of a season's planting. In Kenya, many store sufficient food to survive through a failure of both the long and short rains. In drought-prone regions, many manage their grain stocks in such a way that they can lose yet a third harvest while retaining sufficient seed to replant once again. When the rains fail a fourth time, however, even the most prudential managers of family grain stores face the prospect of famine.

A second measure of magnitude is geographic spread. The broader the sweep of the drought the greater the number of farmers who risk losing their plantings. The Kenya drought of 1984/85 was a particularly dangerous one, for instance, not only because it led to a third loss of crop in the low-lying areas but also because it ranged into areas that lay at higher elevations. It spread into the densely populated Central Province, thereby leading to a far greater loss of harvest (see Figure 5.1).

Vulnerability to Drought

Other factors increase the likelihood that drought will result in famine. These are linked not to the stimulus—i.e., the rainfall—but rather to the population subject to that stimulus.

One is simply the skill of the farmers in managing their food stores or in employing strategies for handling food shortages.[3] Illustrative of the importance of these factors, once again, is the drought of 1984/85 in Kenya. When the drought penetrated the Central Province, it not only placed a larger number of harvests at peril but also attacked a population that was infrequently subject to drought and therefore had fewer skills for coping with shortfalls in the rains.

Also affecting the vulnerability of a population is its technology of food production. Populations that have shifted to arable production are more vulnerable to fluctuations in the supply of moisture than are those that engage in pastoralist production. Pastoralists can shift their enterprises to where rainfall has fallen. In the drought of 1984/85, for example, many herders shifted their "crops" to the coast, where rainfall levels had remained closer to normal levels. Arable production, by contrast, involves standing crops; unless the rain comes to the farm site, the crops are lost. Moreover, where arable has significantly displaced pastoralist production, livestock can no longer wander in search of grazing materials; many are stall fed and special grasses are grown for them. With the onset of drought, such grasses are lost; and because the livestock cannot forage, many perish. Populations are therefore more at risk when arable production replaces herding as the economic basis of rural life.

FIGURE 5.1 Seasonal Rainfall—March, April, and May, 1984

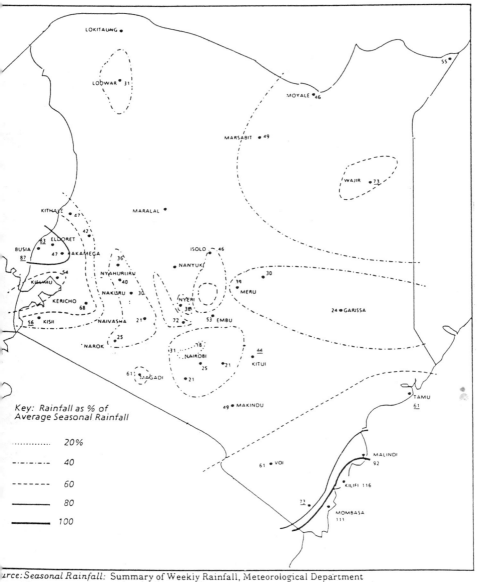

Key: Rainfall as % of
Average Seasonal Rainfall

```
..............   20%

-·-·-·-·-·-   40

----------   60

————————   80

————————   100
```

⌐rce:Seasonal Rainfall: Summary of Weekly Rainfall, Meteorological Department
   Averages: Ministry of Agriculture Farm Management volumes, Climatological Statistics for Kenya,
   Annual Rainfall Summary for 1972

A third factor increasing the likelihood that famine will result from drought is the size of the population and the relative rates of growth of population and agricultural productivity. For a given agricultural technology, population size affects the translation of drought into famine by affecting the drought's magnitude: the larger the size of the population, the greater the number of harvests lost. The relationship between the rates of population and productivity growth affects the population's degree of vulnerability. If the population increases at a rate faster than technical change, farming then must spread from areas of high-quality soils and abundant and reliable moisture supplies to more marginal agricultural regions. In the absence of technical change, the old farming areas cannot produce sufficient food' to support the larger population. This dynamic is reflected in Kenya by the movement of farming from the highlands into the semi-arid zones.[4] The result of population growth and static agricultural technology is thus an increase in the number of people at risk to climatic fluctuation.

As population increases, moreover, there is an acceleration in the shift from pastoral to arable production. Pastoralism requires a low ratio of people to land; population can increase, but the quantity of land remains constant; and population increases therefore render pastoralism more costly to pursue and arable production an increasingly attractive alternative. The result, once again, is an increase in vulnerability to drought.

The impact of these variables can perhaps best be seen by comparing the impact of two droughts of similar duration and geographic spread that take place in two different periods, the first before an increase in population and the second after. If the rate of population increase has exceeded that of the increase in the productivity of farming, then more people are at risk, greater numbers will have shifted to marginal agricultural zones, and arable will have replaced pastoral production. The second drought would thus pose a far greater threat even though the two droughts are of the same spread and duration.

The Management of Food Stocks

For fear of drought, human beings have invested in witchcraft, prayer, and technical innovation; they have yet, however, to control the rains.[5] People can control population growth and invent agricultural techniques; but neither measure in the short run can help to avoid the suffering occasioned by the failure of rains. In the short run the prime factor that can effectively be controlled is the level of food stocks. It is clear that given two droughts of equal magnitude, one of which occurs when stocks are high and the other when they are low, the latter will be more likely to result in famine. As Mbithi (Mbithi and Wisner 1973; 1974) and others have documented, individual farm families in Kenya employ a variety of techniques for managing their food supplies. The concern of this essay is more with national policymakers than with individual farm families, however, and we therefore focus on the way in which government officials manage national food stocks. In understanding how droughts transform into famines, we look for factors which have made it possible for national stocks to be low when the rains fail.

A Fruitful Puzzle

We begin with a puzzle, one pertaining to the behavior of the national bureaucracy charged with the maintenance of national food stocks, which we will call the Maize Board.[6] We focus on the Maize Board because maize is the basic staple grain of Kenya.

It seems plausible that variations in rainfall would have a major impact on the stocks held by the Maize Board. In fact, contrary to expectations, there is *no* apparent statistical relationship between variations in the rainfall and in the level of stocks held by the Board, and no alteration of the lag structure in the measures employed alter this finding[7] (Table 5.1).

It seems plausible that variations in the rainfall would have a major impact on the intake of grain by the Maize Board; that is, that the Board would be able to purchase more grain in years in which farmers experienced abundant rains. Once again, however, expectations are confounded. The data yield *no* apparent statistical relationship between variations in the rainfall and in the level of purchases by the Board. Whether the Board purchases a lot or a little maize is not significantly affected by the weather. Experimentation with a variety of alternative specifications failed to alter this finding (Table 5.2).

How, then, do droughts affect the national food stocks? Almost in desperation, we turn to a third measure of the Board's activities: its sales. And here, by contrast with our previous efforts, we find a large, highly significant relationship. In years of shortfall in the rain, sales by the Board rise dramatically. A 40 percent reduction in the rainfall over the period April to August in Kitale, these estimates suggest, would lead to a roughly 150,000 metric ton (mt) increase in sales by the Board—or over 1.6 million bags[8] (Table 5.3).

Table 5.1 Dependent Variable Changes in Stock ('000 mt)

Constant	-0.334
	(-0.0009)
Rainfall (mm)	-0.001
	(-0.027)

Note: F=0.000; R^2=0.000; t-statistics in parentheses. Ten observations.

Table 5.2. Dependent Variable Purchases by the Board ('000 mt)

Constant	524.008
	(3.041)
Rainfall (mm)	-0.239
	(-0.963)

Note: F=0.830; R^2=0.192; t-statistics in parentheses. Ten observations.

Table 5.3. Dependent Variable Sales by the Board ('000 mt)

Constant	738.685
	(8.239)***
Rainfall (mm)	-0.579
	(-4.362)

Note: F=11.759; R^2=0.77; t-statistics in parentheses. *** significant at .01 level. Ten observations.

The stocks of the Board can stand between the onset of drought and the outbreak of famine. And drought itself influences the activities of the Board. But it does not do so by affecting sales *to* the Board; rather, it affects the volume of sales *by* the Board. The Board can leave Kenya vulnerable to drought by failing to possess sufficient stocks of grain to cover the surge of consumer demand for its stocks at times when the rains fail.

Illustrative is the data contained in Figures 5.2, 5.3, and 5.4, which portray the impact of the drought of 1984. As can be seen in Figure 5.2, despite the drought, purchases by the Board in 1984 initially exceeded those in previous years, although they fell off precipitiously. As seen in Figure 5.3, it was sales by the Board that differed most strikingly from previous years; sales reached the

FIGURE 5.2 Weekly Purchases, 1981–1984

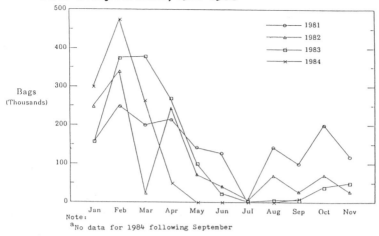

Note:
^aNo data for 1984 following September

FIGURE 5.3 Weekly Sales, 1981–1984

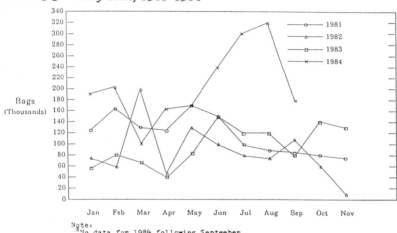

Note:
^aNo data for 1984 following September

FIGURE 5.4 Weekly Stocks, 1981–1984

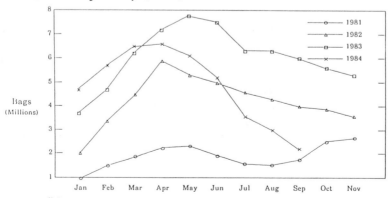

Note:
^aNo data for 1984 following September

unprecedentedly high level of 300,000 bags a week by the end of July. The result, as seen in Figure 5.4, was a rapid drawdown in the Board's stocks, with levels plummeting toward zero by the month of September.

Unscrambling the Puzzle

The data thus present a puzzle. Fluctuations in the rainfall do not affect the Board's stocks. Nor do they affect purchases by the Board. But they do affect Board sales. The reason that the Board's stocks are not significantly affected by variations in the rainfall is straightforward: increases in sales trigger imports by the Board. As seen in Table 5.4, an increase in sales of 100,000 mt (or slightly over one million bags) leads to imports of 46,000 mt (or slightly over one half million bags). Because the Board calls for imports at times of high sales, the impact of drought on stocks is depressed (Table 5.4).

The reasons why droughts affect sales but not purchases are far more informative. They are worth elaborating at greater length, for they underscore important elements of the basic structure of the maize industry and some of the dynamics that transform fluctuations in the rainfall into food shortages.

Some Elementary Structures

The Supply Side

For purposes of analysis, maize producers can be divided into large, intermediate, and small farmers. According to one report, the number of persons falling into each category in the mid-1970s was 20,000, 270,000, and 10,340,000, respectively.[9] The dividing line conventionally employed in Kenya is twenty hectares or greater for large farms; eight to twenty hectares for intermediate farms; and eight hectares or less for small farms. The large farms tend to be located in the former settled areas of the Rift Valley; maize production tends to be located in the western reaches of the valley, concentrating in Trans Nzoia and centering about Kitale. The intermediate-size farms also tend to be located in the Rift Valley or in areas immediately adjacent to it; many are the result of the subdivision of large-scale farms that took place at the time of independence. Small-scale farms are to be found everywhere in Kenya.[10]

Table 5.4. Dependent Variable Imports

Constant	-83.793
	(-1.713)*
Sales	-0.464
	(-3.333)***

Note: F=6.685***; R^2=0.49; t-statistics in parentheses.
* significant at .10 level. *** significant at .01 level. Seventeen observations.

All categories of farms produce maize. Estimates suggest that the large and intermediate farms produce 20 to 30 percent of the total crop, and the multitude of small farms 70 to 80 percent.[11] It is tempting to think of the large and intermediate farmers as "commercial farmers" and the small farms as "subsistence" producers, and many people tend to do so. Indeed, the large farmers market on the order of 75 percent of what they produce; and while representing a very small fraction of the total farming population, the large farmers supply nearly one half of the purchases by the Board. A breakdown of the sources of the 1981-1982 maize crop is presented in Table 5.5.

Nonetheless—and this is crucial—studies also suggest that smallholders vigorously participate in the market, and in particular the market for food. Over 75 percent of the smallholders both buy and sell food (Casley and Merchant 1979: 3, 9). Roughly one half of the food consumed by smallholders is purchased from off the farm, including 19 percent of the starchy staples, which include maize (Central Bureau of Statistics 1977: 62).

The Demand Side

Over 80 percent of Kenya's maize consumers live in the rural areas, the vast majority of which are small-scale farmers; roughly 10 percent live in town. The vast bulk of the maize that is marketed is therefore sold within the rural areas, largely among the smallholder families. Maize sold in the rural areas tends to be purchased in unprocessed form; of the processed maize consumed in the rural areas, less than 50 percent is commercially milled (Casley and Merchant 1979: 3, 9). This percentage rises to over 60 percent in Central Province and falls to 15 percent in Western Province. By contrast, the vast bulk of the maize that is consumed in the urban areas is processed maize, maize that has been ground and/or sifted

Table 5.5. Distribution of Total Maize Harvest by Province and Size of   l Size
Holding, 1981/82 Percentages

Size of Holding	Central	Coast	Eastern	Nyanza	Rift	Western	Total
Small	9	2	7	12	25	12	68
Intermediate	0	0	0	0	9	2	12
Large	0	0	0	0	19	1	20
Total	9	2	7	12	54	15	100

Source: Republic of Kenya, Ministry of Finance, Grain Marketing
Study, Interim Report, Vol. 1 (Nairobi: Githongo and Associates and
Bookers International, July 1983), Appendix 2, Table 1.

in the commercial maize mills, most of which are located in the
major towns: Nairobi, Mombasa, Nakuru, Kisumu, and Eldoret. The
millers receive their consignments from the Maize Board. Should
they purchase from suppliers other than the Board, they would risk
losing their licenses.

Perturbing the System

According to Acland, maize in Kenya requires roughly 200 mm of
rainfall in the planting season. Less than that and yields decline;
much less than that and crops fail (Acland 1971: 125).[12]
    As we have seen, much of the maize that is marketed through the
Maize Board originates from Western Kenya and especially from the
large farmers in and about Kitale and from the intermediate-size
farmers in the former settlement schemes. Kitale lies at roughly 5,500
feet; on average, 650 mm of rain fall during the growing period in
Kitale, a figure that is exceeded in the areas of Western Kenya that
fall in the "rain shadow" of Nyanza Victoria.
    Many smallholders live in regions that lie at lower elevations
and receive lesser amounts of rain. The maize and cotton zones of
Machakos, for example, lie at 3,000–4,000 feet and receive roughly
300–400 mm of precipitation during the growing season (Ministry of
Agriculture II, 1984: 149ff). In these and other smallholder areas, far
more maize is grown than is marketed, as we have seen; and what is
marketed tends to be exchanged in unprocessed form.

A visual portrayal of the system thus outlined might look like Figure 5.5.

But suppose there were a 35 percent reduction in the rainfall. The large and intermediate farmers would then receive roughly 420 mm of rain, which, according to Acland's figures, is enough to produce a crop. But the small farmers would receive only 195-260 mm of rain, barely enough to secure a crop. Being unable to secure unprocessed maize in the rural markets, the smallholders instead begin purchasing processed maize in rural shops. Rural businesses experience a rapid increase in demand for processed maize. Duka owners therefore stream into town and purchase supplies from the maize mills. The mills are supplied by the Board. At times of drought, then, the Board experiences a growth in demand for its stocks of maize, for it has been hit with a shift in demand from Kenya's rural sector—the sector that contains over 80 percent of the nation's consumers.[13]

We can thus comprehend why drought might affect the Board's sales but not its purchases. The model that unravels this puzzle also helps to show how droughts become food crises, because it illustrates how random perturbations in the weather can lead to a rapid run downward of the national stocks as rural people start to purchase their food from the Board. Should the Board's stocks be low at a time of drought, then that drought could result in famine.

In light of this lesson, it becomes critical to understand how the Board manages its stocks. The results of such an examination prove disturbing, because they suggest that problems within the Board—administrative difficulties of managing large physical quantities of stocks, and financial difficulties arising from the holding of large inventories—generate systematic pressures. These pressures convert abundance into dearth and lead the Board to reenter situations in which it holds few stocks and is therefore vulnerable to chance fluctuations in the rains.[14]

A Policy-Induced Maize Cycle?

While fluctuations in the weather may not affect purchases by the Board, the evidence suggests that the prices the Board offers farmers do affect its purchases. (Table 5.6). As will be seen shortly, this fact plays an important role in the behavior of Kenya's maize economy.

On the basis of my own research (Bates, forthcoming; Bates et al., forthcoming) and previous studies of the maize industry in Kenya

114   ROBERT H. BATES

FIGURE 5.5 Schematic Outline of Maize Industry

Western Kenya   Urban Kenya   Eastern and Other Parts

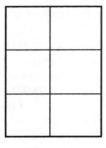

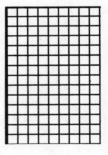

Large and Intermediate
  farmers;
Altitude: 5,500 ft.
Rainfall: 650 mm
Positive trade balance
  vis-a-vis the Board

Consumers of milled
  maize;
Negative trade balance
  vis-a-vis the Board

Smallholders;
Altitude: 3,000-4,000 ft.
Rainfall: 300-400 mm
Few transactions with
  the Board

Table 5.6. Dependent Variable Purchases by the Board   ('000 mt)

Constant	152.635 (2.085)*
Maize Price (Ksh per bag)	10.303 (2.386)**
Wheat Price (Kshs per bag)	-4.309 (-1.821)*

Note: F=4.000**; R^2=0.43; t-statistics in parentheses. * significant at 10 level. ** significant at .05 level. Sixteen observations.

(Republic of Kenya 1966; Kenya National Assembly 1973; Republic of Kenya, Ministry of Finance, 1983) we can document the response of farmers and the Maize Board to problems they confront under different conditions.

Period 1

State: Glut, with warehouses full to overflowing, generally resulting from high prices to farmers and fortuitous growing conditions, combined with stocks of imported grain carried over from a previous food emergency.

Problems of the Board: Physical congestion, money tied up in inventories, and therefore a lack of room to store additional purchases and no money to finance them.

Responses by the Board: A raising of moisture and quality standards as a means of avoiding additional purchases. Delays in payments to farmers.

Responses by farmers: Increased frustration over rejected deliveries and delays in payments for deliveries made. Changes in production plans, substituting other crops for maize.

Period 2

State: Continued glut, as maize intake matches sales.

Problems of the Board: Physical congestion, money tied up in inventories, and therefore a lack of room to store additional purchases and no money to finance them.

Responses by the Board: Continued rejection of deliveries, lowering of prices offered farmers in real and sometimes nominal terms, and the proposal of exports to clear the stores and to generate cash flows.

Responses by the farmers: Cutbacks in plantings in response to delays in payments for maize, reductions in prices, and the rejection of deliveries.

Period 3

State: Reduced inventories, as a consequence of reduced deliveries and export sales.

Problems of the Board: Physical and cash flow problems alleviated.

Responses by the Board: Continued exports, as export contracts signed in the period of glut are honored.

Responses by the farmers: Continued caution in growing maize.

Abundance thus creates problems for the Board: administrative problems of managing physical stocks of grain and financial problems of paying farmers for deliveries to the Board. The response of the Board is to behave in ways that weaken the incentives for farmers and to export, so as to reduce the physical and financial costs of holding large inventories. Because of exports, the Board's stores empty; because of weakened financial incentives, fewer deliveries flow in. Clearly, should nature intervene at this state—i.e., should there be a drought—the Board would lack the stocks to cover the increase in its sales. A food crisis would result, and the nation would be vulnerable to famine.

The evidence suggests that random shocks of drought have impacted at periods of policy-induced vulnerability at several points in the history of the Board. And when they have done so, the Board has reacted by importing maize and by raising the prices to farmers.[15] Once the rains have resumed, however, they find the stores full from imports. Because of higher prices, the farmers return to growing maize and the result once again is glut.

There is thus evidence of a systematic tendency for the Board to manage its affairs in such a way that periods of abundance alternate with periods of dearth, such that the nation's grain stocks reenter situations that leave the nation vulnerable to famine.

Notes

1. Research on this paper was supported by the National Science Foundation (Grant No. SE 582-16870), the Social Science Research Council, the

California Institute of Technology, and Duke University. While conducting field research, I was a Fellow of the Institute for Development Studies of the University of Nairobi. And while writing up this research, I was a Fellow of the Center for Advanced Study in the Behavioral Sciences. My stay at the Center was financed by the Exxon Foundation, the National Science Foundation (Grant No. BNS-801 1495), Duke University, and the Guggenheim Foundation. None are responsible for the contents of this study.

2. Studies of drought and food shortages in Kenya would include: Campbell (1979a, 1979b); Mbithi and Wisner (1973, 1974); Wisner (1976); Hopcraft and Reining (1972); Newman (1975); Dalby and Church (1974); and Herlehey (1984).

3. For a description of these strategies, see the materials collected and reported by Mbithi and Wisner (1973, 1974).

4. See, for example, the data contained in the World Bank, *Kenya: Population and Development*, vols. I & II (Washington, D.C.: The World Bank, 1960).

5. They have succeeded, however, in managing water supplies by other means, as through the construction of catchment basins, irrigation systems, and systems of flood control. For reasons that are becoming increasingly understood, populations in Africa have resisted adopting such techniques to a greater extent than has been the case elsewhere.

6. The Maize Board has gone by a variety of names, the most recent of which is the National Cereals and Produce Board.

7. The measure of rainfall was the level of rainfall April to August in Kitale, as published in Schulter (1984). All the results reported in this chapter have been corrected for first-order autoregressive errors applying the Cochrane-Orcutt procedure.

8. The average rainfall in Kitale, April through August, is 650 mm; there are 11.1 bags of maize per metric ton.

9. See the data in the World Bank, *Kenya: Growth and Structural Change*, (vol. I 1984: 200).

10. For a broader discussion, see R. Bates (forthcoming).

11. This and much of the following discussion are drawn from Schmidt (1979); Casley and Merchant (1979); and Maritim (1982).

12. Note that in this discussion we do not take into account variation in the moisture needs of different maize varieties—something a fuller discussion would require.

13. Interview notes, Kenya, 1982-1984.

14. For evidence of a maize cycle, see as well Masaya (1957). Masaya fails to provide, however, an explanation of his findings or to model how the "maize cycle" might be caused. See as well the analysis done within the Ministry of Agriculture's *Grain Marketing Study*, 9 June 1983.

15. The data in Table 5.7 is apposite and suggests that exports trigger the lowering of prices and imports trigger the raising of prices, thus generating a possible overreaction to abundance and dearth.

References

Acland, J.D. 1971. *East African Crops*. London: Longman.
Bates, R.H. *Beyond the Miracle of the Market*. Forthcoming.

118   ROBERT H. BATES

Bates, R.H., H. Bienen, J. Waterbury, R. Christensen, and E. Frank. *Agricultural Policies in Africa.* Washington, D.C.: World Bank. Forthcoming.

Campbell, D.J. 1979a. Coping with Drought in Kenya Masailand. Working Paper No. 337. University of Nairobi: Institute for Development Studies.

————. 1979b. Responses to Drought in Masailand. Discussion Paper No. 267. University of Nairobi: Institute for Development Studies.

Casley, D.J. and T.M. Merchant. 1979. Smallholder Marketing in Kenya. Project Working Document. UNDP/FAO.

Central Bureau of Statistics. 1977. *Integrated Rural Survey 1974-75.* Nairobi: Ministry of Finance and Planning.

Dalby, D. and R.J.H. Church. 1974. *Drought in Africa.* London: School of Oriental and African Studies, University of London.

Herlehey, T. 1984. Historical Dimensions of the Food Crisis in Africa: Surviving Famines along the Kenya Coast, 1880-1980. African Studies Working Papers, New Series, No. 87. Boston University.

Hopcraft, P.N. and P. Reining. 1972. Arid Lands—Economic, Social, and Ecological Monitoring. Occasional Paper No. 22. University of Nairobi: Institute for Development Studies.

Kenya National Assembly. 1973. *Report of the Select Committee on the Maize Industry.* Nairobi: Government Printer.

Maritim, H.K. 1982. Maize Marketing in Kenya: An Assessment of Inter-regional Commodity Flow Patterns. Ph.D. diss., Technical University of Berlin.

Masaya, T.R. 1975. Special analysis of Coffee, Maize and Wheat Production in Kenya. Working Paper No. 218. University of Nairobi: Institute for Development Studies.

Mbithi, P.N. and B. Wisner. 1973. Drought and Famine in Kenya. *Journal of East African Research and Development* 3:2:113-143.

————. 1974. Drought in Eastern Kenya: Comparative Observations of Nutritional Status and Farmer Activity at 17 Sites. Discussion Paper No. 167. University of Nairobi: Institute for Development Studies.

Ministry of Agriculture (Kenya). 1983. *Grain Marketing Study.* Nairobi: Ministry of Agriculture.

————. 1984. *Farm Management Handbook of Kenya.* Vol. 2. Nairobi: Ministry of Agriculture.

Newman, J.L., ed. 1975. *Drought, Famine and Population Movements in Africa.* Syracuse, N.Y.: Maxwell School of Citizenship and Public Affairs, Syracuse University.

Republic of Kenya. 1966. *Report of the Maize Commission of Inquiry.* Nairobi: Government Printer.

————, Ministry of Finance. 1983. *Grain Marketing Study.* Interim Report, 2 vols. Nairobi: Githongo and Associates and Booker International.

Schmidt, G. 1979. Maize and Beans in Kenya: the Interaction and Effectiveness of the Informal and Formal Marketing Systems. Occasional Paper No. 31. University of Nairobi: Institute for Development Studies.

Schulter, M. 1984. *Constraints on Kenya's Food and Beverage Exports.* Research Report No. 44. Washington, D.C.: International Food Policy Research Institute.

Wisner, B. 1976. Man-Made Famine in Eastern Kenya: The Interrelationship of Environment and Development. Discussion Paper No. 96. University of Sussex: Institute for Development Studies.

World Bank, 1960. *Kenya: Population and Development.* Vols. 1 and 2. Washington, D.C.: The World Bank.
————. 1984. *Kenya: Growth and Structural Change.* Vol. 1. Washington, D.C.: IBRD.

CHAPTER 6

The Production and Marketing of Miraa in Kenya

PAUL GOLDSMITH[1]

Miraa (*catha edulis*) is a tree indigenous to highland forests of eastern Africa (Greenway 1947) traditionally valued in parts of Africa and Asia for its stimulatory and medicinal properties. In the case of Ethiopia and southern Arabia, where miraa is known as *chat* and *khat* respectively, its use is a longstanding social institution. *Catha edulis* domestication may actually predate the domestication of coffee (Peter 1952:25; Greenway 1947:98), and in these countries it has been cultivated on a commercial basis for centuries. The fresh leaves and tender young shoots of the tree are chewed to achieve a state of increased alertness and enhanced concentration, and the nature of the stimulation gives it considerable social value. Because miraa is highly perishable, traditional markets for the commodity were located within a short radius of the areas where domesticated production thrives, and almost always consisted of alcohol-eschewing Muslims. Still, miraa circulated in a remarkably large geographic area of Ethiopia and Arabia prior to this century.

In Kenya, however, the popularity of miraa beyond the geographically restricted areas where it occurs naturally is a relatively recent phenomenon following in the wake of urbanization and the development of transport infrastructure. The popularity of miraa among Kenya's Muslim communities has been the principal stimulus for commercial production since precolonial times, but today its use has outstripped any earlier religious, ethnic, and social boundaries. Kenya's miraa consumption has doubled several times since independence, and its use outside the areas where social controls traditionally limited the potential for abuse often generates heated debate, particularly within Kenya's Muslim community (Troughear 1982; Goldsmith 1985). While this debate is also of some importance from the economic point of view, this paper focuses on production rather than issues of consumption, and concentrates on the role of miraa in rural development. Miraa has slowly but gradually developed into a crop of significant proportions and wide distribution. What makes the growth of the miraa phenomenon so interesting, however, is how radically it differs from other examples of the development of commercial agriculture in Kenya. In contrast to coffee, tea, pyrethrum, cotton, and many other crops produced for the market, miraa is a purely indigenously developed and marketed cash crop.

Miraa is grown for local consumption in several ecologically suited areas in Kenya, Uganda, Tanzania, and Zaire, and its cultivation is said to be spreading as far as Zimbabwe and Madagascar (Shahandeh et al.1983). Miraa production for a larger regional market, however, is exclusively the franchise of smallholder farmers from primarily the Igembe section of the Meru people, who reside on the northeast flanks of Mount Kenya and the adjacent Nyambene Hills. Miraa cultivation is confined to a very small section of the latter area, perhaps no larger than fifty square kilometers, and is distributed efficiently to every corner of the country and beyond. It is a lucrative enterprise that acts as the mainspring of the local Nyambene economy. Even though some of the world's best tea and coffee comes from the same area, miraa is king. Production, packaging, and distribution employs many people in the Nyambenes and many Nyambene people outside the Nyambenes, as well as various non-Meru people who are integrated into the Meru miraa network. Miraa spans ethnic boundaries, especially when the social aspects of consumption are considered along with the commercial linkages, and Meru (primarily Igembe Meru) miraa production is really only the core of a much wider regional industry.

The origins of the miraa trade lie well back in precolonial times but the impressive expansion that has taken place, especially during the past half-century, reflects economic and social change following in the wake of regional integration into the world economy. Consumer demand exists in both urban and rural areas, and the miraa network responds rapidly to technological and infrastructural developments in its quest to surmount environmental and political obstacles that stand between markets and a product that has an economic half-life of forty-eight hours. Miraa is directly subject to the vagaries of supply and demand, and its market value depends on freshness and quality. In comparison, the marketing of tea, coffee, and other cash crops produced for international markets, and controlled by monopsonistic marketing boards, is much less risky.

Still, miraa production has increased since the turn of the century in the face of government response that ranged from laissez-faire to active opposition, and never official support. Although the Igembe consider miraa the "father of development" in their area, it is only recently that Nyambene miraa farmers have received belated praise for their efforts from the government, underscoring miraa's increasing social legitimacy and importance as a cash crop.

The expansion of capital enterprise may very well be the greatest determinant of structural change in rural Africa, although there is little agreement on the specific effects of commercialized agriculture in Africa. The main arguments suggest that development is turning large areas of rural Africa into labor reserves, forcing formerly independent cultivators into a peasant economy dependent on externally controlled markets, and creating class divisions in rural society along capitalist lines. Such a framework, however, cannot totally account for the diversity of African farming systems and rural economies, and grossly oversimplifies the processes at work (Berry 1986:76; Hill 1986). Miraa production and marketing in Kenya is a case in point. By focusing our attention on specific local variations associated with a specific commercialization of smallholder agriculture in Africa, we create the basis for more adequate theory construction. This is especially so when the case does not fit easily into existing assumptions.

Since cash crop production assumes many forms, according to the ecological, geographic, and political determinants present, Kenyan commercial agriculture embodies a number of different strategies, ranging from capital-intensive large-scale production to smallholder production organized by private companies or government parastatals. Although many of these variations produce changes along the lines referred to above, the miraa economy resists classification into conventional categories. As an example of indigenous economic initiative based upon unique social organization, miraa farmers share much in common with Polly Hill's (1974) Ghanaian cocoa farmers. The miraa farming system itself emphasizes a variation of intercropping that marries commercial production with the subsistence production of food and other household needs, including firewood, animal forage, and building materials. The pattern of ecological adaptation combined with regional integration and the utilization of interethnic regional tradeworks shares as much with Kjekshus's (1977) picture of East Africa during the nineteenth century as any descriptions of twentieth century agrarian change. Like the laissez-faire economic growth associated with the kola trade among the Hausa in West Africa during the nineteenth century (Lovejoy 1980:141), miraa has provided the capital for the shift to the full commercialization of agriculture in the Nyambene area, while retaining important aspects of local social organization.

Igembe social organization still involves age-set relations, which remain more important than class distinctions. Economic differentiation tends to be mediated by patron-client ties. Such patrons are usually men who left home at one time to pioneer Meru participation in the demanding and often risky long-distance markets, or to create markets where they did not formerly exist. They exercise control over the local Nyambene wholesale markets only to the extent that the perishable nature of miraa often creates markets favoring large-scale wholesale buyers, and through easily abrogated, short-term agreements with client growers. External markets, in contrast, defy the control of dealers and even entire governments. The virtual absence of land sales in the miraa growing area, the high productivity of a small plot under miraa, and high opportunity for off-farm income in harvesting, marketing, and other aspects of the industry give considerable options to the Nyambene peasant cultivator compared to many other Kenyan smallholders. And free entry of the peasant farmer to the market lessens the power concentrated in patrons' hands. While the emergence of a patron class can concentrate resources in relatively few hands over the long run, and contribute to the perpetuation of rural inequalities (Lemarchand 1986:31), the structure of the miraa economy mitigates against this happening in the same way it has occurred in other parts of Kenya. Because the miraa industry operates largely independent of state control or involvement, politicans, who often manipulate access to the state and its resources, have had little scope for interference. The ultimate impact of changes taking place within the local economy are yet to be seen, but one observation is very clear: the miraa industry is incredibly efficient, is flexible in the face of external changes, is remarkably free of waste and corruption, and bears little resemblance to other agricultural enterprises in Kenya.

This does not mean that miraa provides an easily replicable model for agricultural development in Kenya, or anywhere else. Indeed, the circumstances are altogether too uniquely dependent upon favorable environmental conditions and social circumstances. It does, however, allow us to challenge or qualify some of the assumptions about the nature of rural Africa. The miraa industry, for example, fails to confirm Tosh's view that "the entry of tropical African societies into cash crop production was a more disruptive experience than either liberal economic theory or colonial apologists would show" (Tosh 1978:94). Production of surplus for the market was not always new to African societies, and the transition to market-oriented agriculture can be smooth. Nor can we uncritically accept notions that "the rural social order constituted in itself a powerful blockage restructuring the development of the market as long as its institutions remained relatively undisturbed by outside pressure" (Hart 1982:38). The rural social order actually facilitates the organization of the miraa trade and the distribution of its profits and lends continuity to the development process. Certainly, if and when African economies interfered with colonial design, it was generally the autochthonous that had to give way, often altering itself or being altered against its own interests (see, e.g., Mutiso 1976). But local adaptations to the forces of change in rural Africa did not always upset the prevailing ecological and social balance—and that's the point that is often belatedly understood.

In Kenya, for example, the shift to outside agencies creates a well-documented form of dependence (Moris 1981). The end result is that often outsiders, affiliated with churchs, administration, or nongovernmental organizations, organize local self-help groups. Such groups tend to operate only as long as the external agency provides funding or inputs. On the other hand, the role of indigenous institutions in development is as fundamental to the process and critical to success as either correct prices or structural inputs. In the Nyambenes the internal thrust of the miraa economy fosters an ideology of autodevelopment that carries over to other areas, making it clear that indigenously powered development is a distinct possibility deserving of greater attention.

Conditions in rural Africa resulting from unrestrained international capitalism on the one hand, and the backlash of heavy-handed state policies on the other, should not obscure the real potential of the African social order for change and adaptation. Evidence points to the ability of local societies to reside in poor policies and the lack of, or deterioration of national institutions and infrastructure, than in local social formations capable of combining complex intermixtures of enterprise, equity, and environmental and social controls. This is in a continent where the state is described as the property of personal rulers (Jackson and Rosberg 1984), as a predator, or, in more benign terms, as simply "suspended above society" (Hyden 1983). Clearly, the local social order cannot be held responsible for the fiascos of governments; perhaps it should be accorded some credit for surviving in spite of them.

The Igembe Meru entered the capitalist economy with a full complement of precolonial baggage in the style of Hyden's (1980) uncaptured peasants, and demonstrate that smallholder peasants can exert considerable influence on the course of events in Africa. While the response of such peasants to unfavorable policies and prices is often perceived as withdrawal from markets into subsistence production (see, e.g., Bates 1984), this should not blind us to the range of possibilities and responses offered by alternative markets and parallel economies, be they of an affective (Hyden 1980), magendo (Kasfir 1983), or of some as yet unknown nature. The Igembe Meru parlayed a potential market and unfavorable conditions (or the lack of favorable ones) into a system of production and marketing that supports a major social institution in East Africa. These people show little reluctance, however, to be captured by favorable policies and to sacrifice their autonomy once the proper inducements prevail, despite their success within the parallel economy, which survives as an escape hatch in the case of unfavorable policies regardless. We should be very wary, therefore, of generalizing about the intrinsic nature of African societies and their responses to change.

Studies emerging from different parts of Africa take into account the critical role of the underlying social structure on smallholder production, and "designate certain forms of social organizations that are significant in mobilizing human and material resources, even though largely unrelated to socialist or capitalist options" (Lemarchand 1986:36). Cases of indigenous African capitalism, innovations, and other varieties of local adaptation have important implications for rural development in Africa, as the following case study of the historical development of miraa production and marketing attests to. The question that remains is: are unique local responses, future permutations included, a permanent part of the African landscape, or are they essentially to be included within the rubric of a transient, peasant mode of production?

The Meru People and District

Meru district occupies 3,349 square miles in Kenya's Eastern Province. It extends from the Eastern slopes of Mount Kenya down to the edge of the Somali plateau to the northeast. The drop in elevation encompasses several ecological zones and a variety of geographical features that have had a significant impact on the nature of agricultural development from precolonial times to the present. Oral traditions record the migration of the Meru people's ancestors from an island called Mbwa on the coast (probably Manda island in the Lamu archipelago). Upon arriving in their present region sometime during the early eighteenth century (Holding 1942), the original group separated into five sections, an event the Meru refer to as the *kagairo*. These sections (the Imenti, Miutuni, Igoji, Igembe, and Tigania) were grouped by the British with their Tharaka, Cuka, Mwimbe, and Muthambi neighbors to the south and east and given the appellation Meru. In any event, these people are similar linguistically and culturally. Any strong group identity above the level of clan and section since the *kagairo*, however, is a recent development (Fadiman 1976:151-154).

Several generations of migration brought the proto-Meru to the edge of the forests of Mount Kenya. Groups penetrated the forest in a vertical movement, which increased the isolation and fragmentation that had occurred earlier. There differences were intensified by the specific nature of each section's contact with the Maasai, Oromo, Okiek, Agumba, and other inhabitants who predate their own arrival in the region. Early contact often resulted in hostilities. Meru numerical superiority helped them to prevail over their antagonists, and even to acquire cattle in the process (Fadiman:161-162). The intermingling and resulting forms of interaction led to inter-marriage and the incorporation of valuable new skills and cultural adaptations.

From the Oromo the Meru acquired the Cushitic cyclical age-set system and the practice of circumcision as the group's major ritual of initiation. From the Maasai they adopted the practice of warrior organization, where the alternating generational sets going through the warrior cycle at any given time lived in common barracks called "gaaru." The Meru learned from Okiek hunter-gatherers the witchcraft and supernatural rituals they used to protect isolated fields from intruders (Fadiman 1977). It is altogether likely that they also learned the hunter-gatherers' extensive pharmacopia, including uses of miraa in the tree's wild state, although the Meru, like the Somalis, Arabs, and Swahilis, tell the same legend explaining the discovery of miraa by a herdsman who found his goats happily munching on branches of miraa after an uncharacteristic overnight absence (see Getahun and Krikorian 1973:354-356). The happy-goat story is also invoked to explain the discovery of coffee (Jacob 1935; Hattox 1985:13). A third explanation, although perhaps only remotely possible, is that knowledge of miraa reached the Meru from the Ethiopian highlands through some form of stimulus diffusion. Regardless of how it came about, the Meru eventually domesticated the tree and incorporated it into their social and ceremonial milieu.

The Nyambene Range and The Meru Farming System

The particular determinants of modern-day cash crops are to be found in the traditional zone agriculture practiced by the Meru and outlined in detail by Bernard (1972). The Nyambene range is an island ecosystem that matches the gradations of altitude, soil, and flora of adjacent Mount Kenya beginning at a high bracken zone below the tree line to the semi-arid fringes of the lower parts of Meru District.

This first zone occurs above the altitude of 5,500 feet and is characterized by high rainfall, cool temperatures, and powdery, overacidic, and structureless soil of the brown loam type. Traditionally this zone was used for grazing cattle, but during the past several decades it has given way to tea, wheat, potatoes, and pyrethrum. The more productive "Kikuyu grass" zone overlaps with the bracken zone but is distinguished by volcanic loams and loamy clays. The Kikuyu grass zone supports the same crops as the high bracken zone and occurs between 5,000 and 8,000 feet. A low bracken zone occurs underneath the 5,000-foot contour and is underlain by infertile, acidic soils that nevertheless support the production of bananas, yams, sweet potatoes, and coffee, with heavy manuring and fertilization. The star grass zone, which falls between 4,000 and 6,000 feet, is highly productive agricultural land with fertile soils, adequate rainfall, and moderate temperatures making it ideal for a wide range of traditional and introduced crops. These include bananas, root crops, cereals, and pulses; it is also the prime area for coffee production.

The zones that occur below 4,000 feet have decided disadvantages compared to the higher zones. Malaria poses a threat to humans, and the tsetse fly to cattle. Productive soils occur in some areas, but lower and more variable rainfall and high evaporation limit the agricultural value of these zones to millet, sorghum, and other drought-resistant crops. The grass-woodland zone between 4,000 and 3,000 feet is used for the shifting agriculture of cereals, pulses, and tobacco. Other lower zones are used primarily for goats and sheep, and an area in the northern part of the range that is free of tsetse fly is fit for cattle. The lowest reaches of the Nyambene range fade into the arid plateau of northeastern Kenya. To the west lies the frontier town of Isiolo and to the east the expanses of Meru Park.

The Igembe approached their present home from the Meru Park side via Thagicu and worked their way up through the various zones at an uneven pace, clearing patches of montane forest as they reached the higher zones. A vertical pattern of land-holdings developed over time. Most of the population lived in the temperate middle zones but maintained the fields they had cleared at lower altitudes, augmenting them as they gradually cleared the forest above. As a result, the extended families inhabiting these vertical holdings had access to a wide variety of food crops and cash crops, livestock, forest products, and honey. The vertical pattern also functioned to heighten the fragmentation and isolation of the different sections after the *kagairo*, and led to the *mwiriga* (p. miiriga) as the primary unit of social organization.

A *mwiriga* is essentially one or more biologically related groups that functions as a unit of land organization, government, and communal defense. Sections such as the Igembe, Tigania, and Imenti are made up of different *miiriga*. Governance took place though small councils called *kiama* (pl. *biama*) that operate on each level of the age-set system from warriorhood up to the gerontocracy. Representatives from each council could convene a larger *njuri* council to settle disputes within the *mwiriga* or between *miiriga*, a special *njuri* could be called to settle disputes between the larger sections, which by the nineteenth century had fallen into a pattern of internecine warfare (Fadiman 1982). Immediately following independence the Meru built a large structure to house the *njuri* of all the different sections, but the Kenyan government saw it as a threat to the administration's local government and prevented its operation. The building still stands.

Meru warfare was not engendered by competition for land, which remained plentiful through the colonial period. Rather, it was embedded in the complex structure of social organization that encouraged cattle-raiding as the legitimate avenue to achieve personal security and community status, and to provide the necessary animals for enforcing spiritual harmony though religious ritual. It was regulated by stringent controls (Fadiman 1982:42-47).

Warfare of either an internal or external nature was no obstacle to the regional trade that developed among the Meru and their neighbors. The variety of ecological niches, and ethnically diverse peoples embracing the agricultural, hunting-gathering, and pastoral modes of production, fostered a proliferation of exchange networks linking different economic and social groups (Waller 1985:348). These networks promoted interaction, symbiosis, and a high degree of flexibilty in both mode of production (Zwanenberg 1982) and ethnic identity (Hjort 1974:53-54). The Meru, who had originally fought many of the groups in the area and prevailed, occupied a wealthy corner of the Kenyan highlands, and continued to build upon their success through exploiting the comparative advantage of the different ecological zones. In turn, they developed a military organization that maintained their internal strength and led them to incorporate various client groups in the area, rather than vice versa.[2]

The Igembe and Tigania of the Nyambene Range were situated in an advantageous location to benefit from the expansion of the local precolonial trade, and the long distance trade from the coast in the latter part of the nineteenth century. The range juts out like an island of prosperity into the drier areas on the edge of the highlands, placing the residents of the Nyambenes in a position to profit from trade with their pastoral and agricultural neighbors and with the caravans and trading parties that came later. The Igembe were the only Meru group to use donkeys. These animals, which they acquired from the Oromo, provided valuable transport of agricultural products to the lowlands and of saline earth up into the hills for exchange with other farmers. The Igembe traded with the Kamba who had developed a far-flung trade network linking the coast with central Kenya (Jackson 1976): and even the Rendille from the Lake Turkana region (Chanler 1893:472) visited Nyambene markets. The trade that took place in these markets must have included the full range of agricultural and livestock products, as well as iron tools, weapons, herbal medicines, poisons for hunting, wire, cloth, and miraa. The Nyambenes became a main stop for the coastal caravans that pioneered both the Arab and European exploration of the interior. It is therefore difficult to imagine that miraa escaped the attention of the Arab-Swahili traders and caravan leaders who were familar with "the flower of paradise," at the very least in name, because of their longstanding contacts with Yemen (Moser 1917). Also, recent Somali arrivals in the vicinity knew of and used the Ethiopian *chat* known in the Horn of Africa as early as the fourteenth century (Peters 1952).

The Development of the Miraa Trade

The developments that sapped the strength of regional trade networks also promoted miraa to its unique position as the engine of development in the Nyambenes. Miraa always enjoyed high social and even religious status in Africa (Cassanelli 1986); its present high economic status represents a long but steady evolution since the days of precolonial trade. Some of the more remarkable features of this trade are reflected in miraa's strong pattern of integration with the indigenous social structure from earlier times to the present, a pattern that contrasts with the commercial agriculture that has developed in other parts of Kenya (see, e.g., Buch Hansen 1984; Leys 1974, 1080; Kitching 1984). A few additional comments on the Meru social structure, as based upon the age-grade system, are necessary to understand how the Meru perceive the historical development of the miraa trade.

Age-sets are a structural feature that crosscut the more molecular groupings based on kinship and locality. This form of social organization, hardly unique to the Meru, occurs among pastoral groups throughout eastern Africa and among many of the Bantu peoples who came into contact with those groups (Muriuki 1974; Spear et al. 1982). The system, however, has lapsed among most of the agricultural people who formerly practiced it because of outside influences such as Western education, Christianity, the replacement of indigenous norms of governance (Tignor 1984), and the socioeconomic stratification that has accompanied the development of commercial agriculture. This is certainly the case among the Gikuyu, Embu, and the sections of the Meru who are the Igembe's neighbors in the Mount Kenya region. It remains in operation among the Igembe, who refer to it often when discussing the miraa trade and their internal organization.

The system is distinguished by initiation into a specific *riika*, or age grade, upon circumcision. As warriors, men of one *riika* lived in common barracks until marrying, retaining membership in their *riika* throughout their life cycle as they progressed from the stage of warrior, to adult, to elder. Those who distinguished themselves by their skill in war and leadership during the warrior stage, and by their wisdom and ritual knowledge during adulthood, were elevated to a position of governance by membership in their respective *njuri* council. The system, in short, connected alternating moieties into overlapping alliances, acting to create a system of secular social control that was both part of and in addition to the regular kinship relations (Mahner 1975:404). A third practice known as *gichiaro* further extended the parameters of social organization by adding the element of fictive kinship relationships through blood brotherhood.

The coming of colonial rule halted the growth of regional trade networks as they existed at the time, and led to a restructuring of internal populations in many cases. New avenues of accumulation sapped the strength of old trade networks (Waller 1985:376) and internal relations alike. British-appointed chiefs were imposed on the formerly chiefless societies in Kenya causing a fundamental shift in authority in many of the local societies, although some notable cases proved to be exceptions (Tignor 1979). Economic change had far-reaching effects in many areas and gave rise to new elites who were the result of a process of inversion created by the confrontation between old values and the new order (Mutiso 1976). In agricultural areas, the *riika* system almost universally gave way in the face of new political, economic, and religious institutions. Its survival among Meru of the Nyambenes signifies elements in common with many pastoral peoples (see Rigby 1984), where formal age-grade organization continues to be functional in altered economic circumstances. British settlement ended at Timau on the other side of Mount Kenya, and although the British district administration was centered in nearby Meru town, it exerted limited influence on the Nyambene area. Among the Igembe, social organization based on the *riika* system remained intact, and circumcision along traditional lines still takes place.

Age-sets also provide a convenient scale by which to measure historical developments, and Igembe elders uniformly fall back on the cycle of age-grades to describe the development of the miraa trade. Holding (1942) mentions nineteen generations since the Meru migration from the coast. The names of specific *riika*, however, differ from section to section, consistent with the strong sense of local autonomy that developed among the different Meru groups. The Igembe mention six *riika* in connection with the development of the miraa trade. (See Table 6.1.)

The Igembe credit the Miriti with the initial use and domestication of miraa. This would place the domestication of miraa sometime in the third quarter of the last century, although domestication most likely took place at an earlier date. When a miraa tree becomes old (*uuru*) it begins to "dry out" and no longer produces high quality miraa. This usually happens between seventy and one hundred years, although a tree enjoying optimum conditions may survive longer. Meru report trees as old as two hundred years, but this is probably an exaggeration as the Meru probably didn't enter their present area before then, and *uuru* trees are usually uprooted once they lose their economic value. The oldest miraa tree I personally observed was described as planted "by the father of the father of the father of my grandfather." Counting the owner, the tree would date back six generations, or to the first Miriti domesticators. Anything older is speculation.

Miraa was originally reserved for social and ceremononial functions among the Igembe—indeed, it still is. The Gwantai are credited with being the first *riika* to actively trade miraa dating to before the turn of the century. The Ithalie, a few of whom are still alive, bridged the precolonial and colonial periods. By then miraa had become a regular item of exchange, and the Igembe transported

Table 6.1. The Cycle of Igembe Riika and Approximate Initiation Dates

Miriti	(1870)
Gwantai	(1885)
Michubu	(1900)
Ithalie	(1915)
Ratanaa	(1930)
Lubetaa	(1945)
Miriti	(1960)

Note: The average period of warriorhood between 12 and 15 years could, at times be extended due to circumstances.   In the table above 15 year intervals are specified for the sake of convenience in the absence of exact dates.

it to a halfway point between their area and Isiolo, where they exchanged the miraa for goats and skins. Later the trade shifted to Isiolo, a growing town that served as the "gateway to the northern frontier district." Miraa shifted from a social and ceremonial role to that of a major trade item during the time of the Ithalie *riika*, when social, political, and environmental changes accompanying the inception and consolidation of colonial rule led people to "new ways of livelihood, building on the traditions they knew, but responding to new economics and political realities" (Barker 1984:21). Miraa planting began on a larger scale for the economic rewards it promised.

It was a dynamic period. The Meru's neighbors the Gikuyu, on the other side of the mountain in what became Central Province, underwent profound disruption before the turn of the century when famines and livestock epidemics preceded the imposition of colonial rule. They were already the major provisioners for caravans passing through the central highlands before 1893 when they responded to European presence by cultivating potatoes and European vegetables. The Gikuyu realized considerable profit from these cash crops, and after the turn of the century cultivation was still far more profitable than cash paid for labor (Miracle 1974:23-24). Rapid economic change was not as pronounced among the Meru. They were able to avoid the famines and pestilence of the late nineteenth century by taking refuge at higher altitudes. But the changes in the wake of colonialism removed the Meru from the center to the periphery. Unlike the Gikuyu, they did not see tracts of their lands alienated, and they were only partially influenced by many of the new developments.

External influences, however, were stimulating a reformulation of former trade networks, and small communities like the Igembe Meru sought to maximize their possibilities by specializing and by reinforcing their preexisting links with outsiders and the outside (Ambler 1985:204). In Central Province the Gikuyu were joining the cash economy at the same time competition from the administration and increased pressure on the land restricted the traditional bank: wealth in cattle, and its dividends, and livestock supplies. The Somalis responded to this market by bringing animals in large numbers from the north to trade with the relatively affluent Gikuyu. The Somalis undersold the Maasai and the Kamba, and the livestock trade became a prominent feature of both the Gikuyu economy and that of northern Kenya for the next three decades (Miracle 1974:23-24).

Somali ascendancy in the cattle trade spurred the growth of Isiolo town, on the interface of the highlands and arid regions to the north, as the major commercial and administrative center for the Somali and their pastoral neighbors. The Somalis were relatively recent arrivals in the area, but their appetite for miraa is longstanding and legendary. Isiolo thus naturally became the major destination for Meru miraa. Over the years Isiolo became the major reexport market for miraa sold in northern Kenya and beyond. Revenues from the municipal tax on the reexport of miraa became so important to frontier towns like Isiolo and Garissa by the 1970s that when Somalia banned imports of miraa in 1981, they were described as "the dying towns of the miraa trade" in the local press.

The Ithalie *riika*, who were more oriented toward the market than the Gwantai, propagated the first trees planted for principally commercial reasons. One must nevertheless keep in mind that the Igembe households were essentially self-sufficient and, perhaps more so than the other Meru sections, relatively isolated from the changes taking place in other areas of the Mount Kenya region. The transformation of Igembe traditional markets, however, mirrored the change in Igembe social institutions. Cattle, for example, represented both the traditional bank and the source of the greatest prestige. Wealth and prestige formerly acquired through warfare found an outlet in the miraa trade. The cultural institutions associated with warriorhood appeared to adapt naturally to the miraa trade, which entailed traveling great distances through the bush and dealing with dangerous clients; and like the institution of warriorhood, the miraa trade frequently suffered from administrative disapproval. Smugglers, after all, often maintain a "warrior" mentality. In contrast to the changes among the Gikuyu, the initial period of commercialization represented a gradual transformation of traditional ideology among the Igembe Meru, and eventually led to change in patterns of accumulation.

The Michubu *riika* entered the trade between the wars, when miraa exports to Meru town began. The Michubu, and the Ratanaa *riika* span the troubled times from World War I to Mau Mau. The Nyambene economy was sufficiently detached from the colonial economy to remain unscathed by the depression years. The Second World War stimulated price increases for both settler and African produce. Despite the drought that affected large numbers of Africans in drier areas, it was a period of unprecedented prosperity in the Mount Kenya region and Nyanza (Anderson and Throup 1985:341), and the market for miraa expanded modestly as exports began into Meru town in addition to Isiolo.

The developments that took place during the war period, however, put Africans and Europeans on a collision course that in due course culminated in Mau Mau. The British had failed to implement a policy that would reconcile the conflicts between their African "wards" and the powerful settler interests. The experiment allowing African coffee cultivation in Embu, Meru, and Kisii proved to be a success (Barnes 1979) and pointed to the soundness of certain voices in the British administration who felt the problems in the native reserves could be aided through the development of a landed middle class. This new class would adopt modern agriculture, boost production, and provide a labor market for the growing number of landless peasants. Had coffee production been allowed in Gikuyu country, where the pressures in the native reserve were the greatest, perhaps the developments after the war might not have occurred (Sorrenson 1967:270). Adequate land and the success of miraa as a cash crop created different conditions in the Nyambenes, but the Igembe nevertheless came out in strong support of the Mau Mau.

By this time, miraa consumption in Kenya and other Crown territories had begun to attract the British, who viewed it with a jaundiced eye (e.g., Greenway 1947). Although they did not declare miraa illegal in 1945 as Hjort (1974:29) reports, they did place a tax on each tree. For the Igembe this was an alarming trend. Some people, especially those whose fields were near roads, uprooted their trees; many felt taxation would eventually lead to alienation of land as in other parts of the colony. This threat to their autonomy, and the mass detention of Embu and Meru along with Gikuyu in urban areas when Mau Mau broke out, may at least partially explain the strong solidarity with the forest fighters Igembe express to this day, anti-Gikuyu sentiment notwithstanding. British opposition to miraa, and the curfew imposed in the reserves, frustrated trade. And like the Gikuyu, the Igembe were resentful of government programs that blocked their development (Throup 1985:427). The Igembe rose up in opposition. People lost cattle and land for supporting the rebellion, and this period, associated locally with the Ratanaa *riika*, was in general one of nongrowth.

However, before the outbreak of Mau Mau one major development had occurred. During the late 1940s an Arab named Abdul Saleh started to export Meru miraa to Nairobi. Deliveries were uneven at first, but the miraa found a ready-made market, particularly among Muslims in such neighborhoods as Pumuani, Majengo, and Eastleigh, and miraa consumption increased despite the curfew. Consumers eagerly awaited miraa, making the long trip from Nyambene markets by truck, sometimes skirting the sundown curfew to buy miraa when the truck was late. When the curfew was lifted, the Meru, no longer bottled up in the reserve, gradually became involved in the growing trade, and for the first time miraa became a major source of off-farm employment. The earlier urban traders, however, were often non-Igembe Meru like Daudi Bohora, a Meru from Imenti who is credited with being the first Meru to market miraa in the cities. Enormously successful, he acquired property and beer distributorships in Mombasa and Nairobi; he is also credited as the Meru who introduced European beer to Meru. Igembe entrepreneurs followed in the steps of successful businessmen like Abdul Saleh and Daudi Bohora. By the late 1950s they expanded to Mombasa and other urban areas. The first truly urban entrepreneurs included some Ratanaa, although the majority were mainly members of the Lubetaa age-grade. The Lubetaa generation had purchased their first vehicles by 1960, and they presided over another boom in planting.

Miraa has enjoyed steady growth ever since. Consumption has grown steadily since independence. Miraa dealers I spoke to say that by 1975 the volume was double that of the early 1960s. In 1975 consumers discovered "Big G," a locally manufactured chewing gum that neutralizes miraa's bitter taste while holding the cud of masticated miraa together in the mouth. Big G sparked a major consumer revolution, and some dealers estimate that miraa consumption doubled in the years following its discovery. Although Meru and other miraa purists view it as adulteration, Big G popularized miraa chewing by making it accessible to numbers of people formerly repelled by its bitter and astringent taste, and it has become a standard item wherever miraa is sold.

The Lubetaa *riika* were the main beneficiaries of these

developments. The Lubetaa were the first miraa traders to seriously crack the potential market for local products represented by Kenya's expanding economy. They achieved their success by systematically and efficiently delivering quality and uniformity in an organic wrapper at a fair price. Miraa, the Meru assert, is unstoppable. Indeed, miraa has overcome all the various restraints and obstacles that have intervened between it and an expanding regional market. The miraa network expanded into every corner of Kenya and beyond its borders in the years following independence. Meru miraa began going by air to places it couldn't reach by road, and major markets developed in Somalia and briefly in Saud¨ Arabia (before *khat* possession was placed on the same level as aicohol). Somalia represented the largest external market. During the 1960s, even the Shifta War failed to deter Somali smugglers who defied the miraa ban in Northeastern Province, and the shifta bandits themselves, to run miraa overland through dry acacia bush in landrovers tuned to the performance level of rally cars in Eastleigh garages.

The stigma of British disapproval remained though, and the Kenya government declared miraa illegal at one point after independence. A delegation of Meru elders visited Kenyatta, presented him with a bundle of choice *alele*, and told Mzee that "miraa feeds us, clothes us, and pays our children's school fees." The ban was promptly lifted. Subsequent bans enacted in Northeastern Province following the periodic outbreak of shifta-type violence have also failed to obstruct the flow of miraa. Likewise, Somalia's ban of miraa in 1981, which has only limited, not stopped, imports, upholds the Meru view of "miraa haipingiki" (miraa cannot be blocked).

During the 1970s, miraa received official recognition as an earner of foreign exchange, and the Igembe date 1981 as the year when miraa finally received government recognition for its important role in the local economy—the year the Forestry Department began stocking miraa seedlings. Urban miraa consumption in Kenya, as in other parts of the world where it is chewed, began as an Islamic custom but has spread to include other ethnic groups and religious affiliations. Chewing miraa for work and recreation has become a virtual social institution over the last two decades, and has created controversy in the process (see Troughear 1982; Mungai 1982). The most organized opposition is centered on a faction of the Muslim religious establishment on the coast whose antimiraa campaign is partially funded by Iran. Miraa consumption displays many parallels with the early coffeehouses in England, which became popular alternatives to taverns as centers of intellectual and political intercourse (Aytoun 1956). And the ongoing miraa debate shares strong similarities with legal debates over the status of coffee in the Islamic world during the sixteenth century (Hattox 1985:70). Questions persist, but there is no real question of miraa losing its current status in Kenya, or even becoming subject to legal controls in the near future: miraa has become a sprawling corporate enterprise spanning ethnic blocks, local municipalities dependent on the revenue from its sale, wealthy patrons, and parliamentary representatives.

The risks and the profits of the miraa venture are mediated by a labor-intensive system whose economic logic reflects Hyden's description of the economy of affection: "economic action is not motivated by individual profit alone, but is embedded in a range of social considerations that allow for the redistribution of opportunities and benefits in a manner not possible where modern capitalism or socialism prevails, and formalized state action dominates the process of redistribution (Hyden 1980:19). If such "social considerations" mark the survival of traditional elements, they do not represent obstacles to be overcome. The highly perishable nature of miraa underscores how efficient and responsive to market forces precapitalist elements in affective economies can be. This view is confirmed if we turn from the historic development of the trade to examine how the system operates from the ground up.

The Role of Miraa in the Nyambene Economy

Traders surmount long distances, rough terrain, poor communications and infrastructure, and administrative obstacles on a daily basis. But the foundation of the miraa trade is a core of smallholder farmers who live within the nine-by-nine-kilometer "miraa triangle" that connects the towns of Kangeta, Lare, and Maua. Kangeta, perhaps the most famous miraa town, was the traditional center of Meru miraa culture, and produces the highest quality miraa. Lare, however, produces in quantity what Kangeta produces in quality. Maua falls within the miraa zone, but developed as the main commercial center of the Nyambene Range. The town is one wide boulevard of ships, restaurants, and butcheries. There is a Methodist church, a hospital, and a miniature Barclays Bank symbolizing the rural prosperity of the area. Igembe Division itself is a densely populated region where one cannot distinguish rich from poor on the basis of appearance. Small but permanent streams running down the hillsides belie a natural wealth not common in Africa. Most people live in the scattered homesteads that uniformly dot the landscape. The Meru-Maua is the best road this writer has seen in rural Kenya, but private vehicles are rare except for tourists on their way to Meru Park, tea lorries, and the landrovers that leave like clockwork between three and four every day with the cargos of miraa.

The observer who enters this area in search of miraa is unlikely to spot it against the riot of trees, shrubs, and crops that stand out from the luxurious natural vegetation. More obvious are the ubiquitous plots of tea and coffee. Upon closer inspection, scattered trees of *mbaine* miraa emerge within intercopped systems incorporating maize, cassava, sweet potatoes, peas, bananas, and the leathery sheaths of gomba plants—a cash crop in its own right; six varieties of indigenous and exotic trees cultivated for timber, firewood, and forage border the plots of tea and coffee. Often *mwenjele*, a tall tree used for goat fodder, is planted next to the miraa trees. The *mwenjele* supports jungle-like growths of yam vines, while serving as a ladder for the harvesting of older miraa trees. Once identified, organized plots of the younger, wiry-limbed *muthairo* planted in straight lines can be seen either by itself, or interspersed at times with the tea and coffee. Not all smallholdings are blessed by miraa, which requires very specific soil and climatic conditions to produce a crop of commercial value. The type and quality of miraa can also vary greatly within a very short distance.

Domesticated miraa grows to a height of up to ten meters. It is propagated from root cuttings that take five years to produce miraa of commercial value. Miraa, however, is like fine wine that improves with time. Young trees called *muthairo* produce marketable crops, but the trees called *mbaine* that are twenty or more years older produce the highest quality miraa—the older the better. Very old trees produce a very high quality miraa called *alele*, or "shamba ya wazee," because it was reserved for the elders. Old trees, planted by the Gwantai and Ithalie, are extremely valuable today. The main distinctions in the grade of miraa rests on age (as previously noted) and the area it comes from. The town of Kangeta lies on the edge of the best growing area, and was the principal selling point until the market was moved to nearby Muringene to make room for the food market in the town's square. Kangeta-Muringene miraa is marked by tea and grows in the Kikuyu grass zone. Lare town is the other principal miraa market. Lare miraa is marked by coffee and grows in the star grass zone. There are essential differences between the two markets. Lare miraa may fetch only half the price of most of the miraa sold in Muringene, but it is more plentiful and travels better.

Eight to twelve vehicles leave Lare daily, many of them fanning out into the NFD (Northern Frontier District). Only four vehicles leave from Muringene: two for Nairobi and two for Mombasa.

Official records of miraa exports are spotty and extremely hard to rely on, as the quantities are regularly underestimated to avoid paying the higher tax exacted from each vehicle of miraa, and to conceal the actual value of miraa exports. The value of these exports is even harder to estimate because of the effect on consumer prices of fine gradations of quality, the daily price fluctuations that result from market conditions, the season, and climatic factors. The Muringene market is generally more consistent in quantity and price than Lare, where the market is occasionally glutted with lower-quality miraa, leading to wild fluctuations in both the wholesale and retail markets. The statistics are further complicated by a major shift in the packaging system that occurred in 1965.

Formerly, miraa was packaged in roughly uniform "bundles" exported in units of five per "bunda." The current system was the brainchild of the famous miraa dealer Samwel, who invented the new packaging under the influence of the metric system, which was being promulgated at that time. Samwel popularized the "kilo," which became the main unit of consumption. In his system, one kilo consists of two halves, each consisting of ten small bundles of ten sticks each. The measure has nothing to do with weight; also, the growing popularity of the shorter "*giza*" variety of miraa led to variations in which fewer but larger bunches of the twigs make up a kilo. The average consumer purchases one kilo, a light chewer one half, a heavy chewer two kilos or more. The original twenty bundles in two halves, however, is still the sign of high-quality miraa, both for *giza* and *kangeta*. Ten kilos are packaged in one bunda, which is the standard unit of wholesale trade. Usually eight bunda are sewn into one "gunia" (gunnysack) for transport to retail markets. Samwel's innovation represents a marketing revolution that created a uniform standard of packaging and quantity for the first time.

To get an accurate idea of the economic dimensions of miraa production, it is best to examine the value of production beginning with the smallholder household unit of production. Miraa trees require no cash inputs and little maintenance beyond pruning (which promotes growth by exposing the young shoots to the sun) and a monthly firing to ward off pests or extreme cold when it occurs. In Kangeta, the average estimated produce of a typical shamba (farm) is between five and eight bunda. Miraa produces one harvest a month during the rains, and one harvest every forty-five days during the dry season. When the miraa is ready to be harvested, an overseer is hired at the rate of K Sh 150 per day and several laborers at K Sh 15 per bunda. A good worker can tie up up to two bunda in a half-day's work. The miraa is picked early in the morning and the workers begin the task of tying the twigs into successively larger units using banana fiber string. The twenty gomba leaves that go into a finished bunda add K Sh 25 to the cost. Often the gomba comes from areas in the vicinity that are unsuitable for miraa cultivation. By noon the miraa is usually ready to be taken to the market. Table 6.2 shows a range of the profits that can be realized from a "typical" shamba. This does not include the owner's own labor contribution or that of household members.

A plot can generate up to ten harvests a year. In Lare the labor costs paid are about half those paid in Muringene, but the quantity of miraa is usually greater, as is the amount of miraa one worker can tie up in one day. Traditionally, only elders handled miraa. The development of commercial production, however, created a demand for labor that eroded this injunction and the similar restrictions on consumption. Now even children, particularly in Lare, may earn wages by harvesting. The multiple harvests that take place throughout the year represent a substantial annual income for producers and opportunities for wage labor throughout the year.

People carrying bundles of bundas on their heads converge on the markets after midnight. Wholesalers and agents, skilled at assessing the quality of miraa at a quick glance, barter with the sellers. In Muringene, the average load ranges from twelve bunda to a few kilos of *alele*; most fall somewhere in between. In Lare, essentially the same pattern prevails, although some particularly large holdings produce up to thirty bunda for their owners. Consignments are quickly sewn into gunnysacks (*gunia*), tagged with the names of the destination and receiver, and loaded into vehicles as a single clerk from the Meru County Council keeps records. The transport charge is K Sh 6 per bunda to Nairobi, and K Sh 12 per bunda to Mombasa.

Tables 6.3 and 6.4 represent an attempt to estimate the quantities and approximate value of miraa exported from the two Nyambene markets in 1985.[3] Some Lare miraa is directly purchased by exporters, and it is especially hard to estimate its production and value. One example of this is a depot in the town of Kaelo that purchases miraa for the Somali market. This miraa is sent to the border, smuggled into Somalia by camel, picked up by soldiers in government landrovers, and then sold in urban areas for

Table 6.2. Production Costs and Profits for an Average Kangeta Shamba

Costs	Profits	140sh.	120sh.	100 sh.
10 bunda = 550 sh.		850	650	450
8 bunda = 470 sh.		650	490	330
6 bunda = 390 sh.		450	330	210

Note: 16 ksh. = $1 (1986) U.S.

Table 6.3. Muringene Market

4 vehicles: 1 vehicle carries approx. between 70-100 gunia of miraa.
Daily export of 300 to 400 gunia daily = 2,400 to 3,200 bunda.
Price: 1 bunda mbaine = 140-160 ksh.
          1 bunda muthairo = 70-100 ksh.

Note: If we conservatively estimate the average value of 1 bunda at
sh. 100 over the year, the daily wholesale value of exports fluctuates
between 240,00 and 320,000 ksh., or sh. 80m annually (at 250,000 per
day).

Table 6.4. Lare Market

8-12 vehicles
Daily export = 600 to 1200 gunia daily, 4,200 and 9,600 bunda.
Price: 1 bunda = 30 to 100 ksh.

Note: If we estimate the value of Lare mirra at sh. 50 per bunda, the
estimated daily value of exports fluctuates between 210,000-480,000
ksh., also ksh. 80m annually (at 250,000 per day). These "ballpark"
figures indicate that miraa production is at least 160m ksh. a year
industry (very likely much more), not counting the miraa that is
exported at alternative depots such as the Kaelo location which is the
center of Somalia-bound miraa.

prices as high as 400 Somali shillings (equivalent to K Sh 100) per
kilo.

Vehicles heading for major urban markets arrive in Nairobi by
8:00 P.M., and in Mombasa before sunrise. The Nairobi miraa
terminal is in Majengo, a cramped mass of mud and corrugated iron
houses lined by open gutters whose ankle-deep water is disguised by
a film of dust and garbage that collects on the surface. There is no
electricity, and a pile of trash has marked the middle of the main
intersection for the past three years. The miraa is unloaded in the
darkness and quickly finds its way to the correct owners who share
cramped quarters and a gaaru-like communal existence. The outward
appearance of poverty in Majengo, however, is a facade hiding the

large amounts of cash that these migrating entrepreneurs handle. The miraa will be taken to different parts of the city in the morning by retailers, except for what is sold in the nearby Eastleigh ward where the serious aficionados congregate at night.

Eastleigh, in ways, is East Africa's greatest truckstop. It is also Nairobi's main retail miraa market by day. The *gomba* flag adorns shops, restaurants, lodgings, kiosks, and the boxes of small traders who take up positions on the street. Rivaling the *gombas* in number are the various lorries, trailers, pickups, and landrovers representative of the financial clout that supports miraa consumption on such a level. Areas like Eastleigh and River Road in Nairobi, Mwembe Tayari in Mombasa, and the usual multiethnic *majengo* section of every Kenyan town, provide the social milieu of miraa use. Socially, miraa dissolves lines normally associated with ethnicity, socioeconomic class, and religion. This explains at least part of its popularity and persistence, and participants in the miraa culture are quick to point this out.

The Meru miraa traders form part of this ethnic melting pot, but the miraa trade also reinforces their Igembe ethnic identity. Many miraa dealers are solo operators who may work with an agent at the Nyambene market or purchase their miraa locally from a wholesaler. Wholesalers form what the Igembe refer to as a *kampuni*. The kampuni, the most representative from of successful miraa trading organizations, is usually limited to several members, although older, diversified operations may own vehicles and several shops, and usually form a small chain on one miraa route. Rarely officially registered or incorporated as a formal "company" by law, the kampuni arises around a successful businessman, usually a Lubetaa trader. Originally, firms were kinship-oriented, but dependence on one's kin soon gave way to qualifications based on reliability, integrity, and friendship. Members of kampuni are usually Igembe Meru except for an occasional partnership, although client retailers may be from any ethnic group. In the city and towns, kampuni members usually operate shops where they retail and wholesale miraa in addition to a few other basic items and provisions. Often these shops employ individuals who use the job as an apprenticeship to learn the trade before striking out on their own (Hjort 1974).

Kampuni are representative of the social and economic organization of the miraa trade where deals are based on a person's word. Trust, rather than a contract, is the essential nexus of miraa transactions from field to consumer. Despite the high volume and value of miraa, most dealings are in cash, and there are few written records. The informal basis of both the kampuni and solo operator

allows for miraa traders to return to their Nyambene homes
periodically. Despite the attractions of modern urban life, the
Igembe trader rarely prefers his outside existence to the ambience of
kin and friends, good food, and invigorating climate of the
Nyambenes. This partially explains the great efforts traders make to
minimize their overhead. For example, they share food and shelter
gaaru-style in towns and cities, always a source of wonderment to
their clients who cannot understand why men engaged in a
seemingly lucrative business "utterly lack any sense of self-
improvement." Also, miraa traders working abroad go to great
lengths to minimize their expenses in order to earn the capital to
reinvest back home in land and other enterprises.

In reality, miraa traders see their outside existence as an educational and broadening experience, and as a step towards establishing
themselves back home. Ideally this means getting married and acquiring land. Some try to make a quick killing in miraa, but this is an
extremely risky business for those who attempt it (Hjort 1979:78-79).
Traders who deceive non-Meru clients lower their standing within
their own communities, and risk curtailment of the reciprocity that
acts as an important mechanism ensuring supply and security to
traders living "abroad." Consistency and persistence is the real key to
success in the fluctuating market. Traders provide for each other, and
if one doesn't receive miraa one day, someone will share his con-
signment with him. Many young traders of the new Miriti age-set who
are currently seeking their fortunes until they make enough money to
invest in either land or a business may or may not return to the
miraa trade. But they will plant miraa on the land they acquire to
provide security in old age and a birthright to their children. Those
who are fortunate enough to be involved with a kampuni usually
acquire enough capital to invest in new land; they leave the
management of the rural enterprise to their wives while they return
to the city, rotating with their associates between city and country on
a regular basis.

The miraa business, it must be remembered, entails long hours,
hard work, and personal discipline to maintain a daily clientele. It
has created a class of entrepreneurs who straddle urban and rural
areas, and who, except for shops and other property they may acquire to facilitate kampuni operations, return most of their earnings
to their home areas. Because the work is so demanding, eventually a
man will exit from the export domain to set himself up managing a
farm or small business. Because many Ratanaa and Lubetaa dealers
are now turning over their responsibilities to younger men, the market continues to resist strong monopolies and maintains free entry.

Miraa and Rural Development

The success of Kenya's smallholder agriculture, especially as represented by the large-scale adoption of export crops, is deceptive. Njonjo equates the rapid expansion of agricultural production during the 1960s and 1970s with a rapid deterioration in the real income of farmers, and describes peasant agriculturalists in adjacent Central Province as proletariats on patches of land (Njonjo 1981). To the south of Meru in Embu, Haugerud has shown the consequences of commercialized agriculture and land reform in coffee- and cotton-based rural economy as retarding agrarian enterprise and encouraging investment in land for speculation rather than production. She says: "In brief, peasant agriculture, even in Kenya's relatively prosperous central highlands, provides a meager living for those with very modest material and educational expectations" (1983:83).

At this time, the local Nyambene economy appears to differ from these assessments in important ways. Differences in wealth resulting from the structural inequality of the market are partially redistributed via the social structure; the ecology has been protected by the traditional intercropping system that incorporates food, miraa, and tree crops; and even more important, the local community takes the initiative in setting out its own development priorities. Material prosperity has increased within the setting of social continuity: miraa is a casebook example of the development of peripheral capitalism representing the unique marriage of precapitalist and modern elements. And it demonstrates the ability of local actors to influence the developmental process, as a number of scholars have recently stressed (e.g., Illife 1983).

The nature of the changes has permitted the life cycle embodied in the society's institutions to be transferred into the modern setting with positive results. It may be untenable to assert that the warrior institution has been directly transferred to entrepreneurial activity, and that the role of elders has changed from managing ritual and ceremony to managing enterprises, despite the similarities. Still, there is a correspondence insofar as the age-set system has provided a natural model for the organization of miraa production and trade, including an internal system of checks and balances, and *gichiaro* fictive kinship, which enables Meru to incorporate outsiders into their firms over the demands of less industrious kin. Each generation of the Igembe has gone out into the world to build upon what was established by the preceding generation before "retiring" back to the farm or an individually based enterprise. I do not stress this continuity for its own sake, but for the effect that it has in stabilizing relationships and contributing to what is by any standard a remarkably efficient system of production and distribution—a system built upon local knowledge and characterized by a lack of the conflict that is so conspicuous in many other African enterprises. Miraa has an economic half-life of forty-eight hours, yet it reaches every corner of eastern Africa and beyond with a consistency any government parastatal would be proud of.

This success is due to the market incentives created by a growing urban salaritariat, the lack (or ineffectual nature) of government controls over both consumption and trade, the lack of state involvement through marketing boards and pricing policy, and the ability of miraa to piggyback on the structural developments serving adjacent coffee and tea producing areas. It supports Bates's (1981) thesis of the dysfunctional role of government-managed agricultural development through parastatals, price controls, and other policies that generally favor urban consumers over rural producers. No doubt consumers would suffer higher prices for lower-quality miraa under state management, and the Meru success probably never could have occurred under Tanzania's center-directed development policies, which resulted in rural stagnation under the increasingly incapable and corrupt state apparatus (Ergas 1982). The miraa farmers' brief experience with cooperative marketing during the short life of the Meru Traders Society, between 1969 and 1971, has set them against any suggestion of such a policy again, and highlights the problems of centralization on even a small scale.

The cooperative was the project of the local parliament minister, Joseph Muturi, who was a miraa dealer himself before he was elected to parliament. The cooperative was designed to control prices and protect producers' profits. Because miraa is such a perishable commodity, the Nyambene markets are de facto buyer's markets most of the time. If a farmer does not get the price he wants, there is little he can do with the miraa except watch it go to waste. The society, however, could not organize marketing efficiently. Miraa spoiled in the society's depot in Meru town, farmers rebelled, the cooperative collapsed, and Muturi was voted out of office. Farmers don't want anything to do with another cooperative, or any form of outside interference designed to protect their equity, and they accept the importance of traders and middlemen in the development process (Bauer 1984). Although middlemen might realize a higher profit from miraa, at the same time they operate a network that provides opportunities for their children and kin, while wealthy individuals still pay the material costs of maintaining social relationships. It would be extremely difficult for any kind of outside agency to duplicate their role in all aspects.

Miraa plots represent an extremely valuable long-term resource and are virtually not sold. Most of the miraa (especially the valuable *mbaine*) is actually controlled by elders who may belong to the Ithalie or the Ratanaa *riika*. Few of these elders, unlike the Lubetaa generation that followed them, grew up within the cash economy. These elders are accused by younger generations of mismanaging the petty cash from miraa payments; in fact, a certain percentage of miraa earnings by elders are lost to beer consumption. With the growth of cash requirements for school fees and other modern expenses, a patronage system has developed where farmers rent their miraa to wealthy traders in return for cash advances. The farmers get cash, and the traders get a steady supply of miraa at lower prices. Some young men see themselves victimized by a pattern of dissipation of exploitation, and as in other places in Africa, the pattern of conflict does not crystallize on class but on generational differences.

Until the early 1970s, miraa fueled a natural economy that developed according to its own internal logic, which was largely supported by indigenous social institutions and social relations. Expanding economic opportunity has kept up with the growing population, and as overcrowding at home increases the new Miriti *riika* has tended to supplant traditional clients as traders (Dahl 1979). The symbolic significance of contemporary conditions and the full-cycle inscribed from one Miriti *riika* to the new one is not lost upon the Igembe Meru: elders tell the new Miriti generation that they will have to engineer a breakthrough during their generation equivalent to that of the old Miriti's discovery of miraa. The failure to do so will no doubt result not in marginalization of peasant farmers, but a "share the poverty" strategy following agricultural involution (Geertz, 1963).

The three-fold expansion of coffee holdings that took place in Meru District during the 1960s largely bypassed the Nyambenes, and farmers who did plant coffee received half of what their Mount Kenya counterparts received during the same period (Bernard 1972:123). After a slow start, smallholder tea production began at a later date and took off during the 1970s. Miraa farmers began planting other cash crops on a large scale only after the shift to the cash economy was accompanied by the shift of the comparative advantage of coffee and tea over food (despite price fluctuations). By the time this happened, the higher reaches and edges of the traditional zones had been purchased by wealthy individuals, usually

Meru but from outside the division, and put under moderately large-scale tea and coffee cultivation. This, more than any other factor, has put a ceiling on the expansion of smallholder agriculture. The combination of large- and smallholder tea and coffee production has resulted in more acreage actually under these crops, although they don't approach miraa's role as the local engine of development. Nevertheless, the longstanding bias against miraa leads to it, rather than other cash crops, absorbing the blame for the fall in local food production.

The diversification into tea and coffee represents a social shift also. Tea and coffee are land intensive where miraa is labor intensive; and tea and coffee payments are disbursed in two large payments a year. From the viewpoint of household management, these crops function as a bank in a way similar to the traditional role of cattle, which they have replaced on a practical level in terms of labor and land, at least to some degree. The commercialization of local agriculture has two contrary effects locally: on the one hand, it increases individual actor-type tendencies within the system; on the other hand, the greater risk created by the fact that food production has been replaced by reliance on international markets and government marketing underscores the importance of miraa production and the group affiliations that go with it (Berry 1984:91). The Miriti generation, the first *riika* to have significant contact with Western education, continues to rally around the miraa flag while pursuing greater intensification of smallholder agriculture.

Despite the conventional view that development projects are the "cutting edge" of development (Moris 1981:47), the evidence from the case of miraa indicates that the African farmer and the adaptability of African social organization actually hold the key to development. Critical questions, however, remain to be answered. Is the unique Meru adaptation a transitory phase of the peasant mode of production that will in time follow the same pattern as other highly productive areas of the central highland as the local economy becomes incorporated in the larger national economy? Is the peasant mode of production too overgeneralized to remain a productive concept (Hill 1986)? More complex field research is required before such questions can be addressed.

Notes

1. This research was partially funded by the Center for African Studies at the University of Florida. A briefer version was presented at the 1986 African Studies Association Meetings in Madison, Wisconsin. I extend special thanks

to Dr. Ronald Cohen and Dr. Art Hansen of the University of Florida, and to Marehemu Elias Maitheta and Ezekial Maingi, among the many helpful individuals from Igembe location.

2. Among the Meru, warriors of one *mwiriga* live in a *gaaru*, or common barracks, until they collectively graduate to adulthood and marry. Two alternating groups go through warriorhood at one time, a term of service that lasted from twelve to fifteen years but could vary according to circumstances. The age-set system also creates classificatory relationships between different *riika*: member of one *riika* call each other "bamingo," a term referring to patrilineal parallel cousins, but call members of the *riika* immediately above or below themselves "baite," a term referring to cross-cousins. Members of one *riika* marry daughters from the adjacent set above them, and marry their daughters to the adjacent set below them, creating a chain of alliances marked by ritual and political authority of one *riika* over the younger one, and which becomes offset over time as the younger *riika* assume authority of the same nature over the elder *riikas'* daughters and grandchildren.

3. These are conservative figures both in terms of quantity and value of exports, but nevertheless indicate that the value of miraa production is double that listed in government records. The following chart, compiled from *Meru District Agricultural Reports* for the representative years in the 1970s and 1980s, demonstrates the erratic nature of miraa records, and provides ample evidence for Polly Hill's case concerning African statistical information.

Table 6.5. Miraa Production in Meru 1973-1984

Year	Hectares	Growers	Bundles (millions)	Cess (millions)	Value (pounds)
1973	750 .829		3767	100	21
1974	750 1.350		4000	200	27
1975	750 1.164		4000	150	64.4
1976	800 1.231		----	---	63.3
1977-80	--- -		----	---	---
1981	2000	----	260	---	66.0
1982	2100	----	250	---	70.0
1983	2200	----	270	---	?
1984	3050	----	208	---	?

Note: According to miraa dealers these figures are based on guesses by government officials. The category 'bundles' does, however, give an indication of the growth of miraa production.

REFERENCES

Ambler, C.H. 1985. Population Movement, Social Formation and Exchange: Central Kenya in The Nineteenth Century. *International Journal of African Historical Studies* 18:2.

Anderson, D. and David Throup. 1985. Africans and Agricultural Production in Colonial Kenya: The Myth of the War As a Watershed. *Journal of African History* 26:327-345.

Aytoun, E. 1956. *The Penny Universities: A History of the Coffee Houses*. London: Secken and Warburg.

Barker, J. 1984. *The Politics of Agriculture in Sub-Saharan Africa*. Beverly Hills: Sage Publications.

Barnes, C. 1979. An Experiment With Coffee Production by Kenyans, 1933-1945. *African Economic History* 8:198-209.

Bates, R. 1981. *Markets and States in Tropical Africa: The Political Basis of Agricultural Policies*. Berkeley and Los Angeles: University of California Press.

————. 1984. Some Conventional Orthodoxies in the Subject of Agrarian Change. *World Politics*.

Bauer, P.T. 1984. Remembrance of Studies Past. In *Pioneers in Development*. Gerald M. Meier and Dudley Seers, eds. London: Oxford University Press.

Bernard, F.E. 1972. *East of Mt. Kenya: Meru Agriculture in Transition*. Munich: Weltforum, IFO-Institute.

Berry, S. 1984. The Food Crisis And Agrarian Change In Africa: A Review Essay. *African Studies Review* 27:2.

————. 1986. Social Science Perspectives On Food In Africa. In *Food In Sub-Saharan Africa*. Art Hansen and Della McMillan, eds. Boulder, Colo.: Lynne Rienner.

Buch, H., M. Marcussen, and H.S. Marcussen. 1982. Contract Farming And The Peasantry: Cases From Western Kenya. *Review of African Political Economy* 23:9-36.

Chanler, A. 1893. Mr. Chanler's Expedition to East Africa. *Geographical Journal* 1:533-534.

Coquery-Vidrovitch, C. 1978. Research On An African Mode Of Production. In Gutkind and Waterman, eds. *African Social Research*

Dahl, Gudrun. 1979. *Suffering Grass*. Stockholm Studies in Anthropology.

Dale, I.R. and P.J. Greenway. 1961. *Kenya Trees and Shrubs*. Buchanan's Kenya Estates.

Ergas, Z. 1982. The State and Economic Deterioration: The Tanzanian Case. *Journal of Commonwealth and Comparative Politics* 20:3:286-308.

Fadiman, J.A. 1976 *Mountain Warriors: The Pre-colonial Meru of Mt. Kenya*. Athens: University of Ohio Center for International Studies.

————. 1977. Mountain Witchcraft: Supernatural Practices and Practitioners Among the Meru of Mt. Kenya. *African Studies Review* 20:1:87-101.

————. 1978. The Meru Peoples. In *Kenya Before 1900*. B.A. Ogot, ed. Nairobi: East African Publishing House.

————. 1979. *The Moment of Conquest, Meru, Kenya 1907*. Athens: University of Ohio Center for International Studies.

————. 1982. *An Oral History of Tribal Warfare: The Meru of Mt. Kenya*. Athens: Ohio University Press.

Geertz, C. 1963. *Agricultural Involution.* Berkeley and Los Angeles: University of California Press.

Getahun, A. and A.D. Krikorian. 1973. Chat: Coffee's Rival From Harar, Ethiopia. Botany, Cultivation, and Use. *Economic Botany* 27:4.

Greenway, P.J. 1947. Khat. *East African Agricultural Journal* 13:98-102.

Hart, K. 1982. *The Political Economy of West African Agriculture.* Cambridge: Cambridge University Press.

Hattox, R.S. 1985. *Coffee and Coffeehouses.* Seattle and London: University of Washington Press.

Haugerud, A. 1983. The Consequences of Land-Tenure Reform Among Smallholders in the Kenya Highlands. *Rural Africana* 15-16:65-89.

Hill, P. 1974. *Migrant Cocoa Farmers of Ghana.* Cambridge: Cambridge University Press.

————. 1986. *Development Economics On Trial.* Cambridge: Cambridge: Cambridge University Press.

Hjort, A. 1974. Trading Miraa: From School-leaver to Shop-owner in Kenya. *Ethnos* 39:1:27-43.

————. 1979. *Savanna Town: Rural Ties and Urban Opportunities in Northern Kenya.* Stockholm Studies in Social Anthropology.

Holding, M. 1942. Some Preliminary Notes on Meru Age Grades. *Man* 42:31:58-65.

Hyden, G. 1980. *Beyond Ujamaa in Tanzania: Underdevelopment and an Uncaptured Peasantry.* Berkeley: University of California Press.

————. 1983. *No Shortcuts to Progress.* Berkeley and London: University of California Press.

Illife, J. 1983. *The Emergence of African Capitalism.* Minneapolis: University of Minnesota Press.

Jackson, K. 1976. The Dimensions of Kamba Pre-Colonial History. In *Kenya Before 1900.* B.A. Ogot, ed. Nairobi: East African Publishing House.

Jackson, R. and C. Rosberg. 1984. *Personal Rule in Subsaharan Africa.* Berkeley: University of California Press.

Jacob, H.E. 1935. *The Saga of Coffee: The Biography of an Economic Product.* London: Allen and Unwin.

Kasfir, N. 1983. State, Magendo, and Class Formation in Uganda. *Journal of Commonwealth and Comparative Politics* 21:3:84-103.

Kitchings, G. 1977. "Modes of Production in Kenya." *Review of African Political Economy.* Jan.-Apr.: 56-74.

Kjejshus, H. 1977. *Ecology Control and Economic Development in East African History.* London: Heinemann.

Lemarchand, R. 1986. The Political Economy Of Food Issues. In *Food In Sub-Saharan Africa.* Art Hansen and Della McMillan, eds. Boulder, Colo.: Lynne Rienner.

Leo, C. 1984. *Land and Class in Kenya.* Toronto: University of Toronto Press.

Leys, C. 1974. *Underdevelopment in Kenya.* Berkeley: University of California Press.

Lovejoy, P.E. 1980. *Caravans of Kola.* Zaria, Nigeria: Ahmed Bello University Press.

Mahner, J. 1975. The Outsider and Insider in Tigania, Meru. *Africa* (London): 45:4:400-409.

Miracle, M. 1974. Economic Change Among The Gikuyu, 1895-1905. Working Paper No. 158. Nairobi University: Institute for Development Studies.

Moris, J. 1981. *Managing Rural Development.* Bloomington, Ind.: International Development Institute.

Moser, C. 1917. The flower of Paradise: The Part Which Khat Plays In The Life Of The Yemen Arab. *National Geographic* 32:173-1886.

Mungai, J.M. 1982. Use And Abuse Of Miraa. *Daily Nation,* 27 May.

Muriuki, J. 1974. *The History of the Gikuyu.* Nairobi: East African Publishing House.

Mutiso, G. 1976. *Kenya: Politics, Policy, and Society.* Nairobi: East African Publishing House.

————. 1978. Kitui Ecosystem, Integration And Change. In *History And Ecology In East Africa.* Bethwel Ogot, ed. Nairobi: East African Publishing House.

Njonjo, A.L. 1981. The Kenya Peasantry: A Reassessment. *Review of African Political Economy* 20:27-39.

Peters, D.W.A. 1952. Khat: Its History, Botany, Chemistry, and Toxicology. *Pharmaceutical Journal* 15 July:15-16 and 12 July:36-37.

Rigby, P. 1985. *Persistent Pastoralists: Nomadic Societies in Transition.* London: Zed.

Shahandeh, B. et al. 1983. *The Health and Socio-economic Aspects of Khat Use.* Lausanne: International Council on Alcohol and Addictions.

Sorrenson, M.P.K. 1967. *Land Reform in Gikuyu Country.* Nairobi and London: Oxford University Press.

Spear, T. 1982. *Traditions of Origin and Their Interpretation.* Athens: Ohio University Center for International Studies.

Throup, D. 1985. The Origins of Mau Mau. *African Affairs* 84:336:399-433.

Tignor, R. 1979. Colonial Chiefs in Chiefless Societies. In *Bureaucratic Corruption in Sub-Saharan Africa.* Monday U. Ekpo, ed. Washington, D.C.: University Press of America.

Tosh, J. 1980. "The Cash-Crop Revolution in Tropical Africa: An Agricultural Reappraisal." *African Affairs* 79:3/4Z:79-84.

Troughear, T. 1982. Miraa, The Not So Strange Addiction. *The Standard,* 6 October.

Waller, R. 1985. Ecology, Migration, and Expansion in East Africa. *African Affairs* 84:336:348-370.

Zwanenberg, . 1982. Hunting-Gathering: Way of Life or Mode of Production? *African Economic History* 2:12-21.

CHAPTER 7

Food Surplus Production, Wealth, and Farmers' Strategies in Kenya

ANGELIQUE HAUGERUD[1]

Theories of agrarian change differ sharply in explanatory focus. Some center on "rational" individual actors, while others examine culture, social structure, mode of production, nation-state, or world economic system. One persistent division is that between individual rationality or entrepreneurship on the one hand, and society or social structure on the other. This split is associated with the 1960s formalist-substantivist controversy in economic anthropology (LeClair and Schneider 1968; Cancian 1968; Dalton 1969), with neoclassical versus "institutional" economics (Mann 1960; Veblen 1934, 1961), with moral economy versus rational peasant approaches (Scott 1976; Popkin 1979), and with oppositions within anthropological theory in general (Ortner 1984).

Implicit ideological differences underlie explicit theoretical divisions such as those of formalism and substantivism (see Sahlins 1972:xiv and Orlove 1986).[2] Some scholars address this issue explicitly in their own work, while others attack their opponents' analyses for being inappropriately influenced by political values.

Studies of Africa's agrarian crisis do not escape such conflicts. To what extent theoretical and empirical disagreements in this area arise from noncomparable data, methods, or definitions; from ideological attachment to particular paradigms; or from some combination of these and other sources is uncertain. Two recent reviewers of the literature on African agrarian change each suggest (for different reasons) that the prevailing paradigms and the special interests they serve have produced misleading interpretations of Africa's agrarian crisis (Berry 1983; Cohen 1986b; and Chapter 1, this book). Competing theories and interpretations are translated into contradictory policy recommendations.

Much theoretical debate about agrarian evolution has been stimulated by the opposing views of A.V. Chayanov (1966) and V. I. Lenin (1899) concerning differentiation among the Russian peasantry late in the nineteenth century. While Chayanov's theory is based on marginal utility principles and depicts the microeconomic logic of peasant household differentiation as determined by household demographic characteristics (especially the ratio of consumers to workers),[3] that of Lenin portrays long-term processes of social class formation involving the ultimate demise of the peasantry under expansion of commodity production and capitalism. In the latter view, the middle peasantry is a group eroded at opposite extremes by the land-hungry poor and by wealthy land accumulators. Chayanov has been criticized for ignoring class differentiation in peasant agriculture, and for not addressing the dynamics of a system in which rich and poor farmers are linked to middle peasants via labor, land, and capital markets and exchanges (see Patnaik 1979). Lenin had earlier emphasized the predominant role in Russian agriculture of a minority (20 percent or fewer of all farmers) of capitalist farmers or peasant bourgeoisie who hired labor and whose importance was reflected in their shares of the total quantity of means of production and produce grown (Thorner in Chayanov 1966:xx).

Recently, scholars such as Lehmann (1982) have suggested the need to transcend this debate, pointing to agrarian structures and paths of change that depart from both Chayanov's and Lenin's models. A differentiated peasantry, for example, often coexists with large-scale holdings. Differentiation within the peasantry does not necessarily imply an inevitable demise of family farms and emergence of a proletariat and bourgeoisie. Rather, agrarian evolution involves the differential survival of a complex array of farm types and modes of domestic organization. Large holdings, for example, do not always rely most heavily on hired labor, but instead are operated by family, cooperative, and hired labor in variable combinations. Small farmers are not necessarily subsistence oriented, but differ in the percentage of income received from export cash crops, food crops, and nonagricultural economic activities. Rural household organization and composition sometimes seem to defy classification since a single farm household, for example, may simultaneously include individuals who work as casual laborers for other farmers, who are employed as teachers or clerks in the civil service, who operate small businesses, who engage in livestock trading, who cultivate export crops such as coffee or tea, and who cultivate food crops for both home consumption and for sale. In short, food self-sufficiency; production for markets; participation in formal and informal labor markets; and use of hired, cooperative, and family labor in agricultural production all are related in complex and diverse ways to one another and to the scale of agricultural production. This empirical diversity and complexity are easily overlooked in debates that force choices between large- and small-scale agricultural development strategies. Policy interventions in the name of either strategy are unlikely to produce consistent outcomes.

Debate over the merits of large- versus small-scale agriculture in Africa focuses in part on farmers' capacity to produce sufficient output to satisfy both national foreign exchange requirements and domestic market demand for food crops. The notion that Africa's agrarian crisis is one of acute underproduction, however, lacks a sound statistical foundation:

> Aggregate production data are too unreliable to warrant firm conclusions about continental production trends, and arguments that agricultural output is declining or stagnating in Africa are too much in the interests of the authors to warrant unquestioning acceptance. (Berry 1983:1)

The available data simply do not permit accurate determination of the extent to which crop output has actually declined, or has gone into parallel rather than official markets or into higher rural consumption standards. Agricultural supply crises arise from poor distribution and a number of other causes, as well as from declining production. Inadequate statistics weaken arguments premised on important productivity differences between large- and small-scale agriculture.

Poor aggregate statistics also undermine assertions that small farmers' supposed "subsistence orientation" makes them unwilling to market food crops. We really don't know, for example, to what extent they are willing to (and do) market crops in parallel rather than in official markets. Nor should farmers' willingness to market food crops be confused with their capacity to do so.

This paper examines variation across seasons and among households in small farmers' food production levels. It highlights the economic complexity and diversity masked by such terms as "subsistence orientation," and argues that small farmers' subsistence orientation, if present at all, is neither a tradition-bound absence of response to market incentives, nor a reflection of uniformly low productive capacity. Rather, it is in part a direct and variable response to the uncertainties of market and state institutions and policies (cf. Bates 1983; Hyden 1980; Little and Horowitz 1987). An economically crucial aspect of this institutional uncertainty is that it encourages *both* large and small farmers to reduce their risks by diversifying their economic pursuits rather than specializing in one or two products for the market. The preference for diversification in turn limits local market demand for food crops, except in years when poor weather causes widespread production shortfalls (and except where a large and rapidly expanding urban labor force stimulates demand for marketed food crops).

Evidence to support these arguments comes from Kenya, one of Africa's economic and administrative successes, and a country about which scholars hold contradictory views concerning both actual and desirable courses of agrarian change.

Change in Kenya's Agrarian Structure: The Rise of Smallholders[4]

Policy rhetoric and practice are often inconsistent. Kenya, for example, is officially committed to a strategy of smallholder development, and is widely praised as a success in this regard (e.g., World Bank 1981). Observers of the country recognize, however, that many state policies and agricultural services in practice have not been reoriented from large-scale to small-scale farmers' needs (Cox 1984; Bates 1981, 1983). Nevertheless, the relative contributions of large- and small-scale farms to marketed agricultural output in the last three decades have shifted dramatically in favor of smallholders.

Kenya's agrarian structure has been distinctly multimodal since the colonial period, when Europeans began to settle and to farm the country's fertile highlands. Large-scale European and small-scale African agriculture coexisted under a system of "apartheid regulations in commodity production" (Njonjo 1981:13). In particular, the colonial state placed restrictions on African cultivation of cash crops such as coffee, tea, and pyrethrum. Racial restrictions on commodity production were eased in the late 1950s and early 1960s, when the colonial government began a land tenure reform program that involved consolidation of fragmented holdings and registration of individual freehold titles (see Sorrenson 1967).

After political independence in 1963, some of the large European farms were subdivided into African settlement schemes; some were transferred intact to African owners, partnerships, and public and private corporations; and some remained in European hands (see Heyer, Maitha, and Senga 1976; Hunt 1984; Kitching 1980; Leys 1975; Sorrenson 1967; Wasserman 1965).

The late-colonial tenure reform began in the African small-holder areas of the central highlands, where anticolonial political protest over land alienation and other issues had been particularly strong.[6] Land consolidation and title registration in these areas were intended to foster an agrarian revolution along nineteenth-century European lines, and to encourage the emergence of a class of commercial farmers who would gradually buy out smaller subsistence-oriented production units of "uneconomic" size. Cultivators made landless by this process were to be a source of labor for the larger commercial farms and later for a growing industrial sector.

Today—twenty-five years after the tenure reform was completed in the central highlands—neither the agricultural nor the industrial sector has grown at a rate sufficient to absorb an increasing landless population. Kenyan land tenure reform has been less important as a means of capitalizing agriculture and encouraging agrarian entrepreneurship than it has been for institutionalizing rural inequalities associated with nonfarm income and access to state resources.[7] Moreover, in spite of the formal system of titled ownership, and the program to consolidate fragmented holdings, use of multiple parcels persists off the land register in association with cultivation and grazing rights based on relations of friendship, patronage, and kinship.

While land transactions have become monetized (that is, cash purchases and sales do occur), land is by no means a commercial commodity whose allocation is determined by market forces. For example, there are still strong informal sanctions against sales to "outsiders" (e.g., beyond the owner's kin or ethnic group), and there are both informal and official sanctions against sales that would preclude household food self-sufficiency (see Paterson 1984; Shipton 1985; Haugerud 1984). The growth of a landless proletariat in some regions of Kenya has been slowed by the persistence of socially defined channels of access to land, that is, by continued lending and borrowing that in part reflect a disinclination on the part of the wealthy to specialize in agricultural expansion and modernization.

The Kenyan tenure reform showed that there is no necessary connection between institutionalizing individual freehold tenure and achieving a capitalist agrarian revolution (see Okoth-Ogendo 1976; Smith 1976). Nonetheless, land consolidation and registration have remained for the last twenty years major recipients of agricultural development funds and are still the foundation of Kenya's smallholder development program.

Today, competition for land is keen in Kenya. With an area approximately the size of the state of Texas, the country supports about 20 million people, 85 percent of whom occupy the 20 percent of the country's land that is arable. Land in Kenya is unequally distributed to the extent that "0.1 percent of farm holdings (2,227 large farms and plantations) contain 14 percent of the arable land area" (Livingstone quoted in Hunt 1984:252).

Although the growth of small-scale agriculture in Kenya has been praised widely, many observers now recognize that the success was build on "soft" development options whose potential had nearly been exhausted by the mid-1970s. These options include the expansion of cultivated land in fertile regions (where some of the former large-scale farms were transferred to small farmers); removal of earlier restrictions on African dairy production and on cultivation of export cash crops such as coffee, tea, and pyrethrum; and the widespread adoption of hybrid maize (see Gerhart 1975; Lofchie 1986; World Bank 1982).

Since the mid-1970s, Kenya's annual agricultural growth rates have fluctuated, but on average have fallen below the population growth rate (estimated to be the highest in the world). Important external influences on Kenyan agricultural growth in the last decade include a doubling of world tea prices in 1984 (which helped Kenya pay for its food imports during the 1984 drought); coffee booms associated with poor weather in Brazil and with high coffee prices on the world market in 1986 and in 1977 (when world coffee prices increased tenfold); a decline in world coffee prices in the late 1970s; droughts in 1979 and 1984; and rising oil import costs in the 1970s (world oil prices doubled in 1979).

Recent national policies affecting Kenyan agriculture include increases in the 1980s in producer prices of important food crops such as maize; a 40 percent currency devaluation between 1978 and 1981; and an additional 50 percent devaluation by 1986.

Use of the "soft options" (expansion of cultivated area, cash crops, and hybrid maize) contributed to a dramatic shift in the relative contributions of the large and small farms sectors to marketed agricultural output between 1958 and 1975. Whereas large farms contributed 81 percent of the value of marketed agricultural output in 1958, by 1975 they contributed just 45 percent and small farms accounted for 55 percent (Njonjo 1981:31). Small-scale agriculture grew faster than the large-scale in the first decade after independence, and smallholder development remains a stated emphasis in the current Development Plan.

In practice, however, many state policies and services continue to favor large-scale farmers. While large-scale coffee estate farmers, for example, receive at least 90 percent of the world market price for

coffee, small-scale coffee farmers receive no more than 66 percent (Bates 1983:114). Programs that subsidize agricultural inputs such as fertilizers tend to benefit large-scale farmers at the expense of small-scale farmers (Bates 1983:116). Agriculture's share of the total development budget is less in the 1980s than it was earlier, and "a large percentage of the agricultural budget has gone to parastatals with only limited benefit to most smallholders" (Cox 1984:170). Kenya's small farmers have become heavily dependent on off-farm income sources; an estimated 41 percent of their income is derived from such sources (Miller 1984:56).

Although small farmers depend increasingly on nonagricultural economic pursuits, and although the "soft" development options have nearly been exhausted, the World Bank (1982:1) argues that in Kenya "smallholder development in high-potential areas offers the most promising prospect for increased production, labor absorption and equity." The Bank cites the growth in small-scale agriculture, and evidence of the superior productivity per unit of land of small farms to support its smallholder development emphasis (see, for example, World Bank 1981:51). Some scholars, such as Hunt (1984:302), go even further in arguing for a switch to an exclusively small-scale agricultural development:

> Available evidence on the efficiency of land, capital and labor use in agriculture shows that it would be possible to raise both output and employment by switching to an entirely small-farm based development strategy.

The data commonly cited to make such points, however, are subject to multiple interpretations. As Hunt herself notes (1984:257), for example, "a large proportion of the very small farms (under 0.5 hectares) are in the most fertile areas." Kenya's multimodal agrarian structure, its politics, and the special circumstances that created the current highly productive small farm sector suggest to others that it would be inappropriate to eliminate alternative development options. The World Bank (1981:52) states: "Priority to smallholders does not mean that *only* they warrant attention."

In addition to the varied normative assessments of Kenya's agrarian structure, there are divergent views about what actually *is* happening to middle-income smallholders in that country. Njonjo (1981), for example, argues that the Kenyan peasantry offers the "illusion of a property owning class . . . with relations to patches of land," but that it is in reality dissolving. Kitching (1980) also finds the Kenyan peasantry to be an eroding group; Anyang-N'yong'o (1981) argues that it is stagnating; Leys (1971) states that it is expanding geographically at the (expense) of the capitalist sector; and Collier and Lal (1984) argue that its economic well being is improving. Collier and Lal (1984) also recognize, however, that existing data are inadequate to assess whether economic inequality (e.g., in income and land ownership) has increased or not among Kenyan smallholders over the last two decades. In short, there is substantial disagreement (and much more complex debate than is represented here) over both what is and what should be the fate of the Kenyan smallholder.

The disagreement arises in part from the empirical diversity of agrarian structures and the complexity of the interactions among them. For example, in Kenya today there are small family farms; both foreign and local corporations that oversee contract farming and estates; and urban bureaucrats who maintain farms operated both by family members and by hired managers. Such variation is of course the essential raw material of evolutionary change, and policy interventions are one of the mechanisms of such change. Each of the observers cited above may be right about processes occurring somewhere in Kenya.

Can Small Farmers Help to Feed a Nation?

Policy debate about the role of smallholders centers in part on their supposed unwillingness to sell food crops. Cohen's (1986b) analysis of Nigerian agricultural development, for example, asserts the promise of large-scale farming and notes small farmers' reluctance to sell food crops unless the next year's harvest is almost mature and is seen to be adequate. In his view, the national agricultural contribution of smallholders is unreliable and is limited by their subsistence orientation or emphasis on safeguarding food security and self-sufficiency. The small farmers Cohen (1986b) interviewed said that both recent droughts and customary practice made them wary of possible food shortages. Large farmers in the same study, however, state that one reason for increasing their agricultural investments is to "achieve market independence for basic food grains under extraordinary inflation" (Cohen 1986b:25). In other words, the so-called "subsistence orientation" of African farmers must apply to both large- and small-scale farmers.

Some (e.g., World Bank 1981) argue that better producer incentives (especially higher producer prices) would increase smallholders' marketed output. Others such as Berry (1983) have argued persuasively that the notion that it is possible for economists or for African states to determine which prices are right and which are wrong is a misleading and inadequate approach to the agrarian crisis.

If small farmers have a conservative stance vis-á-vis food-crop marketing, it arises not only from price incentives, but also from the unreliability of food marketing institutions. The risks of depending on national food-crop markets and institutions are strikingly illustrated in Kenya, where the state has since the 1940s regulated private trade in maize between districts, purchases from farmers, sales to wholesalers, and producer and consumer prices. During the 1980 famine, maize and bean prices on unofficial or parallel markets were six to eight times the official producer prices. Prices and margins that are fixed in the formal markets under parastatal (state marketing board) control tend to lag behind prices and margins in the informal system. Between 1976 and 1982, official producer prices of maize did not rise as quickly as the consumer price index, the input price index, or the price index of purchased goods in rural areas (Cox 1984:162). The official marketing system repeatedly fails to stabilize maize supply or to maintain strategic food reserves to meet higher demand in years of poor weather and low output. In years of good weather and bumper harvests (such as 1978 and 1983), the Kenyan grain parastatal had to curtail or to suspend buying food crops from farmers because crop output exceeded the agency's purchasing and storage capacity. The board's action was associated with unstable and declining prices on unofficial markets. Although the storage problem had been addressed in the 1981 Sessional Paper Number 4 on National Food Policy, little action had been taken to correct it between the 1978 and 1983 bumper harvests (see *African Business* 1983:25).

Under such circumstances, when unofficial market prices fluctuate widely, and when official state agencies are unable to protect consumers or producers from alternating cycles of gluts and deficits, it is not surprising if small farmers keep their options open by using food production as just one of many diversified economic pursuits, rather than specializing in production of one or two crops for the market. In short, the frequent incapacity of state agencies and markets to handle agricultural surpluses and deficits encourages small farmers to diversify their economic activities and to reduce their dependence on food-crop markets and official programs (cf. Hyden 1980, 1983).

Seven commissions of inquiry into the Kenyan maize marketing system between 1946 and 1972 recommended reduction in state involvement as a means of lowering consumer prices, encouraging regional specialization, and making the large parallel market redundant (Moseley 1986:110). Political interests prevented enactment of the recommendations of each commission. Decontrol would mean losses for large and politically influential maize farmers, whose superior access to maize trading licenses allows them to earn substantial personal profits through interdistrict trade in times of shortage. Locally perceived disadvantages of decontrol also included a reduction in food security and an increase in the economic role of Asian traders.[8]

If oversupply as well as undersupply of food crops to the market is a cyclical problem in Kenya, and one against which existing state and market institutions provide no buffer, we would expect large as well as small farmers to reduce their economic risks by practicing diversification rather than specialization. For both large and small farmers, off-farm incomes from salaries or trade subsidize agricultural investment, cover some of its risks, and supplement subsistence food production. The same forces that discourage individual specialization also discourage regional specialization, so that in Kenya consumers prefer to grow maize themselves, however unsuitable the soil and climate, rather than to depend on markets to purchase maize (Moseley 1986:110).

Neither diversification nor specialization, of course, offers any guarantee against poverty; specialization, for example, can bring some farm households short-term prosperity but long-term decline as their market opportunities are changed by successful imitators or monopolizers (Berry 1983:74). Scholars such as Hart (1982) argue, however, that the possibilities for sustained economic growth in Africa remain limited unless there is a significant structural shift from diversification to specialization of individual production units. Such a shift would require more reliable state and market institutions and costly guarantees to farmers to reduce the risks of farm specialization. It is, of course, easier to change the agricultural practices of a small elite of educated, large-scale farmers than it is to influence thousands of dispersed, small-scale producers of maize and beans. However, the success of capitalized large-scale farming itself requires reliable and timely provision of credit, inputs, and marketing and storage services, all of which remain costly and difficult to accomplish reliably in Africa.

Finally, though specialization is commonly assumed to be essential for economic growth, growing crises in industrial agriculture point again to the advantages of retaining some diversity (see Barlett 1987, 1984; Gladwin and Zabawa 1987; Norgaard 1987; and Rogers

1987). Caution must be exercised in the exportation to developing countries of capital- and energy-intensive agricultural techniques that create food supply systems that are neither stable nor sustainable in the long run.

Large- and Small-Scale Food Production in Kenya

Little is known about the proportion of Kenya's total maize crop that is directly consumed by small-scale producers, or the percentage marketed informally rather than through the official grain parastatal. Schmidt and Mbugua (1976) estimate that about half of Kenya's marketed maize is traded through informal channels, though the percentage that is legal or illegal interdistrict trade is uncertain.[9]

Kenyan smallholders contribute over 90 percent of the total output of maize and beans, the country's principal food staples. Maize itself contributes 50 to 70 percent of caloric intake in rural as well as urban areas (DeWilde 1984). Most wheat, which is still a luxury food, is grown primarily on large farms (Schmidt and Mbugua 1976:3).

Many small farmers both buy and sell maize, selling some immediately after harvest to meet urgent cash requirements and purchasing it again later in the season when the harvest has been consumed. Small farmers often depend on informal markets for both sales and purchases of maize, in part because official marketing agents require payments of unofficial fees and are not well distributed throughout producing areas (DeWilde 1984). While small farmers probably sell a larger proportion of their maize crop in local and parallel markets than do large-scale farmers, about half of the maize output officially marketed through the grain parastatal nevertheless comes from small-scale farmers (Schmidt and Mbugua 1976).

Economists such as Gsaenger and Schmidt (1977) state that sources of instability in Kenya's maize output differ for large- and small-scale producers. Large producers, they believe, show a high price-supply response with respect to acreage planted,[10] while variability in smallholder maize production is more closely tied to rainfall and input prices. Gsaenger and Schmidt (1977:4) state that smallholders decide what acreage to plant in maize less on the basis of producer prices than according to home consumption needs. This view of small farmers' motives is not uncommon among analysts of agrarian Africa (Berry 1983:32-33), and is related to Chayanov's theory of peasant economy (see note 20). If Gsaenger and Schmidt's assertions are correct, we would expect to find among smallholders a strong relationship between food-crop output and household size and composition.

Data from central Kenyan smallholders suggest, however, that variation in their food crop output is much more than a product of differences in rainfall and household consumer needs. The remainder of the paper focuses on this and other issues citing a case study of small farmers in Embu District, in Kenya's productive central highlands.

Farming in Embu[11]

The fertile uplands of Embu District on the southeastern slopes of Mount Kenya are occupied by the Embu ethnic group, who numbered 180,000 in 1979 (Kenya 1979). They are a Bantu people who are closely related linguistically and culturally to the Kikuyu on the southern and western slopes of the mountain, and to the Meru subgroups on its northeastern and eastern sides.[12] Each of these three groups has long had important trading ties to neighboring lowland societies more dependent on livestock (e.g., the Kikuyu with the Masai, the Meru with the Tharaka, and the Embu with the Mbeere). The Kikuyu with 21 percent of the national population (Kenya 1979), are the country's largest ethnic group and have long dominated the national political economy. While the Embu people represent just 1.2 percent of the country's population, their political, economic, and social ties to the Kikuyu and Meru have helped to give Embu District more influence in Nairobi than its relatively small population size alone might suggest.[13]

Embu District did not include large-scale European farming in the colonial period, and was one of the first areas to undergo the smallholder land tenure reform discussed earlier. By the early 1960s, small farms in the most agriculturally productive uplands of the district were titled and registered under individual freehold tenure. Unlike their Kikuyu neighbors, the Embu people did not lose to European farmers their natural frontier for population expansion, an intermediate altitude grassland zone (locally termed *weru* and here referred to as the cotton zone) between the densely settled uplands and the lowlands occupied by the Mbeere ethnic group.

The Embu population has more than tripled in the last sixty years, while emigration from the district has increased slowly, and is far below rates found, for example, in the Kikuyu districts (see Haugerud 1984:41-44). Population density in Embu has increased rapidly, and per capita land availability today is less than a third of what it was early this century (see Mwaniki 1973 for early twentieth-century population estimates). Between 1969 and 1979, the average population density of upper Embu (Runyenje's Division) increased from 570 to 861 persons per square mile (Kenya 1969, 1979).

Some Embu farmers were permitted to cultivate coffee earlier than the Kikuyu, in part because the Embu lived farther away from and were less involved than the Kikuyu as migrant laborers in the large-scale European farm sector. Their distance from European farming, together with the region's high agrarian potential (fertile volcanic soils and good rainfall) helped to make highland Embu one of the first African areas to receive a number of colonial government programs to improve smallholder agriculture (see Moris 1970).

Agricultural opportunities in Embu District are defined in part by a pronounced ecological gradient that extends from the tropical alpine zone of the Mount Kenya forest down through a tea and dairy zone, a mixed coffee and tea zone, a coffee zone, a sunflower and maize zone, a cotton zone, and a livestock and millet zone. The present study focuses on farmers in contiguous coffee and cotton zones.

Embu, Kikuyu, and Meru farmers in the Mount Kenya region practice vertical ecological strategies similar to those used in the more extreme mountain environments of the Andes (Brush 1977, Guillet 1981, Murra 1970, Orlove 1977) and the Swiss Alps (Netting 1976). In spite of the tenure reform's attempted consolidation of fragmented holdings, Embu families today often maintain access to land in two or more agroecological zones, which allows them to diversify their production, reduce the risks of crop loss, and distribute labor requirements more evenly throughout the annual cycle.

Individuals acquire access to land in more than one zone either through formal ownership of multiple parcels or through informal relations of monetary and nonmonetary land exchange among relatives and acquaintances. Cultivating land in two or more zones is made practicable by the geographic compression of the district's environmental diversity. The portions of the coffee and cotton zones included in the present study, for example, comprise a decline from about 1,525 meters to 1,160 meters above sea level across a distance of less than eight kilometers. At the upper end of this altitude gradient, soils are more fertile and rainfall significantly higher and more reliable than at the lower end. (Rainfall averages just over 1,270 millimeters per year at the top of the gradient and about 760 to 890 millimeters per year at the lower end.)

The Embu people recognize that this environmental variation

crucially affects their economic prospects. The local terms *ruguru*, *iveti*, and *weru* correspond roughly to the tea, coffee, and cotton zones. The geographic referents of the terms vary somewhat in relation to the zone of origin of the speaker, but they are consistently associated with a progression from more hilly, better-watered terrain to flatter and drier country. Since the colonial period, the altitude zones in which one farms have determined what cash crops (tea, coffee, or cotton) one can legally cultivate. The differences in cash returns and labor requirements of these crops are pronounced.

About 90 percent of the population of Embu District live in dispersed farmsteads rather than in villages or urban centers. Numerous small trading centers have regular market days, one to three times per week, when farmers sell their produce at bartered prices.

There is wide variation in the size of the eighty-two sample households' land holdings, which range from less than a half hectare to sixty one hectares, with a mean of five and a median of three hectares.[14] There is little evidence that the largest landholders are more likely to invest in agricultural improvements, although they are somewhat more likely to have superior access to additional means of production, such as animal traction plows (in part because plows are more suited to the flatter terrain of the cotton zone, where parcels are larger). Use of hybrid maize and chemical fertilizers, and ownership of improved cattle are not significantly related to land-holding size. Indeed, smaller landowners appear slightly more likely than large landowners to use chemical fertilizers (though these are applied in quantities well below recommended dosages and on selected crops in small field areas).

Agricultural expansion is not the primary motivation for land accumulation. More than half of the sample households who increased their land holdings through purchases (in the first two decades after land registration was completed in the area) have under cultivation by themselves and by borrowers less than two-thirds of the total land they own. Land is accumulated for speculation, for the future subsistence security of sons, and for the increase in cash-borrowing power that each additional title deed confers.

Most crop production is carried out by hand with hoes and machetes. A fifth of the households sampled own animal traction plows. Farmers plant at least twice per year in association with a bimodal rainfall distribution, which includes a long rainy season between April and June and a short rainy season in October and November. There is also some dry-season cultivation in marshy valley bottoms. Coffee-zone farmers devote an average ten to twenty percent of their land (about .2 to .4 hectare) to coffee. The fifty percent of the cotton-zone residents who do cultivate cotton (a less profitable and less widely grown cash crop than coffee) devote five to fifteen percent of their land to cotton. The remaining acreage is used for food crops such as beans, maize, bananas, sorghum, sweet potatoes, Irish potatoes, and cassava. In both zones, maize and beans are the principal staples, with most households growing one-half to one hectare of these crops in mixed and single stands. A larger proportion of land is left fallow or used for grazing in the cotton zone, where for historical and environmental reasons, population density and intensity of cultivation are much lower than in the coffee zone.

Major changes in land use among Embu smallholders in the last quarter-century or so include the expansion of tea, coffee, and to a lesser extent cotton production, and the diminution of land available for grazing as the population expanded and cultivation intensified. Earlier changes in the second quarter of this century include a reduction in tubers, sorghum, and millet in favor of beans and maize.

Agricultural production in Embu is organized around family labor, supplemented during peak work periods by occasional cooperative labor and hired labor. Land preparation and planting are the points in the agricultural cycle when both hired and collective labor are most often used (Haugerud 1984:285-288). Nonmonetized exchange labor (*irima* or *ngwataniro*) includes both organized reciprocal work groups of two to a half dozen or more friends and relatives who rotate from one participant's home to the next, and also the more common situation in which a household simply calls together neighbors and relatives for a day to help with land preparation, weeding, planting or harvesting. The former corresponds to Sahlins' (1972) concept of balanced reciprocity and the latter to generalized reciprocity. In both cases, participants are given food or home-brewed beer or both, and workers expect wealthier households to provide more food than poorer ones.

Hired laborers are usually casuals paid on a daily or piecework basis, while a few wealthier households employ full-time laborers on monthly salaries. During the 1980 long-rains season, about two-thirds of the sample households hired some agricultural labor, though only 17 percent of them spent more than K Sh (Kenyan shillings) 300 ($40 in 1981 prices), the equivalent of no more than about thirty person days of weeding or planting labor, or many fewer days of land preparation labor (for which wages are higher).

Cultivation is supplemented by small-scale production of sheep, goats, cattle, and poultry. Mean livestock holdings per household are about four cows, two or three goats, and one or two sheep.

Like farmers elsewhere on the continent, Embu farmers earn incomes from a number of sources in addition to agriculture. Over a quarter of the sample households include at least one salaried employee, and 9 percent operate small businesses. Other income sources include casual agricultural and urban wage labor, charcoal production, beer brewing, tailoring, clothing and grain trade, making sisal ropes, and carpentry. Only 10 to 15 percent of the households receive no nonagricultural income from any of these sources. The median annual cash income from all sources is approximately K Sh 4,500 per household, the equivalent of about K Sh 500–555 ($65-75 in late 1980 prices) per individual.

Although coffee cultivation became an important source of rural differentiation during the colonial period, today wealth differences among Embu farmers arise primarily through nonagricultural activities. Education, salaries, trade, and small businesses are the means of accumulating wealth in land, cash, and material possessions.

Average incomes from salaries are much higher than those from export cash crops. The average annual salary of employed individuals in the survey sample (most of whom work in the services sector) is five times the coffee income produced by 350 mature trees (the sample mean number of coffee trees). While at one end of the wage scale, employment permits accumulation of land and other forms of wealth, at the opposite end of the scale, it is part of a cycle of rural impoverishment that removes crucial adult labor from the farm without producing sufficient cash income to compensate for the loss.

Coffee, which is marketed officially through local producers' cooperative societies and unofficially through local and nonlocal traders, is the most important income source for most of those farmers in the coffee zone who do not have regular salaries or small businesses. Over half of the coffee-zone sample earn 40 percent or more of their incomes from coffee. Coffee farmers remain diversified producers, however, in that no farmer in the sample has more than 1,200 coffee trees; most have just two or three hundred coffee trees; and everyone grows staple food crops such as maize and beans.[15] Average annual coffee earnings in the study area are barely sufficient to send just one child to a nongovernment secondary school.[16]

Cotton, on the other hand, is the most important income source for no more than about 16 percent of the sample households in that zone. Slightly more than half of the cotton-zone residents grow the crop, but they earn no more than about 20 percent of their total incomes from cotton. Charcoal production is an economically attractive (but environmentally destructive) alternative to cotton production. A farmer who makes charcoal just twice in one year earns more income from that source than he does from a well-tended one-fifth hectare of cotton. With poorer returns from their export cash crop and poorer access to food crop markets, cotton-zone residents rely more heavily on income from charcoal production and casual wage labor than do their coffee-zone neighbors.

Market vagaries and the relatively poor rewards of agricultural investment slow technical improvements in farming. The wealthy invest in more attractive economic alternatives outside of agriculture, but continue to practice farming and to retain a social and political stake in the rural economy. One of the largest landowners and largest users of hired farm labor in the study area, for example, has an accounting business and university education, but still has a firm foothold in the rural "economy of affection" (Hyden 1980); he lends out several portions of his land and he pays secondary school fees for two of his nonresident brothers and for the son of one of his permanent farm laborers. Most of the largest landowners (seven of the eight households who own eight hectares or more) lend land to others. Land is lent in exchange for token gifts such as a kilo or two of sugar, for labor, or for political support. Cash rentals are still rare.

In sum, important aspects of Embu District's rural economy include a pronounced ecological gradient that defines unequal agricultural opportunities; an individual freehold tenure system in which ownership of and informal access to multiple land parcels across ecological zones is common; increasing land scarcity associated with rapid rural population growth; household diversification strategies that combine income from a number of different sources, including export cash crops, a wide array of food crops, trade, salaries, and other enterprises; and combined use of hired, cooperative, and family labor in farming. With this as the context of smallholder economic activity, we turn now to the causes of variation in household food production levels and to the heterogeneous "subsistence orientation" of small farmers. To unravel sources of variation in smallholder food-crop output requires attention to production differences both within and across seasons.

Seasonal Variation in Household Food Production

Small farmers are well accustomed to the dramatic effects on their crops of weather and other environmental hazards such as pests and diseases. William Allan (1965) pointed out over two decades ago that the precarious existence of African cultivators requires production at levels that yield a surplus in years of average weather, so that production is sufficient to meet consumption needs in years of poor weather.[17] In other words, farmers learn how to manage the production risks posed by variable rainfall.

Independent of seasonal variation in rainfall, however, in a wide range of societies (see Sahlins 1972) there is substantial household variation in food-crop production levels. Household production differences may exceed variation between villages (Sahlins 1972:67-68) and that between seasons. That some farm households produce less food than required to meet their customary subsistence needs, while others produce more food than required, is in part a consequence of the nature of kin-based economic organization:

> Insofar as production is organized by domestic groups, it is established on a fragile and vulnerable base. The family labor force is normally small and sorely beset. . . . Households will show a considerable range in size and composition, range that may well leave some susceptible to disastrous mischance. (Sahlins 1972:74)

How households that underproduce survive depends in part on sociopolitical structures that link them to households that overproduce. We return to this point later.

First, let us examine four consecutive and highly varied seasons of maize and bean production in Embu. The seasons covered range from abundant rainfall (1978 short rains), to somewhat below-normal rain (1979 long rains), to drought (1979 short rains), to moderate rainfall (1980 long rains).[18]

As Tables 7.1 and 7.2 show, striking seasonal differences exist in both mean household production and in the proportion of households whose output is sufficient to satisfy their consumption requirements. As would be expected, in the worst rainfall season (1979 short rains), mean output was lowest, and the largest percentage of households report harvests below consumption requirements. In that season, only 8 percent of the households produced more than their maize consumption requirements. On the other hand, in the favorable 1978 short-rains season (when nationally there was a bumper crop), nearly three-quarters of the households produced maize in excess of their consumption

Table 7.1. Embu Households' Maize and Bean Harvests in Four Seasons

Season	Crop	Mean Household Production in Kilograms (Number of Households)	
1978 Short Rains	Maize	655	(N=70)
(Abundant Rainfall)	Beans	258	(N=70)
1978 Long Rains	Maize	281	(N=76)
(Below-average Rainfall)	Beans	174	(N=78)
1979 Short Rains	Maize	113	(N=82)
(Drought)	Beans	50	(N=82)
1980 Long Rains	Maize	293	(N=81)
(Moderate rainfall)	Beans	234	(N=81)

requirements.[19] Fluctuations in output of beans proved less risky to household subsistence (often with smaller percentages of households producing below consumption requirements and with a narrower range of variation in output), though relative seasonal differences are consistent with those of maize. (Absolute differences in maize and bean harvests are related to the Embu preference for a consumption ratio of about two to one of maize to beans in their diet.)

In short, the Embu data show that in seasons of good or average rainfall, many households produce maize and bean surpluses beyond their consumption requirements. In other seasons, they must survive by consuming smaller quantities of maize and beans and larger quantities of other crops they produce, or by acquiring additional maize and beans as purchases, as in-kind payments for labor performed, or as gifts. To what extent, however, are households' production levels in any given season related to their consumption requirements?

Household Composition and Food-Crop Output

Table 7.3 shows the relationship between maize and bean harvest size and number of consumers per household in the Embu study. The relationship is positive and statistically significant in six of the eight crop seasons (four maize seasons and four bean seasons).[21] Most of the correlation coefficients are less than .3, however, suggesting that there are important additional influences on crop production decisions and output.

It might be expected that favorable household ratios of consumers to workers (dependency ratio) would contribute to differences in output. As Table 7.4 shows, however, the household

Table 7.2. Maize and Bean Production in Relation to Subsistence Requirements in Four Seasons

Season and Crop	Harvest in Excess of Consumption Requirements		Harvest Below Consumption Requirements		Harvest Equal To Consumption Requirements	
	Number of Households	Percent of Households	Number of Households	Percent of Households	Number of Households	Percent of Households
1978 Short Rains[b]						
Maize	53	74%	12	17%	7	10%
Beans	34	48%	28	39%	9	13%
1979 Long Rains[c]						
Maize	23	30%	46	61%	7	9%
Beans	34	44%	32	41%	12	15%
1979 Short Rains[d]						
Maize	6	8%	66	84%	7	9%
Beans	8	10%	66	83%	6	8%
1980 Long Rains[e]						
Maize	32	41%	35	45%	11	14%
Beans	34	43%	32	40%	14	18%

[a]Consumption requirements used here are those reported by each household and are not standardized to the same level across households.

[b]Abundant rainfall.

[c]Below-average rainfall.

[d]Drought.

[e]Moderate rainfall.

Table 7.3. Relationship Between Harvest Size and Number of Consumers in Household

Season	Crop	Spearman Correlation Coefficient[a]
1978 Short Rains (Abundant Rainfall)	Maize Beans	.35** .27**
1979 Long Rains (Below-average Rainfall)	Maize Beans	.14 .14
1979 Short Rains (Drought)	Maize Beans	.34** .22
1980 Long Rains (Moderate Rainfall)	Maize Beans	.24* .19*

Notes: ** Significant at .01 level (one-tailed test).
  * Significant at .05 level (one-tailed test).
[a]Spearman's rho is a nonparametric rank-order correlation coefficient that varies from +1.0 to -1.0.
The table shows the correlation between the following two variables:
1) household maize or beans output (in kilograms), and 2) number of consumer equivalents in the household.
Weights used for individual age categories to compute consumer equivalents are as follows:
  61+ years of age = 0.50
  16 - 60 years   = 1.00
  11 - 15 years   = 0.75
  11 years   = 0.50

Table 7.4. Relationship Between Household Dependency Ratio and Crop Output per Producer in Four Seasons

Season	Crop	Kendall Correlation Coefficient[b]
1978 Short Rains (Abundant rainfall)	Maize Beans	.28** .11
1979 Long Rains (Below-average rainfall)	Maize Beans	.07 .05
1979 Short Rains (Drought)	Maize Beans	.12 .03
1980 Long Rains (Moderate rainfall)	Maize Beans	-.07 .16*

Notes: [a]Dependency ratio is the ratio of consumers to producers in a household, using the following age weights:

Consumer Coefficients		Producer Coefficients	
61+ years of age	=0.50	61+ years of age	=0.50
16-60 years	=1.00	16-60 years	=1.00
11-15 years	=0.75	11-15 years	=0.50
<11 years	=0.50	<11 years	= -0-

[b]Kendall's tau is a nonparametric rank-order correlation coefficient that varies from +1.0 to -1.0, and whose absolute value tends to be smaller than that of Pearson's r.
The table shows the correlation between the following two variables:
1) household maize or beans output (in kilograms) per producer equivalent (as defined in note 1 above), and 2) the ratio of consumers to producers (dependency ratio) in each household.
** significant at .001 level (one-tailed test).
 * significant at .05 level (one-tailed test).

ratio of consumers to workers is not strongly correlated with output of maize and beans per producer, and the correlation is statistically significant in only two of the eight maize and beans crop seasons. The coefficients suggest that the relationship is strongest in those crop seasons when the physical conditions of production were most favorable (e.g., 1980 long rains for beans and 1978 short rains for maize). The seasonal differences in the strength of the correlations are related to differential access to hired and cooperative labor (discussion follows), which is especially important in dealing with uncertain weather conditions, such as early, late, or interrupted onset of rains. Households that have unfavorably high dependency ratios (few workers per consumer) and that cannot readily recruit hired and cooperative labor would be most disadvantaged in seasons when rainfall conditions delay land preparation and planting, and when weather conditions shorten the period of time in which these tasks must be accomplished (such as 1979 short rains—see note 18).

How characteristics other than household composition influence food crop production becomes strongly apparent when we examine the minority of households (15 percent of the eighty-two households sampled) who produced beyond their consumption requirements in at least six of the eight crop seasons. The sizes of the "surpluses"[22] in the moderate 1980 long-rains season (when maize did not recover as much of its 1978 high as did beans) ranged from about 45 to 540 kilograms of maize, and from about 45 to 1,080 kilograms of beans. Household composition as reflected in the ratio of consumers to producers (dependency ratio) does *not* differ for the minority of surplus producers as compared to the majority (nonsurplus producers). The mean dependency ratio of each of the two categories of households is exactly 1.5. What characteristics, then, do separate these two categories of household?

Household Wealth and Food-Crop Output

Smallholders are not a homogeneous category. In the Embu sample, household land-holdings range from less than one-half hectare to sixty-one hectares[23]; annual cash incomes range from under K Sh 2,500 to well over K Sh 15,000; cattle herd sizes range from zero to two dozen; and the number of mature coffee trees owned by coffee zone residents ranges from 30 to 1,200. Some small farmers are, whether by choice or by force of circumstance, more subsistence-oriented in their agricultural activities than are others. The capacity of smallholders reliably to produce food-crop surpluses for the market is not uniform enough (either within or between seasons) to warrant their treatment as an undifferentiated category for purposes of agricultural policy formulation.

While most farm households produce at least occasional food surpluses, some regularly produce less food than they need to meet their consumption requirements, while others consistently overproduce. The deviations from subsistence levels are not random and are not independent of one another. Household failures and successes constitute an interrelated "social system of production" (Sahlins 1972:114-115). The survival of households who usually underproduce is linked to the existence of a set of households who consistently produce beyond their consumption requirements. Social relationships among households help to define access to any surplus product, whether the producers make that product available to others as a purchasable commodity, as a gift, or as in-kind payment for labor.

Table 7.5 summarizes distinctive characteristics of the households whose food production in most seasons exceeds their customary consumption requirements. Their mean wealth score (which is not statistically related to household dependency ratio) is significantly higher than that of the majority. The surplus producers have more than twice as many mature coffee trees, own nearly twice as much land, spend more than five times as much cash on hired labor, *provide* cooperative labor to other households *less* often, and *receive* or use cooperative labor *more* often and in greater quantity.[24] All of these relationships, with the exception of land ownership and collective labor provided to other households, are positive and statistically significant. Table 7.5 suggests a pattern of deviation from subsistence production that is defined by both commercial and noncommercial relations of production.

The Social and Economic Context of Surplus Production

Farmers who consistently produce food surpluses use them both to earn cash and to build and maintain political support through clientage. They use some of the extra food they produce as payments in kind for agricultural labor and as "gifts" to kin and others. Food surplus producers can better feed their visitors, which enhances their prestige. They tend to be better-placed than the majority in the wider patronage networks that channel access to education, jobs, and improved agricultural inputs such as hybrid seed and fertilizers. As local patrons, their superior access to both hired and cooperative labor increases their productive capacity.

Table 7.5A. Characteristics of Households That Usually Produce Food Surpluses and Those That Do Not

	Household Surplus Production		Mean of Total Sample
	Usual[a] (N=12)	Not Usual[b] (N=70)	(N=82) (Range)
Mean dependency ratio (C/P)[c]	1.5	1.5	1.5 (1.0–2.3)
Mean wealth score[d]	7,564	2,648	3,368 (0–50,605)
Mean number of mature coffee trees	423	211	242 (0–1,200)
Mean number of hectares of land owned	9	5	5 (0–61)
Mean cash expenditure on hired labor in 1980 long rains (in Kenya shillings)	337	61	99 (0–898)
Mean number of occasions exchange labor given during 10 months in 1979/80	2.5	3.7	3.6 (0–13.0)
Mean number of occasions exchange labor received during 10 months in 1979/80	5.2	3.1	3.4 (0–14.0)
Mean number of person days exchange labor received during 10 months in 1979/80	17.5	7.8	9.2 (0–47.0)

Table 7.5B. Kendall Correlation Coefficients[e]

	Surplus Production[f]
Dependency ratio	.02
Wealth score	.23**
Mature coffee trees	.21**
Land ownership	.09
Hired labor expenditure	.21**
Occasions exchange labor given	-.03
Occasions exchange labor received	.15*
Person days exchange labor received	.20**

** Significant at .01 level (one-tailed test).
* Significant at .05 level (one-tailed test).   (N=82 households)

[a]This category includes households that produced maize/beans in excess of consumption requirements in at least six of the eight crop seasons monitored (counting four rainfall seasons x two crops each season). See text note number 13 on defining subsistence requirements.
[b]Households that do not usually produce food surpluses are those that produced maize/beans in excess of consumption requirements in fewer than six of the eight crop seasons monitored.
[c]Dependency ratio is the ratio of consumers to producers in a household, using the following age weights:

Consumer Coefficients		Producer Coefficients	
61+ years of age	= 0.50	61+ years of age	= 0.50
16–60 years	= 1.00	16–60 years	= 1.00
11–15 years	= 0.75	11–15 years	= 0.50
11 years	= 0.50	11 years	= 0.00

[d]The wealth score is an additive scale of 14 assets (automobile, motorcycle, bicycle, ox cart, plough, gas cooker, sewing machine, sofa set, radio, pressure lamp, kerosene stove, hurricane lamp, charcoal stove, wood chairs) weighted according to their cash value when new. The median wealth score for the 82 sample households is 1,803.
[e]Kendall's tau is a nonparametric rank-order correlation coefficient that varies from +1.0 to –1.0, and whose absolute value tends to be less than that of Pearson's r. This table shows correlations between the dependent variable (surplus production) and each of eight independent variables. A correlation matrix of all of the independent variables is given in Appendix A.
[f]Surplus production of each household is here coded as one of three ranked classes: 3 = usually produce maize/beans surplus (did so in at least six of the eight crop seasons monitored); 2 = occasionally produce maize-beans surplus (did so in at least one and fewer than six of the right crop seasons monitored); 1 = never or seldom produce food surpluses (did not do so in any of the eight crop seasons monitored). Twelve households fall in class 3, 56 in class 2, and 14 in class 1.

Access to labor on demand improves a farmer's capacity to adjust, for example, to rainfall uncertainty at crucial points in the agricultural cycle by allowing him or her quickly to organize a second planting if late onset of the rains causes seed from the first planting to fail to germinate. Poorer households are less likely to be able to afford the extra seed required for a second planting, or to command the resources to hire labor or to organize large or frequent work parties.

One of the largest users of cooperative labor is a household headed by an important local political figure (an elder appointed as assistant to a subchief). That household used forty-seven days of cooperative labor between August 1979 and March 1980, while the sample mean is 9.2 person days. Another heavy user of cooperative labor is a household whose head is a retired civil servant and whose wife is a primary school teacher. Such families are called upon to assist with food or cash needs in poor seasons; with dealings with bureaucrats to secure land title deeds, agricultural inputs, and credit; with school headmasters to gain secondary school admission for children; or with potential employers of those children once they leave school.

The wealthy Embu smallholders who consistently produce more food than they require for home consumption are not specialized farmers who have cut themselves off from rural sociopolitical relationships and obligations. Rather, they owe their positions to successful negotiation of these relationships. Most of the surplus producers who fall in the top quartile of land ownership, for example, lend out some land to others—investing in the local social system and not just in expanded production. While this pattern by no means suggests a "moral economy" in action, the continued importance of socially defined channels of access to land and labor in one of Kenya's most commercialized smallholder regions is striking.

This pattern is not a peculiarity of Embu or even of Kenya, but rather confirms the need to understand the dynamics of local communities, even as they are increasingly affected by wider national and international systems (see Cancian 1985). A small rural locality defined by face-to-face interactions among neighbors and kin remains for most Kenyans (whether Nairobi bureaucrat, politician, businessman, or farmer) a crucial point of reference in individuals' competition for rank, acceptance, and security. The social relationships described above, however, do not necessarily guarantee security to either the poor or to the wealthy, and their persistence does not signal the dominance of collective over individual needs.

The social context of agricultural production and exchange does not mean that farmers avoid food-crop markets. After the relatively poor 1979 short-rains harvest, about half of the sample households bought maize and 60 percent purchased beans before the next harvest. By September 1980, after a better harvest, about a quarter of the households had sold some maize and about half had sold some beans. In the worst harvest season (1979 short rains), only 10 percent of the sample households sold maize. In short, the number of households who purchase or sell maize or beans and the proportion of subsistence requirements purchased vary markedly from one season to the next.

Given the large seasonal fluctuations in food-crop output and in market prices, an average figure for income from this source would have little meaning. The cash earned from selling two bags of maize, for example, ranges from a couple of hundred shillings in a year of abundant harvest to six or seven times that amount in a drought year. While food-crop sales as a proportion of total income fluctuate substantially from one season to the next, fewer than 10 percent of the sample households usually earn 1,500 shillings ($200 in 1981 prices) or more from this source. This amount represents about a third of the total sample's median annual cash income, and a considerably smaller income percentage for most households that have high food-crop (and other) incomes.

Although a minority of wealthy smallholders are capable of regularly producing food surpluses for the market, and although many more produce occasional surpluses, the uncertainties of national market institutions discussed earlier encourage the wealthy minority as well as the majority to avoid market-dependent specialization in just a few crops. In contrast to the approximately specifiable risks associated with rainfall variability, the seasonal uncertainty of the official grain parastatal's producer prices and of its purchasing behavior involves probabilities of gains and losses farmers cannot even approximately predict. Instead, their production enterprises include a number of different food crops for consumption and sale, as well as export cash crops, livestock, trade, and salaried employment. Such diversification increases the likelihood that losses in one enterprise will be compensated for by gains in another. In addition, in Kenya, as elsewhere in Africa, farmers often obtain better returns if they "invest in trade, urban real estate, or their children's education rather than in expanded agricultural production" (Berry 1983:69). The risks of market-dependent agricultural production and the more favorable returns from nonagricultural investments pose formidable long-term challenges to the development of large-and small-scale agriculture alike.

Conclusion

In the study of African agrarian change, concepts such as the supposed "subsistence orientation" of small farmers conceal more than they reveal. They can be misleading if used, for example, to justify concentration of development resources on large- rather than small-scale farmers because they ignore the serious inadequacies of aggregate agricultural statistics, the highly varied production and marketing activities of smallholders, and the uncertain market and state conditions to which both large and small farmers respond.

We have seen that independently of seasonal variations in rainfall, some small farm households do consistently produce more food than required to meet their customary consumption needs. At present that "surplus" food is distributed both through markets and through nonmarket channels of clientage and local exchange. While more than two-thirds of the Embu sample households produce at least occasional food surpluses, special characteristics enable and encourage an additional 15 percent of them to produce surpluses regularly. Particularly important is the consistent surplus producers' superior access to both hired and cooperative labor, a reflection of their greater wealth and patronage resources. They tend to be well-placed in the patronage networks that channel access to education, jobs, commercial loans, and other economic opportunities. The consistent surplus producers also have substantial nonagricultural incomes, and their wealth depends on successful diversification, rather than on agricultural specialization (Haugerud 1984). Although the surplus producers do own more land on average than do other small farmers, land ownership in Embu is highly skewed and has no statistically significant relationship with surplus production (see Table 7.5).

It is true, of course, that a larger proportion of the food crop output of small than of large farmers is likely to be destined for home consumption. The uncertainties of African markets and state institutions, however, encourage both large and small farmers to produce food for home consumption and to diversify their economic activities to include nonagricultural as well as agricultural pursuits. Kenyan farmers' food-crop diversification and subsistence strategies are related to the wide fluctuations in unofficial consumer prices of food crops (and hence the high risk of depending on the market to purchase food); to the unofficial fees charged by and the uneven geographic distribution of official food-crop marketing agents; and to the inability of the state marketing board to protect consumers or producers from alternating cycles of gluts and deficits. Of considerably more importance to African agrarian transformation than the supposed willingness or not of small farmers to sell their food crops is the capacity of African states to create reliable and favorable food-crop production and marketing conditions for both large and small farmers.

Domestic supply of and demand for marketed food crops in Kenya has been highly volatile. Cyclical domestic overproduction of maize is as much a problem as is underproduction. We saw, for example, that Kenya's 1980 maize shortfall and food imports rapidly followed a 1978 bumper harvest that exceeded the grain parastatal's purchasing and storage capacity. The 1980 drought and maize shortages in turn were succeeded in 1983 by another abundant harvest and new suspension of maize purchases by the grain parastatal. Food imports and drought followed in 1984, and in the first half of 1987 there was once again a bumper harvest which the parastatal and national markets could not absorb. This type of volatility and institutional uncertainty invites, but cannot be resolved through, simple increases or decreases in state intervention (cf. Berry 1983, Leonard 1984, World Bank 1981).

Given the political and economic conditions that in Africa favor economic diversification and clientage among both large and small farmers, policies focusing only on production increases or on substantial expansion of large-scale agriculture could intensify the kinds of food-crop market problems and cycles of gluts and deficits Kenya already experiences. The policy issues are complex and knotty, involving international trade barriers, domestic currency valuations, possibilities for industrial versus agricultural expansion, and a host of other issues that lie beyond the scope of this paper.

Our purpose here has been to highlight some of the complexities of small farmers' economic strategies, and to indicate the importance of understanding local food production patterns in the context of rural sociopolitical structures and the particular links of the latter to the wider economy and society. This empirical complexity is not captured by paradigms that focus only on the microeconomic logic of individual production decisions; or those centered on the presumed self-sufficiency or "subsistence orientation" of small farmers; or those focused on relationships between farm size and productivity.

Table 7.6. Matrix of Spearman Correlation Coefficients For All Independent Variables

	(2)	(3)	(4)	(5)	(6)	(7)	(8)
(1) Wealth score	.06	.39**	.39**	.36**	-.18*	.09	.13
(2) Dependency ratio		-.21*	0	-.18	.04	.02	.02
(3) Mature coffee trees			.22*	.30**	.02	.12	.14
(4) Land owned				.16	.15	.20*	.25**
(5) Hired labor expenditure					-.24*	.20*	.23*
(6) Number occasions exchange labor given						.45**	.30**
(7) Number occasions exchange labor received							.91**
(8) Number person-days exchange labor received							

Notes: **Significant at .01 level (one-tailed) test.
        *Significant at .05 level (one-tailed) test.

(N=82 households)

aSpearman's rho is a nonparametric rank-order correlation coefficient that varies from +1.0 to -1.0.

Notes

1. The field research upon which this paper is based was carried out between August 1978 and May 1981 in Embu District, Kenya, with brief revisits in 1985 and 1986. I am grateful for funding received from the Social Science Research Council, the American Council of Learned Societies, Northwestern University, and the National Science Foundation (Grant No. BNS 7902715). This paper does not necessarily reflect the views of any of these institutions.

I thank Michael Chibnik and Ronald Cohen for comments on an earlier version of this paper, and Eileen M. O'Brien for comments on the tables. They do not bear any responsibility for the paper's shortcomings.

2. Compare the following three statements. (1) Sahlins (1972:3) in criticizing formalist approaches in economic anthropology states: "The existing business economy, at every turn an ideological trap from which anthropological economics must escape, will promote the same dim conclusions about the hunting life." (2) Berry (1983:16) in a review of the literature on African agrarian issues says: "The task of generalization has been hampered not so much by the proliferation of case studies, as by the prevalence of certain paradigms of social change. In particular, studies which seek to explain agrarian change in terms of individual rationality and/or social or technological imperatives often fail to account for the complexity of actual cases, giving rise to generalizations which are unconvincing or readily subordinated to the defense of special interests." (3) Cohen (1986a:359) states: "Anthropology, if it is to survive in its present form, cannot afford to carry out empirical analyses of social change, then go on to argue for improvements whose only basis is the uncritical, often unconscious, acceptance of one among a number of possible value/ideological positions."

3. For discussion of controversial aspects of Chayanov's theory among his contemporaries and in current scholarship, see Harrison 1977, 1979; Patnaik 1979; Hunt 1979; Ennew, Hirst, and Tribe 1977.

4. In Kenya, large farms are those greater than fifty hectares in size; medium farms are twenty to fifty hectares, and small farms are under twenty hectares.

5. A unimodal as opposed to a multimodal strategy is one based on small farms and a relatively egalitarian distribution of land under individual ownership (see Johnston and Kilby 1975).

6. By 1984, over 5.26 million hectares, covering most of Kenya's high potential agricultural land, were under individual freehold titles (Lofchie 1986:224). The registration process is still under way in more marginal agricultural zones.

7. Haugerud 1983 and 1984 discuss in detail issues summarized in this paragraph and the next.

8. In spite of Kenya's history of unsuccessful internal attempts to privatize or restructure its maize markets, the World Bank in the early 1980s again recommended that the Kenyan government privatize maize marketing, and tried to make such action a condition of its structural adjustment loan (Moseley 1986).

9. As of September 1983, private traders have been allowed to transport up to ten bags of maize (just under one ton) out of the district of origin without an official permit. Previously (from the 1940s until 1983), the ceiling for private and unofficial interdistrict trade was two bags of maize (about 180 kilograms).

10. See Berry (1983:24-26) for discussion of why the relationship between crop prices and production or supply response cannot be tested conclusively.

11. The remainder of the paper is based on field data collected through formal surveys, participant-observation, and structured and unstructured interviews during two and one-half years of residence in Embu District. For details on research methods and sampling procedures, see Haugerud 1984. Briefly, data are presented from a sample of eighty-two households made up of 739 individuals. The study sample is close to population parameters (as reported in national census data) in such characteristics as age and sex structure, education, and per capita land availability (Haugerud 1984).

The household here includes those individuals who occupy and manage a given farm parcel and who share production and consumption activities associated with that and sometimes additional parcels. Fluctuations in household membership during the research period were monitored, and the consumer/producer figures used in this paper represent the household membership that prevailed during most of the fifteen months (June 1979 to September 1980) when the bulk of the economic survey research was conducted.

12. The present study excludes the lower altitude portions of Embu District, which the Mbeere ethnic group occupies (see Brokensha and Glazier 1973; Brokensha and Riley 1980; Glazier 1985; Hunt 1979).

13. The Kikuyu, Embu, and Meru peoples have from time to time formed political and economic alliances, as, for example, during the 1950s Mau Mau rebellion (see Rosberg and Nottingham 1966 and Barnett and Njama 1966), and later in the Gikuyu, Embu, Meru Association (GEMA), a nationally prominent association of political and economic interests that along with other "tribal organizations" was disbanded by presidential directive in 1979.

14. In per capita land availability, the sample households are close to the population parameter. Per capita land available in the survey sample (N=82 households composed of 739 individuals) is .59 hectare, and that of the population of the two administrative sublocations (which had a combined total population of 7,899 in 1979) from which the sample was drawn is .52 hectare (Kenya 1979).

15. Nutritional data were not collected in this study, but see Fleuret and Fleuret (1983) for discussion of the effects of cash cropping and wage labor on child nutrition in Kenya.

16. The timing of cooperative society payments to farmers is uncertain. Delays of several months are not uncommon, though cooperatives often extend credit to member farmers to cover school fees while awaiting the coffee payout.

Farmers' coffee incomes vary from one cooperative society to the next in accordance with the quality of processing, and the honesty, efficiency, and skills of cooperative society officials; in some areas of Embu District, returns to coffee farmers were five to ten times higher than those in the study area.

17. As Berry (1983:33) discusses, "Allan implies that the possibility of technical progress in agriculture is limited."

18. The year 1978, for example, was one of record-high rainfall, averaging 1,798 millimeters at the 1,490-meter contour in the study area, as compared to a sixteen-year average of 1,334 millimeters (Embu District Annual Reports). In the 1979 short-rains season, rainfall was low and poorly distributed; it began in the second half of October, but then stopped for several weeks in November when it should have been heaviest, and did not begin again until late in December, when it should have ended. The 1980 long rains were moderate, but ended early, which reduced the maize harvest more than that of beans because of the longer growth cycle and greater water requirements of maize.

19. These figures on rate of household underproduction accord approximately with those Sahlins (1972:71) cites, for example, from Freeman's (1955) study of the Iban of Borneo.

20. Chayanov (1966) examined in detail the relationship between peasant households' total output and their demographic characteristics (especially the ratio of consumers to workers). He argued that peasant farm output is ultimately limited and defined by the internal structure of the family itself as represented in the number of consumers and by the increasing drudgery attached to labor expenditure beyond that needed to satisfy basic needs. The Embu case does not strictly accord with Chayanovian farm conditions, since labor is hired and exchanged between households, and since population density restricts household expansion of cultivated area. A number of scholars, however, argue that Chayanov's theory can be applied where farmers hire some labor (see Chibnik 1987 for discussion of the wider applicability of Chayanov's theory).

21. The only season for which there is no significant correlation between harvest size and number of household consumers is the 1979 long rains. This may be because farmers tend to use previous season's rainfall as a predictor of current season's rainfall, and the abrupt change from the abundant rainfall of the 1978 short-rains season to the below-normal precipitation of the 1979 long rains caught them by surprise. In addition, however, land preparation for the March planting of the 1979 long-rains crop was delayed by unusual rains in January and February (normally relatively dry months), which means that labor availability had a strong effect on extent and timing of land preparation for the 1979 long-rains crop (and hence on the size of the subsequent harvest). Since access to extra-household labor is associated with wealth (see later discussion in paper), the capacity to recruit hired and exchange labor could override consumption requirements as determinants of area planted (and size of harvest) in the 1979 long rains.

22. Although there are well-known difficulties in determining minimum subsistence requirements (see, e.g., Orans 1966; Pearson 1957), this analysis is based on sample households' own stated consumption requirements, which are not standardized to the same level across all households. Mean preferred per capita consumption levels of maize and beans calculated from Embu households' stated consumption requirements yield figures of approximately 120 kilograms of maize and 60 kilograms of beans per consumer equivalent per year. These are nutritionally reasonable figures for such a population (see Latham 1981). Deviations from mean consumption levels, of course, occur as poorer households that produce food deficits substitute other foods such as bananas, sweet potatoes, and cassava for maize and beans; and wealthy households consume more wheat, meat, and rice as purchased substitutes.

23. In absolute acreage owned, about 4 percent of the Embu sample farmers own more land than the twenty-hectare maximum commonly used to define smallholders in Kenya.

24. Embu informants note that work performed by cooperative as well as hired labor is of poorer quality than that done by household members. The contribution of cooperative labor in particular should not be overemphasized. As Saul (1983:91) argues in the case of a Voltaic village, growth and accumulation through work parties are limited because organizational and other costs increase in proportion to the scale and frequency of such parties.

In an Ethiopian market village, Donham (1981) found a net transfer of cooperative labor from poorer to wealthier households. In Embu, wealthier households *contributed* significantly less cooperative labor to other households, but the data do not show a significant positive correlation between wealth and cooperative labor *received* by a household (see Table 7.6).

Heavy users of hired labor are also heavy users of cooperative labor in Embu. The correlation between hired labor expenditure and use of cooperative labor is positive and significant ($p=.05$), while that between hired labor expenditure and cooperative labor contributed to other households is negative and significant ($p=.02$) (see Table 7.6).

Cooperative labor use and land ownership are positively related, and cooperative labor use and household dependency ratio are unrelated (see Table 7.6).

References

African Business. 1983. Kenya: What Future? *African Business* 84:23-68.

Allan, W. 1965. *The African Husbandman.* London and Edinburgh: Oliver and Boyd.

Anyang' N'yong', P. 1981. The Development of a Middle Peasantry in Nyanza. *Review of African Political Economy* 20:108-120.

Barlett, P.F. 1984. Microdynamics of Debt, Drought and Default in South Georgia. *American Journal of Agricultural Economics* 66:5:836-843.

――――. 1987. Industrial Agriculture in Evolutionary Perspective. *Cultural Anthropology* 2:1.

Barnett, D. and K. Njama. 1966. *Mau Mau From Within.* New York: Monthly Review Press.

Bates, R. 1981. *Markets and States in Tropical Africa: The Political Basis of Agricultural Policies.* Berkeley and Los Angeles: University of California Press.

――――. 1983. *Essays on the Political Economy of Rural Africa.* London: Cambridge University Press.

Berry, S. 1983. Agrarian Crisis in Africa? A Review and an Interpretation. Paper prepared for the Joint African Studies Committee of the Social Science Research Council and the American Council of Learned Societies, and presented at African Studies Association annual meetings.

Brokensha, D. and J. Glazier. 1973. Land Reform Among the Mbeere of Central Kenya. *Africa* 43:3:182-206.

Brokensha, D. and B. Riley. 1980. Introduction of Cash Crops in a Marginal Area of Kenya. In *Agricultural Development in Africa: Issues of Public Policy*. R.H. Bates and M. Lofchie, eds. New York: Praeger.

Brush, S. 1977. *Mountain, Field, and Family: The Economy and Human Ecology of an Andean Valley*. Philadelphia: University of Pennsylvania Press.

Cancian, F. 1968. Maximization as Norm, Strategy, and Theory: A Comment on Programmatic Statements in Economic Anthropology. In *Economic Anthropology: Readings in Theory and Analysis*. E. LeClair and H.K. Schneider, eds. New York: Holt, Rinehart and Winston.

———. 1985. The Boundaries of Rural Stratification Systems. In *Micro and Macro Levels of Analysis in Anthropology: Issues in Theory and Research*. B.R. DeWalt and P.J. Pelto, eds. Boulder, Colo. and London: Westview Press.

Chayanov, A.V. 1966. *The Theory of Peasant Economy*. Homewood, Illinois: Irwin.

Chibnik, M. 1987. The Economic Effects of Household Demography: A Cross-Cultural Assessment of Chayanov's Theory. In *Household Economies and Their Transformations*, Monographs in Economic Anthropology, No. 3. New York: University Press of America.

Cohen, R. 1986a. Comment on "Smallholder Settlement of Tropical South America: The Social Causes of Ecological Destruction." *Human Organization* 45:4:359-360.

———. 1986b. Agricultural Transformation in Northern Nigeria: A Macro-Micro Analysis. Manuscript revision of paper presented at the 1985 annual meeting of the American Anthropological Association, Washington, D.C.

Collier, P. and D. Lal. 1984. Why Poor People Get Rich: Kenya 1960-79. *World Development* 12:1007-1018.

Cox, P. 1984. Implementing Agricultural Development Policy in Kenya. *Food Research Institute Studies* 19:2:153-176.

Dalton, G. 1969. Theoretical Issues in Economic Anthropology. *Current Anthropology* 10:63-102.

DeWilde, J.C. 1984. *Agriculture, Marketing and Pricing in Sub-Saharan Africa*. Los Angeles: African Studies Center, University of California and African Studies Association.

Donham, D. 1981. Beyond the Domestic Mode of Production. *Man* 16:515-541.

Ennew, J., P. Hirst, and K. Tribe. 1977. "Peasantry" as an Economic Category. *Journal of Peasant Studies* 4:4:295-322.

Fleuret, P. and A. Fleuret. 1983. Socioeconomic Determinants of Child Nutrition in Taita, Kenya: A Call for Discussion. *Culture and Agriculture* 19.

Freeman, J.D. 1955. *Iban Agriculture*. Colonial Research Studies, No. 18. London: H.M. Stationery Office.

Gerhart, J.D. 1975. *The Diffusion of Hybrid Maize in Western Kenya*. Mexico city: CIMMYT.

Gladwin, C.H. and R. Zabawa. 1987. Transformation of Full-Time Family Farms in the U.S.: Can They Survive? In *Household Economies and their Transformations*, Monographs in Economic Anthropology, No. 3. New York: University Press of America.

Glazier, J. 1985. *Land and the Uses of Tradition Among the Mbeere of Kenya*. New York: University Press of America.

Gsaenger, H.G. and G. Schmidt. 1977. Decontrolling the Maize Marketing System in Kenya. Discussion Paper No. 254. University of Nairobi: Institute for Development Studies.

Guillet, D. 1981. Land Tenure, Ecological Zone and Agricultural Regime in the Central Andes. *American Ethnologist* 8:1:139-156.

Harrison, M. 1977. The Peasant Mode of Production in the Work of A.V. Chayanov. *Journal of Peasant Studies* 4:4:323-336.

———. 1979. Chayanov and the Marxists. *Journal of Peasant Studies* 6:1:86-100.

Hart, K. 1982. *The Political Economy of West African Agriculture*. London: Cambridge University Press.

Haugerud, A. 1983. The Consequences of Land Tenure Reform Among Embo Farmers in the Kenya Highlands. *Rural Africana* Winter/Spring:15-16:65-90.

———. 1984. Household Dynamics and Rural Political Economy Among Embu Farmers in the Kenya Highlands. Ph.D. diss., Northwestern University. Ann Arbor: University Microfilms International.

Heyer, J., J.K. Maitha, and W.M. Senga, eds. 1976. *Agricultural Development in Kenya: An Economic Assessment*. Nairobi: Oxford University Press.

Hunt, D. 1979. Chayanov's Model of Peasant Household Resource Allocation. *Journal of Peasant Studies* 6:3:247-285.

———. 1984. *The Impending Crisis in Kenya: The Case for Land Reform*. Brookfield, Vt.: Gower.

Hyden, G. 1980. *Beyond Ujamaa in Tanzania: Underdevelopment and an Uncaptured Peasantry*. Berkeley: University of California Press.

———. 1983. *No Shortcuts to Progress: African Development Management in Perspective*. Berkeley and Los Angeles: University of California Press.

Johnston, B. and P. Kilby. 1975. *Agriculture and Structural Transformation*. London: Oxford University Press.

Kenya (Government of). 1962. *Population Census*. Nairobi: Government Printer.

———. 1969. *Population Census*. Nairobi: Government Printer.

———. 1979. *Population Census*. Nairobi: Government Printer.

Kitching, G. 1980. *Class and Economic Change in Kenya*. New Haven and London: Yale University Press.

Latham, M.C. 1981. *Human Nutrition in Tropical Africa*. Rome: FAO.

LeClair, E. and H.K. Schneider, eds. 1968. *Economic Anthropology: Readings in Theory and Analysis*. New York: Holt, Rinehart and Winston.

Lehmann, D. 1982. After Chayanov and Lenin: New Paths of Agrarian Capitalism. *Journal of Development Economics* 11:133-161.

Lenin, V.I. 1899 (1964). *The Development of Capitalism in Russia.* Moscow: Progress Publishers.

Leonard, D. 1984. Disintegrating Agricultural Development. *Food Research Institute Studies* 19:2:177-185.

Leys, C. 1971. Politics in Kenya: The Development of Peasant Society. *British Journal of Political Science* 1:3:307-337.

———. 1975. *Underdevelopment in Kenya: The Political Economy of Neocolonialism.* London: Heinemann.

Little, P.D. and M.M. Horowitz. 1987. Subsistence Crops *Are* Cash Crops: Some Comments with Reference to Eastern Africa. *Human Organization* 46(2); 254-258.

Livingstone, I. 1981. *Rural Development, Employment and Incomes in Kenya.* I.L.O.: J.A.S.P.A.

Lofchie, M. 1986. Kenya's Agricultural Success. *Current History* May:221-331.

Mann, F.K. 1960. Institutionalism and American Economic Theory: A Case of Interpenetration. *Kyklos* 13:307-322. Reprinted in *Readings in the History of Economic Theory.* I.H. Rima, ed. New York: Holt, Rinehart and Winston, 1970.

Miller, N. 1984. *Kenya: The Quest for Prosperity.* Boulder, Colo.: Westview Press.

Moris, J. 1970. The Agrarian Revolution in Central Kenya: A Study of Farm Innovation in Embu District. Ph.D. diss., Northwestern University. Ann Arbor: University Microfilms International.

Moseley, P. 1986. The Politics of Economic Liberalization: USAID and the World Bank in Kenya, 1980-84. *African Affairs* 85:338:107-119.

Murra, J. 1970. Current Research and Prospects in Andean Ethnohistory. *Latin American Research Review* 5:1:3-36.

Mwaniki, H.S.K. 1973. A Political History of the Embu: C.A.D. 1500-1906, M.A. thesis, University of Nairobi.

Netting, R. 1976. What Alpine Peasants Have in Common: Observations on Communal Tenure in a Swiss village. *Human Ecology* 4:135-146.

———. 1977. *Cultural Ecology.* Menlo Park, California: Cummings.

Njonjo, A. 1981. The Kenya Peasantry: A Reassessment. *Review of African Political Economy* 20:27-40.

Norgaard, R.B. 1987. Risk and Its Management in Traditional and Modern Agricultural Systems. Paper presented at the annual meeting of the Society for Economic Anthropology, Riverside, California.

Okoth-Ogendo, H.W. 1976. African Land Tenure Reform. In *Agricultural Development in Kenya.* J. Heyer, J.K. Maitha, and W.M. Senga, eds. Nairobi: Oxford University Press.

Orans, M. 1966. Surplus. *Human Organization* 25:24-32.

Orlove, B. 1977. Integration Through Production: The Use of Zonation in Espinar. *American Ethnologist* 4:1:84-101.

———. 1986. Barter and Cash Sale on Lake Titicaca: A Test of Competing Approaches. *Current Anthropology* 27:2:85-106.

Ortner, S. 1984. Theory in Anthropology Since the Sixties. *Comparative Studies in Society and History* 26:1:126-166.

Paterson, D. 1984. Kinship, Land, and Community: The Moral Foundations of the Abaluhya of East Bunyore (Kenya). Ph.D. diss., University of Washington. Ann Arbor: University Microfilms International.

Patnaik, U. 1979. Neo-Populism and Marxism: The Chayanovian View of the Agrarian Question and its Fundamental Fallacy. *Journal of Peasant Studies* 6:4:375-419.

Pearson, J.J. 1957. The Economy Has No Surplus. In *Trade and Markets in the Early Empires*. K. Polanyi, C.M. Arensberg, and H.W. Pearson, eds. Glencoe, Ill.: Free Press.

Popkin, S. 1979. *The Rational Peasant: The Political Economy of Rural Society in Vietnam.* Berkeley and Los Angeles: University of California Press.

Rogers, S.C. 1987. Mixing Paradigms on Mixed Farmings: Anthropological and Economic Views of Specialization in Illinois Agriculture. In *Farm Work and Fieldwork: American Agriculture in Anthropological Perspective*. M. Chibnik, ed. Ithaca and London: Cornell University Press.

Rosberg, C. and J. Nottingham. 1966 *The Myth of "Mau Mau": Nationalism in Kenya.* New York: Praeger.

Sahlins, M. 1972. *Stone Age Economics.* New York: Aldine.

Saul, M. 1983. Work Parties, Wages and Accumulation in a Voltaic Village. *American Ethnologist* 10:1:77-96.

Schmidt, G. and E.S. Mbugua. 1976. Aspects of Marketing Effectiveness for Selected Food Crops in Kenya. Working Paper No. 287. University of Nairobi: Institute for Development Studies.

Scott, J. 1976. *The Moral Economy of the Peasant: Rebellion and Subsistence in Southeast Asia.* New Haven and London: Yale University Press.

Shipton, P. 1985. The Kenyan Land Tenure Reform: Misunderstandings in the Public Creation of Private Property. In *Land Concentration in Africa*. S.P. Reyna and R. Downs, eds. Forthcoming.

Smith, L.D. 1976. An Overview of Agricultural Development Policy. In *Agricultural Development in Kenya*. J. Heyer, J.K. Maitha, and W.M. Senga, eds. Nairobi: Oxford University Press.

Sorrenson, M.P.K. 1967. *Land Reform in the Kikuyu Country: A Study in Government Policy.* Nairobi and London: Oxford University Press.

Veblen, T. 1899 (1934). *The Theory of the Leisure Class.* New York: Modern Library.

———. 1961. The Limitations of Marginal Utility. In *What Veblen Taught*. W. Mitchell, ed. New York: Augustus Kelly Reprint.

Wasserman, G. 1965. *The Politics of Decolonization: Kenya Europeans and the Land Issue 1960-65.* London: Cambridge University Press.

World Bank. 1981. *Accelerated Development in Subsaharan Africa: An Agenda for Action.* Baltimore: The Johns Hopkins University Press.

———. 1982. *Growth and Structural Change in Kenya: A Basic Economic Report, Annex II, Issues in Kenyan Agricultural Development.* Baltimore: The Johns Hopkins University Press.

CHAPTER 8

Coping with Structural Adjustment: The Nigerian Experience

AKIN L. MABOGUNJE[1]

No discipline in the social sciences can today remain indifferent to the economic crisis that has enveloped virtually all the countries of sub-Saharan Africa. Nor can any of them shy away from confronting the imperatives of structural adjustment that alone hold the prospect of getting these economies out of their present malaise. Therefore, in this chapter, I intend to address six issues. First, I shall briefly describe the economic situation in Nigeria, emphasizing, however, that it is only a special case of the pervading economic pathology of sub-Saharan Africa. Second, I shall present in broad terms the characteristics of the structural adjustment measures of the type usually prescribed for such ailing economies by the International Monetary Fund (IMF). Third, I shall attempt to discuss why, although Nigerians and Nigerian leaders accepted the need for such measures, they rejected having to do it on conventional IFM terms. Fourth, I shall examine the implications of this decision on economic and social life in urban centers and, in a fifth section, consider its rural impact. Finally, I shall proffer some ideas as to what the current situation is likely to do to the country by way of the emergence of a new national ethos.

The Economic Situation in Nigeria

According to Reginald Green, "to speak of development in most sub-Saharan African economies today is to speak of the past, not the present nor the currently foreseeable future. The world's poorest region is rapidly becoming poorer—in a number of these economies, real resource availability measured in physical gross domestic product adjusted for terms of trade is lower than in 1970. In extreme cases, such as Ghana, Uganda and Zaire, it is probably lower than in the early 1960s" (Green 1985).

The World Bank had become so alarmed at the situation that within the short space of four years it issued three reports on the challenging prospects of the region (World Bank 1981; 1983; 1984). In the last of these reports, it described the situation in the following terms:

> Africa's economic and social conditions began to deteriorate in the 1970s, and continue to do so. Gross domestic product (GDP) grew at an average of 3.6 percent a year between 1970 and 1980, but has fallen every year since then. With population rising at over 3 percent a year, income per capita in 1983 is estimated to be about 4 percent below its 1970 level. Agricultural output per capita has continued to decline, so food imports have increased: they now provide about a fifth of the region's cereal requirements. Much industrial capacity stands idle, the victim of falling domestic incomes, poor investment choices, a failure to develop export opportunities, and inadequate foreign exchange for materials and spare parts. After the impressive start the newly independent African nations made in building infrastructure, education and health services, progress is faltering and may be reversed by a shortage of funds. Many institutions are deteriorating, both in physical capacity and in their technical and financial ability to perform efficiently. Although the picture varies form country to country, even those with good records in the 1970s now face serious difficulties. In short, the economic and social transformation of Africa begun so early and effectively in the early years of independence could be halted or even reversed (World Bank 1984).

The factors responsible for this state of affairs, according to a recent commentator, have been the four Ds: Drought, Desertification, Demography, and Debt. For most sub-Saharan African countries, their economic malaise has been the product of two or more of these circumstances. However, it is fair to admit that many of the countries are small in size and limited in resources. The same cannot be said of Nigeria, even though it has ended in much the same plight. Nigeria is a country of some 100 million people, occupying nearly a million square kilometers of land. Being easily the most populous country in Africa, it has been claimed that every fifth African is a Nigerian. The country extends from the Atlantic Ocean to the borders of the Saharan Desert. It embraces within its territorial limits a wide range of ecological zones, from tropical forest to Sahel savanna. The implication of this is that nowhere within the country is there any serious obstacle to agricultural production. The number of harvests and the volume of yield of crops can, of course, be increased with improved water management and irrigation development. Enormous variety of agricultural produce characterize the economy, ranging from root tubers such as yam, cassava, and cocoyam of the forest belt to cereals such as millet, sorghum, and benniseed in the grassland areas. Maize and rice can be grown all over the country. Palm produce, cocoa, rubber, cotton, groundnut, and soyabeans have been produced for export. The domestic market accounts for other crops and vegetables such as plantains, bananas, potatoes, onions, tomatoes, legumes of various types, mangoes, oranges, and so on.

Clearly, Nigeria is preeminently an agricultural country. Indeed, up to the 1960s agriculture was the mainstay of the economy, providing the bulk of both government revenue and the nation's foreign exchange earnings. Yet, since 1970s, agriculture has suffered severe neglect, during the period of the so-called oil boom. The country developed an almost insatiable appetite for imported goods and commodities. Even food items such as maize, rice, and vegetable oil, which the country used to produce in abundance began to be imported. The import bill for food items rose from under 2 million in 1962 to over 2 billion by 1984, a more than 1,000 percent increase. In that last year, wheat alone accounted for over 20 percent of total food import. The share of food in total imports varied around 9 percent, rising from 7.6 percent in 1970 to 11.3 percent in 1980.[2]

Despite its low contribution to the total gross domestic product, accounting for only between 5 and 9 percent during the period 1960-1980, the industrial production performance had risen dramatically over the period, based as it was on massive importation of raw materials, machinery, and spare parts. For the manufacturing sector, total paid employees rose from 58,000 in 1962 to over 320,000 in 1983. In monetary terms, gross output rose from 1.5 billion in 1974 to over 10.2 billion in 1983. Much of this was accounted for by distillery and brewery industries, motor vehicle assembly, and textiles. The main component of industrial costs, however, was that of raw materials, most of which were imported. In most years, this accounted for more than 75 percent of total cost of production. Capital investment in manufacturing also grew astronomically, going from 64 million in 1975 to nearly 900 million in 1980. Much of this was accounted for by such traditional subsectors as breweries, textile, vehicle assembly, cement, sugar refining, and flour milling, as well as by state-directed efforts in iron and steel, pulp and paper, petrochemicals, and liquefied natural gas.

All of these heavy investments were, of course, made possible by the phenomenal growth in petroleum export dating particularly from 1973. Petroleum production in Nigeria dates from 1958 when 1.9 million barrels were produced and most of it was exported. Production rose to nearly 100 million barrels in 1965, to nearly 400 million barrels in 1970, and to over 840 million in 1979, since when production has generally been declining. However, in monetary terms, the year 1973, the year of the Arab-Israeli War, was a turning point. Up to then, government revenue from oil was never more than 1 billion. It was 735 million in 1972, jumped to 1.4 billion in 1973, and to 4.2 billion in 1974. It rose to over 10 billion in 1979 and to over 13 billion in 1980.

By the following year, 1981, the drop to 9.6 billion was the first sign of the fragility and nosediving decline of the economy. Total foreign exchange earnings of the country dropped from 14.2 billion in 1980 to 10.9 billion in 1981, to 8.2 billion in 1982, and to 7.6 billion in 1983, although it rose to 9.1 billion in 1984 and 11.6 billion in 1985 before its current sharp fall. However, so engrossed was the country in pandering to its taste for imported goods that in 1981, total imports still stood at 12.6 billion, dropping to 10.1 billion in 1982 and then more drastically to 6.6 billion in 1983, 4.5 billion in 1984, and 5.5 billion in 1985.

As a result of these developments, the balance of payments position swung from a surplus of about 2 billion in 1980 to a deficit of nearly 3 billion by 1984. The problems of the external sector were compounded by high debt service burden and accumulation of short-term trade arrears on documentary credit and bills on open account. The total external debt of the country, which had stood at only 175 million at the end of the Civil War in 1970, rose to just over 1 billion by 1979. This was due largely to medium- and long-term loans of the World Bank and the jumbo-size eurodollar loan of 627 million contracted in 1978 by the regime of General Obasanjo. However, between 1979 and 1984, the total loan outstanding against Nigeria escalated to 12.8 billion, of which 62.5 percent belonged to the federal government, 25.1 percent of state governments collectively, and 12.4 percent to the private sector.

By that time the situation had become so critical that the country was having real difficulties in raising the necessary credit to cover its foreign trade transactions. These difficulties were not very noticeable in the agricultural sector, which has remained more or less stagnant over the preceding ten-year period. But it had dramatic impact on the manufacturing sector. Industrial output suffered a sharp decline of 21 percent between 1983 and 1984 because of a drastic shortage of industrial raw material imports, a result of the tight administrative controls on imports. These controls were imposed from 1982 onwards as a means of dealing with the increasingly acute shortage of foreign exchange. As the global market for crude oil worsened with the deepening oil glut and the drop in price, more stringent administrative control measures and levies were imposed to curb the Nigerian penchant for spending foreign exchange prodigally. But by then the economy was in no position to respond positively to these measures.

The Nature of Structural Adjustment

It was in these circumstances that, on 18 April 1983 Nigeria approached the International Monetary Fund for a three-year extended fund facility of between $1.9 and $2.4 billion. This was essentially to satisfy a condition set by some of its creditors for refinancing its trade arrears. Because of the brazen economic mismanagement that had characterized the rule of the particular national government that was seeking this accommodation, the International Monetary Fund quite naturally insisted on reforms of a wide-ranging nature, more commonly referred to as structural adjustment.

In its broadest sense structural adjustment implies the removal of operational bottlenecks and institutional rigidities that militate against the efficient and competitive performance of an economy.[3] However, while there is no conflict as to definition, considerable controversy surrounds the general direction and instruments of policy designed to bring this adjustment about. From the point of view of international financial institutions and donor countries, the general direction of structural adjustment policy should have two objectives. First it should promote strong international interdependence by opening the economy of the structurally adjusting country to the free flow of goods and capital investment on the basis of the principle of comparative advantage. Second it should inculcate a free-market approach to production organization and economic transaction.

To these ends, certain policy instruments are to be preferred. These include the use of indirect monetary and fiscal policies rather than direct administrative controls; the maintenance of realistic, flexible, and responsive foreign exchange rates, especially at levels that facilitate export promotion; the erection of only very low and uniform rates of effective protection to domestic producers in any given sector, or in relation to any given product; the establishment of factor prices such that real wage increases are justified only by rising productivity, while interest rates are kept positive in real terms; the minimization of taxation, subsidies, and general governmental expenditure through the application of cost-recovery principles in pricing infrastructural services; the eschewing of inflation-inducing budget deficits at all times; and the avoidance of underpricing agricultural produce.

In specific terms, structural adjustment is thus seen as involving moving real resources to agriculture in order to correct the prevailing urban bias of development policies. It also entails redressing price distortions by eliminating quotas and import licenses, reducing tariffs considerably, pursuing tight money, credit, and fiscal policies, containing capital flight, dampening inflation, rationalizing parastatal enterprises through closing down or privatizing inefficient ones, deregulating the marketing of agricultural commodities, realigning the exchange rate to international equilibrium level by devaluing the domestic currency, and liberalizing trade generally.

These prescriptions, if implemented, would mean a drastic reorientation of national economies along strictly capitalist lines. Given the nascent nature of the economies of most African countries and their inherent vulnerability, it is understandable that many African governments have had real difficulties accepting this new orthodoxy of the International Monetary Fund. The feeling that, under the guise of structural adjustment, countries are being made to sacrifice preferred social values, cultural self-esteem, and authentic humanist vision, which their leaders have striven to develop and propagate, have led to a certain reluctance and resistance in accepting all of what is now commonly regarded as "the shock treatment" of the IMF.

In the particular case of Nigeria, the country had, in fact, accepted as reasonable a good number of the "conditionalities" attached to the IMF loan. It had, for instance, begun the process of reducing aggregate capital expenditure as well as cutting down its budget deficit from 6.2 billion in 1983 to only .3 billion in 1984. It had also imposed greater budgetary discipline on itself. It was willing, for instance, to reduce the subsidy on fertilizer but not on petroleum products. It would rather "commercialize" than privatize most of its parastatals. It was prepared to simplify and rationalize its customs tariff structure and to abolish the Approved User Scheme. It was willing to vigorously promote export and boost agricultural production through adjustment of producer prices.

On two issues, however, the Nigerian government was unyielding.

The first was the adjustment of the rate of exchange of the naira to correct for its overvaluation; the second was the liberalization of its trade policy abolishing administrative controls in the area on international trade. The IMF had considered that the Naira was overvalued by about 60 percent as of May 1984 and had recommended a 25-30 percent initial devaluation to bring the naira to parity with the U.S. dollar. This would be followed by quarterly reviews and possible further devaluation depending on the performance of the economy after the adoption of the structural adjustment program and until the element of overvaluation had been removed. The Nigerian government doubted the expected benefits from devaluation. It noted that Nigeria's export prices, notably those of petroleum, were usually quoted in foreign currencies, that locally manufactured goods had high import content, and that there was generally a high propensity of demand for imported goods. With regard to trade liberalization, the government maintains that in a situation of mounting trade imbalance, it would be economically suicidal to open the floodgates to unbridled importation of all sorts of goods into the country.

The Rejection of the IMF Loan and the Selective Closing of the Economy

This was where matters stood when on 27 August 1985 the country experienced a change of leadership in the military administration. Mistakenly as ever, the western press came out to acclaim the coup as a strike in favor of taking the IMF loan. However, the new leadership justified its accession to power on the grounds of rejecting the autocratic tendencies of its predecessor and announced its own preference for wide-ranging consultations in matters of major national import. The issue of whether Nigeria should or should not accept the IMF loan on the basis of final agreement to the remaining conditionalities was seen as a matter of grave national significance and was therefore thrown open to public debate between September and November 1985.[4]

All segments of the Nigerian population participated in the public debate. They included bankers, businessmen, university professors, trade unionists, politicians, journalists, small-scale industrialists, professional groups, market women, farmers, and students. Arguments were marshaled for and against accepting the loan. By the end of the debate, there was no doubt that the overwhelming view was against taking the loan, even when it was agreed that rejection was bound to result in serious hardship and would call for great sacrifice on the part of the populace. According to Oyejide and others, the issues that had swung the majority against the loan included those of upholding the sovereignty of the country, commitment to self-reliant development, fear of additional loan repayment burden, fear of further economic mismanagement, and the lessons of international experience, especially of African countries that has accepted the IMF loans. Consequently, the Nigerian government decided to reject the loan and to seek, in the words of President Babangida, solutions to the social and economic problems of the country "through our own efforts, at our own pace and on our own volition, consistent with our long-term national interest."[5]

The 1986 budget speech, from which the above quotation was taken, stressed the determination of the government to harness homegrown efforts to solve the nation's problems and to chart a new path for the future. It also emphasized that the real issue in rejecting the IMF conditionalities was not so much a refusal to accept the compelling necessity for structural adjustment as it was a conscious preference for achieving this in a manner that would not compromise the long-term interest of the country. For instance, there was considerable reservation as to whether the IMF insistence on trade liberalization was not designed to perpetuate the largely import-dependent consumption pattern in the country, when its long-term interest dictates that this be circumscribed and altered as rapidly and effectively as possible to bring the country more in line with its productive capacity and resource endowment.

At any rate, the 1986 budget went on to spell out the implications of the new regime. It banned immediately further importation of food items such as rice, maize, and vegetable oil and served notice to ban wheat importation by January 1987. It imposed a 30 percent levy on all imports and reduced the level of government subsidy on petroleum products by 80 percent. This last decision was expected to generate a revenue of over 900 million naira. This was to be made available to a newly created Directorate of Food, Roads and Rural Infrastructure based in the Office of the President and headed by a member of the Armed Forces Ruling Council. The directorate is expected principally to promote a framework for the grassroot social mobilization of the rural population and to mount a virile program of engaging them actively in the expansion of food and other agricultural raw material production as well as in the construction of roads and other rural infrastructures.

But perhaps the most crucial decision of the new economic

package was to reject a simple devaluation of the Nigerian currency and opt instead for the introduction of a second-tier foreign exchange market (SFEM) through which the currency is expected to find its own level. With very special and limited exceptions, all categories of imports are to be financed through this second window. Apart from easing government control of the economy and reducing bureaucratic hassle with its attendant corruption, this development is expected to reinforce the trend towards curbing the import orientation of consumption patterns among Nigerians and encouraging industrialists to look more seriously for local sources of raw materials for their plants. In other words, what the new economic package has done is to redirect the growth of the economy along certain lines while closing the door selectively against certain types of imports. Although it is perhaps too early to regard 1986 as a watershed year in Nigeria's economic history, it is already possible to identify a certain impact it is starting to have on the social and economic conditions in Nigerian cities and rural areas.

The Urban Impact of the New Package

In looking at the impact of this development on urban residents, it is useful to consider both their consumption patterns and their productive activities. With regard to their consumption patterns, the most immediate impact had been on food preferences. In a sense, the country has been fortunate in that the last three years have been years of good harvests. Hence, local staples have been abundant in the market and relatively cheap. Manufactured food items based on imported raw materials are still testing out the limits of consumer price resistance. That such price limits exist was well illustrated in the case of wheat bread when, because of shortages, prices were hiked up to unrealistic levels. Consumers simply shifted away from eating bread to making do with other local substitutes.

At the same time, government is trying to encourage product substitution of various types. For example, the research institutes are now under pressure to see how well wheat bread can be replaced by corn bread or cassava bread. This possibility had been considered for some years. But the wheat lobby had not taken the government seriously so that little industrial progress had been made. With the decision to ban wheat importation from January 1987, feverish efforts are now being undertaken to make the necessary adjustments. Similar efforts are being directed at finding local sources of malting material for beer brewing. The use of sorghum as a substitute for barley is now generally accepted, and one or two brands of beer already boast of being made from this raw material. Imported wine and sparkling wines like champagne are also being substituted for with products made from local raw materials such as kolanuts. In short, with regard to food and beverages, we can expect some very interesting shifts of taste over the next few years.

The other area where some agonizing reappraisal is currently being undertaken is transportation. In the heyday of the oil boom, the Udoji Commission set up to review the performance and compensation of the Public Service not only recommended substantial increases in salaries and wages but also extended downwards the categories of officers for which government should provide low-interest loans to buy personal cars. At the same time, in a world of rising petroleum prices, the government resolutely stuck to a policy of subsidizing gasoline and other petroleum products. The result, as was only to be expected, was the phenomenal increase in the volume of vehicles on Nigerian roads. In the case of Lagos, the capital city, the traffic congestion that resulted became so intolerable as to earn international notoriety for the city. All of that situation is changing very fast. The sharp reduction of petroleum subsidy from 100 to only 20 percent has curbed the easy mobility of the class for which personal car ownership was only of marginal importance. The high cost and restricted availability of spare parts have also meant withdrawal of vehicles from the road. With the introduction of the second-tier foreign exchange market, the situation is that, at least for the moment, new cars, including even the small Volkswagen "beetle" which the country assembles, are priced well above the means of the executive cadre in the public service.

The same thing has happened with regard to international travels. At the height of the oil boom, it was no problem for a young female secretary to fly to London for a weekend visit. The cost of such a flight could be easily recouped if during her brief stay she could purchase dresses, fabrics, jewelry, shoes, leather goods, and toiletries, which she could sell to her colleagues on her return. The overvaluation of the naira and the administrative difficulties of getting import licenses to bring in certain goods in large quantities encouraged such sideline activities to thrive. But this is becoming a thing of the past. The rise in the naira value of air tickets has sharply reduced the number of traveling Nigerians. The effect of these changes on the appetite for consuming the latest in foreign fads and fashions, particularly among the young, is going to be interesting to watch.

All this, of course, means that, in turn, for the first time in about two decades Nigeria is going to be a relatively cheap place to visit and to live in for foreigners, especially from developed countries. Despite frequent declarations to the contrary, Nigeria, as a country, was never really interested in international tourism. Large sums of money were spent on building hotels, but these were more with a view to attracting business travelers rather than tourists. If the various travel agents and the National Tourist Board were now to exert themselves, significant development could be expected in this sector.

The possibility of growth in tourism leads naturally to a consideration of the impact of the new dispensation on urban productive activities in general. Until now, manufacturing industries have had to confront a government whose basic predisposition was towards mercantile capitalism. The quickest road to wealth in the country was to get a distributorship of some manufactured product such that the agreement with the assembly firms stipulated that they could sell their products to consumers only through distributors. Since the prices at which cars could be sold was controlled, and it was easier to monitor the sales of large firms such as the assembly firms but not of the myriads of distributors, a situation was created whereby the latter were reaping large profits while the former could barely break even.

The result was that many manufacturing firms tried to stay afloat by using various underhand methods to divert funds to their foreign accounts. The most important of these was overinvoicing for imported goods. Such practices were facilitated by the massive corruption resulting from the administrative control of importation through the issuance of licenses. Sometimes licenses were issued to nonexistent enterprises, which then hawked them around and sold them at a premium to firms that desperately needed them. The net effect of all these practices, especially as the economy entered the difficult period after 1981, was to sharply increase capital underutilization in the economy. Many factories were producing at less than 40 percent of installed capacity with the result that prices were kept high and the rate of inflation shot up. Government parastatals, some of which were set up precisely to moderate such a development, were so inefficiently run that they became part of the problem. With SFEM, the expectation is that some of these tendencies may be halted and reversed. Although the value of the naira has fallen sharply, the fact that enterprises can directly purchase foreign exchange through their banks and import raw material and other necessities without the hassle of import license could mean a higher rate of capital utilization. It could also mean that, with time, these enterprises can produce at costs that will make prices more reasonable and bring down the rate of inflation. Certainly, given the effectiveness with which the Central Bank has been monitoring to ensure that foreign exchange purchases mainly for raw material and spare parts, the prospect that things may change for the better does not appear totally unrealistic.

The Rural Impact of the New Policy

The rural impact of the new policy presents us with diverse and interesting perspectives. As life became more difficult in the cities, many urban families turned to part-time agricultural production to supplement their income. Around every major city we now find an expanding zone of cultivation, largely worked by urban residents. Some of these cultivators are organized groups of young school leavers or graduates whom various state governments are trying to attract back to agriculture as a means of coping with the growing urban unemployment among these categories of educated youth. The Rivers state government, for instance, launched its School-to-Land Programme around Port Harcourt in 1984. Since then, other state governments have come out with similar schemes addressed to graduates and other unemployed youths.

In general, government has also encouraged the major Nigerian and multinational companies, as well as wealthy Nigerian businessmen, to go into large-scale agricultural production. With the banning of the importation of various agricultural produce, such ventures are proving less financially risky than they used to be. Besides, owning and managing a big farm is now becoming the in thing to do for wealthy Nigerians, among whom are numbered most of the retired generals of the Nigerian army. The most impressive, and one of the most successful, of this new type of agricultural enterprise is the farm established by the former head of state, General Olusegun Obasanjo. The expanding urban market for poultry and other products has meant in particular an insatiable demand for such crops as maize, rice, and cassava for which farmers can now get very good prices.

Of considerable importance in this respect has also been the dissolution of the various commodity marketing boards. These are boards which, in the colonial days, were set up to protect farmers against the wild fluctuations of prices on the international market for export crops such as cocoa, palm produce, cotton, groundnuts, and rubber. These boards had gone through a checkered history of increasing unresponsiveness to the real needs of farmers and had reached a point of actually depressing farmers' productivity when they were taken over by the federal government in 1974. Following the takeover, similar boards were set up for domestic crops, especially grains. But by 1984 it was already clear that these boards were not only being managed incompetently but were of little value to the needs of farmers. Situations were described where farmers would sell crops to the board at Ilora, near Oyo, some 180 kilometers north of Lagos, and would be given slips of paper to go and collect their money at Minna, headquarters of the board, which is some 500 kilometers farther away.

At any rate, the dissolution of the boards has meant that for export crops farmers are now getting close to the full international market price, while for domestic crops, especially those like maize and rice which are becoming industrial raw materials, they are not doing badly. There is, however, no doubt that some form of institutionalized marketing arrangements will be required. The issue is how to create an organization that would be close enough to the farmers and very responsive to their needs. There is also the question of how intimately farmers should participate in the running of such an organization. These matters are currently being examined at various forums and there can be no doubt that some new level of resolution will be achieved. The resolution being most actively canvassed is one that links marketing with the provision of credit and farm inputs at the level of, say, a state-managed cooperative bank.

But perhaps the most important impact of the new dispensation is the establishment of the Directorate of Food, Roads and Rural Infrastructure based in the Office of the President and with enormous power to coordinate all activities connected with rural and agricultural development. As already mentioned, the directorate's activities are funded through a major diversion of resources from urban to rural areas by ways of the removal of subsidies on petroleum products. For this year, the directorate has been concentrating on increasing and improving the mileage of rural road and providing hand-pumped boreholes for many rural communities. A target of 60,000 kilometers of rural road was set by the president in his 1986 budget. However, because of the time it has taken for the directorate to establish itself and to get its *modus operandi* generally understood, it is very unlikely that that target will be met until well into 1987.

Four elements of considerable interest characterize the operations of the directorate to date. First, there is the concern to involve grassroot participation in its activities through community mobilization. Although community organization and community governance are real facts of life in rural Nigeria, present administrative arrangements accord them hardly any recognition. The formal administrative structure in the country goes down to the level of local government, which territorially can be very extensive and which embraces numerous communities whose leadership and territoriality are only vaguely appreciated. The directorate plans to change this situation, especially as it intends that its activities with regard to infrastructural development be seen more as assistance to individual communities. The communities are expected to make their own contribution to the effort, either in kind (through providing free labor input) or in cash. For this reason, the directorate is engaged in identifying the number of communities in each local government area and listing the settlements belonging to each community. This is meant also to facilitate its major commitment to monitoring all activities in the rural areas for which it is responsible.

The second element in the operations of the directorate is its decision to concentrate on the use of existing facilities in the country. This has meant an emphasis on the maintenance of available machinery and equipment by providing funds to procure spare parts and undertake repairs. It has also meant a certain commitment to the use of direct labor or, more correctly, that of government agencies, such as the state Ministries of Public Works, which were set up to undertake such assignments. Over the years of the petroleum boom, a practice had developed whereby every task was contracted out to private individuals or companies without any appreciable reduction in the staff of the government agencies concerned. Naturally, this aspect of the directorate's operation has not been uniformly popular.

The third element is the close involvement of all existing institutions and organizations in the directorate's activities. This is particularly noticeable with respect to the directorate's plans for expansion of food-producing capacity in the country. It is clear that for this to happen, tremendous effort must be directed to seed multiplication and the production of other inputs necessary to facilitate the adoption of each of the food programs being promoted by the directorate. This has meant, therefore, the mobilization of all research institutes, of state Ministries of Agriculture and of large-scale private sector operations.

Finally, there is the element concerned with the promotion of technology. It was found, for instance, that little attention had been paid in previous programs to disseminating in the rural areas technology of a type that rural residents can relate to. A case in point is the rural water supply scheme. The earlier program was based on a capital-intensive and technologically sophisticated program involving the use of electrical generating plants to pump water into large "Braithwaite" overhead tanks from which a reticulation system distributed water to a number of villages and homes. However, once the generating plant breaks down, which is not infrequent, the whole scheme collapses. For the directorate, therefore, a more viable option is to promote the provision of hand-operated pumps, which can be made by many fabricating companies in the country and maintained by trained villagers. The same strategy is being developed with respect to the fabrication of various agricultural processing machinery and equipment, especially as it is being increasingly realized that processing is as crucial as storage for stimulating higher levels of agricultural productivity.

Conclusion

Clearly, Nigeria today, as it tries to cope with the strains and stresses of structural adjustment, is a country in travail. The pains are all there for everyone to see. High prices, high rates of unemployment, high rates of urban crime, and high levels of personal insecurity are facts of everyday life. Given that all these changes are taking place under a military regime, no one can guarantee the stability of the political system. We have, in fact, had one attempted coup, which was nipped in the bud, but no one can say that it was the last.

Yet, there are straws in the wind indicating that whatever the future holds, the prospects are likely to be very different and probably much better, in the sense of being more enduring, than the recent past. A new ethos is emerging whose essential indication is a concern with production and individual productivity. This is very different from the emphasis on dealership and distributorship that was more characteristic of the preceding decade. It is also a change from the days of the petty and not-so-petty contractors of both sexes. This development is a function partly of the stringent economic situation in the country and partly of the unsettled fiscal and monetary policies of government. But to the extent that the new ethos is encouraging a trend towards increasing self-employment and enhancing the image of the private sector as providing a more viable and satisfying opportunity for self-fulfillment, the present effort at structural adjustment holds the prospect of setting the country on a new course of development.

Dissenting and alarming voices have, however, been raised as to what the present tendencies portend. The emphasis on reducing administrative controls in various aspects of national economic life, and allowing instead the operation of free market forces, appears to a very vocal section of the Nigerian populace as trying to throw away the baby with the bath water. The objectives of state, as enunciated both in the constitution and in every development plan since the Second National Development Plan (1970-1974), emphasize the role of the state in ensuring the equal access of all citizens to opportunities of self-improvement. This has meant the state's concern with the provision of free primary education and highly subsidized secondary and tertiary education. It has also meant free or highly subsidized access to health care, especially maternal and child health care. All this is being threatened by the new dispensation. The threat is brought forcibly home to many by the number of agencies, such as the various commodity boards and the Nigerian National Supply Company, that the government had simply closed down. The air is also filled with plans to "privatize" or "commercialize" one parastatal or the other. Is Nigeria, so the question goes, now trying to become a capitalist country with all the insensitivity, the lack of humane compassion for the weak and the poor, and the heavy wastage of human resources that go with this?

Despite the outcome of the national debate on the IMF, there is a widespread feeling that the country is accepting and adopting the structural adjustment conditionalities almost with a vengeance. It is my view, however, that form should not be confused with substance. The essence of the present structural adjustment program in Nigeria is to achieve a greater measure of integration within the national economy and a higher degree of self-reliance in dealing with the ensuing social and economic problems. It is thus not without interest that for the first time since independence there is a widespread concern with family planning, and the government itself is in the process of formally adopting a national population policy. By the same token, after the acrimony surrounding the discovery that an attempt had been made to formally align the country with the Organization of Islamic Conference, in contravention of the secular status of the state, there is genuine concern to engender stronger accord among the different religious groups. So far, although the general lines along which efforts at structural transformation are progressing are clear, the pervasive feeling is that of a nation in turmoil. What is also very patent is that a new consensus is emerging around which the whole country can be rallied. The days of blaming our ills on our former colonial masters or on foreign advisers and agencies are over. Nigerians are now starting to feel that they are the architects of their own fortune. More than ever before that fortune is being appreciated in a national context against which sectional interests need to be contained. This is the basis for the new consensus. It is no longer one defined largely on ethnic terms. For one thing, the economic debacle has spared no group in the country. All segments of the population have had to accept a sharp fall in real income and are realizing that the situation is not likely to change for the better too soon. They have all watched the government, out of necessity, having to withdraw at least some of the subsidies and commitment to important areas of social welfare such as education and health, whose virtually free public services they had almost come to take for granted. The search for a new consensus, therefore, would tend to draw together the government, the business communities, the workers, the farmers, the professionals, the intellectuals, and the cultural leaders of various persuasions. For the moment, the old political leadership is in quarantine.

The future in Nigeria remains uncertain but challenging. The present difficulties and deprivations hold out promise of raising national consciousness to a new level and making economic progress the centerpiece of national preoccupations. They induce a greater commitment to consolidating the increasing gains the country is making through the fuller exploitation and utilization of its resources. They encourage the hope that these will be used as the basis for striving for a more enduring and more sustainable pattern of growth and development. More importantly, they raise the expectation that out of the present efforts to cope with problems of structural adjustment may emerge a country more united in the appreciation of its goals and more realistic about its capabilities and the means available to achieve those goals.

Notes

1. I feel highly honored and privileged to be invited to contribute to the *Carter Studies on Africa*. I had the singular advantage of meeting Gwen Carter some twenty years ago when, as a young university teacher from the University of Ibadan, Nigeria, I was spending my sabbatical leave at Northwestern University. Gwen had just taken over the directorship of the program of African Studies at that institution, and it was clear that she was going to give it a new sense of purpose and commitment and take it to greater heights of achievement. I felt very privileged to be associated with the program then, and it is from that sense of appreciation that I am delighted at the invitation to contribute to this book.

I have chosen as my subject structural adjustment in Nigeria, aware of course that in her professional field Gwen is quintessentially a scholar of the political scene in southern Africa. This, however, was never allowed to mean an indifference to events and developments in the other major regions of the

African continent. Indeed, Gwen traveled everywhere on the continent, meeting the leaders of most African countries both in the political and the intellectual fields. Her interest in the political situation of the different countries was, of course, a function of the fact that problems of national unity were so much the privileged challenge of those eventful years of the 1960s and early 1970s. Today, there is no denying the fact that overwhelmingly the most significant problems of the African continent are in the economic realm. And it is no mere speculation that if Gwen were to be young again and beginning a research career in Africa, her field of interest would undoubtedly be in political economy.

2. Information on the Nigerian economy has come from *Nigerian Economic Review* 1, 1986, and my own research materials.

3. Much of this section is based on an unpublished monograph by O. Oboyade (n.d.).

4. For an analysis of this debate, see Oyejide, Soyode, and Kayode (1985:119).

5. *Address to the Nation on the 1986 Budget* by Major-General Ibrahim Babangida, President, Commander-in-Chief of the Nigerian Armed Forces, Lagos, 31 December 1985.

References

Green, R.H. 1985. From Deepening Economic Malaise Toward Renewed Development: An Overview. *Journal of Development Planning* 15.

Oboyade, O. n.d. Policy Re-Structuring in the Manufacturing Sector of the African Economies.

Oyejide, T.A., A. Soyode, and M.O. Kayode. 1985. *Nigeria and the IMF.* Ibadan: University of Ibadan Press.

World Bank. 1981. *Accelerated Development in Sub-Saharan Africa: An Agenda for Action.* Baltimore: The Johns Hopkins University Press.

———. 1983. *Sub-Saharan Africa: Progress Report on Development Prospects and Programs.* Baltimore: The Johns Hopkins University Press.

———. 1984. *Towards Sustained Development in Sub-Saharan Africa: A Joint Program of Action.* Baltimore: The Johns Hopkins University Press.

CHAPTER 9

Adversity and Transformation: The Nigerian Light at the End of the Tunnel

RONALD COHEN[1]

The bad news of accelerating food deficits dominates the thinking, the mass media, and a great deal of the research on African rural development. Policies that have proven ineffective and projects that have failed or stalled, strew the literature, creating a dismal note of monocultural consensus. This does not mean to imply that it is therefore possible or accurate to paint over the present picture with a Pollyanna quick fix derived from any single case study. many recent analyses have concentrated on evaluating and recapitulating what went wrong. Once some agreement is reached about the deepening food deficits in Africa and their causes, scholarly efforts move to what Hyden (Chapter 3) calls a "monocultural"—therefore safe—position. This consensus then guides policy recommendations because of the underlying agreement about causal relations responsible for these unwanted outcomes.

Unfortunately, panaceas based on the analysis of failure do not have the epistemological force of those stemming from success. Knowing what went wrong in particular situations may or may not be generalizable, even if valid for the case in question. Furthermore, because food production and distribution are complex biosystems, many factors, indeed myriads of them, are related to outcomes. Unfortunately, this makes most models valid, at least to some extent, while adding credibility to often quite contradictory theories and advice. Nevertheless, predicting failure—which is what most empirical analyses now do—cannot contribute a great deal to success; to wit, determining which among the many potential policy mixes is the correct one on any particular situation. A tiny fraction are eliminated through the analysis of failure. But many, indeed most, are also quite viable solutions. Good news: the mix of factors associated with success is more instructive—and, unfortunately, much more difficult at present to come by.

What is apparent in this complex situation is the cacaphony and variety of scholarly writings, explanations, and recipes for improvement. Often as not these are associate with value positions, or theoretical paradigms, and periods of greater and lesser popularity (cf. Staatz and Eicher 1986; Cohen 1987).

Believers in Marxoid dependency theory find data galore to support their doctrines and the associated recommendations to withdraw from international financial and commodity markets. Similarly so do those holding neoclassical views who argue for more foreign investment and for greater interaction (dependency?) within a world system. There is support for demographic intensification and for theories about its causes and effects, and support as well for the belief that intensification alone is unrelated to agricultural development. People in search of moral economies—especially in precolonial contexts—discover them. Others looking for rational peasants who calculate risks and choose logically to maximize outcomes observe these behaviors and record them. An entire tradition of research is based on a definition that separates growth and development as two quite separate processes. However, a few researchers (cf. Mellor et al. 1987; Cohen 1987) are now beginning to examine or to preach the very opposite idea.

Meanwhile, food deficits continue. It is becoming clear that contexts—locally determined factor relations—underlie much of the confusion. General formulae may or may not be apposite in specific instances, although there are by now, after several decades of sifting and winnowing of theories and policies, some generalizations that are broadly valid, albeit with few if any specifics. Clearly there is a need for better technology, better infrastructure, the "right" prices, water management, and so on, but the mix for any particular place is still illusive. It is in this light that the analysis of a successful case can provide insights into how decisions about specific contexts are made and put into practice.

One caveat is essential before we turn to the analysis. The conclusion that Nigeria's food policies are successful is, so far, a minority position. Discussions and publications by outside experts generally assert the opposite. One of the most recent works (Andrae and Beckman 1985) describes the Nigerian food deficits in awesome terms and concludes with deep pessimism that the country's dependence on cheap imported foods, especially wheat, is so profound and ingrained into its nutritional culture and economy that things cannot be changed under any foreseeable circumstances. This is particularly true of soft white bread which is by now (the 1980s) a fast food in the nation's diet. The conclusion, widely held, is that the galloping demand for food-grain imports, especially wheat, sentences Nigeria and other poorer countries to cadet membership in a world economic system where the cards are stacked against them.

It is sobering to realize how far events have proven such well-researched conclusions to be wrong. There is every indication, in my view, that Nigeria's food supply problem is on the way to being solved. Production was up 31 percent in 1984, 14 percent above 1984's total in 1985; and 1985/86 bids fair to be another good year or an even better one than previous growing seasons (*The Economist* 1985, 1986). As of this writing (February 1987) all imports of maize, rice, and wheat have been stopped, and ample food stocks are available for both rural and urban populations. In the process there have been ups and downs that have fueled the fires of the pessimists. Like many African countries, Nigeria has gone from pre-independence self-sufficiency to accelerating post-independence per capita food deficits, and thence to a rapidly increasing per capita production in the late 1980s. This quite short period of history has witnessed a Toynbee-like challenge and successful response—partly planned, partly accidental. In the process the country has matured in ways important for its overall economic and political development.

Throughout these turbulent times, Nigeria's policy responses have been—like the country itself—plural or multimodal rather than unimodal (Johnston 1985; Cohen 1987). Resources have been allocated to smallholder farm development, large-scale commercial farming, and vast bureaucratically managed irrigation schemes. Costs do not reflect the numbers involved. The bulk of the Agricultural Bank loans have gone to the large commercial farms. In Borno, where several millions were available, only N80,000 was given to small farms on a revolving fund basis (in 1984). The large-scale irrigation scheme, South Chad Irrigation Project (SCIP), served 7,500 farm households at a start-up cost of somewhere between N300 and N500 million, while the smallholder farm program which at that time (1984) served 55,000 farm units had spent N12 million. The obvious inequities of development resource allocations have stimulated criticism by writers who stress their belief that food production can be increased significantly, including surplus sales, only if those who produce most of the food—the smallholder farmers—are given the bulk of the rural development investments (cf. Johnston 1985; Forrest 1981; Matlon 1981; Delgado, Chapter 3 in this book). Generally this argument is buttressed by the assertion that small farm units are more efficient than large commercial farms (World Bank 1981:54; Staatz and Eicher 1986:56).

In the following sections I wish to briefly examine relevant aspects of Nigeria's macrolevel food policies and then summarize and discuss the relevant programs that have been put into place and that we examined in Borno State. These include development efforts directed at smallholders, large commercial farms, and irrigated state-run holdings for former rain-fed smallholders.

The Historical Context

As with much of Africa, food supplies were a nonproblem for most of the twentieth century. The major exception was a devastating drought during the First World War, along with several milder episodes up to the 1950s. In general, those who have looked at the problem in detail conclude that rainfall conditions have been similar to those in the past (Watts 1983), or have actually been worse in the twentieth century than in any other period over the past 500 years (Nicholson 1984). In other words, up until quite recently, Nigeria has been able to produce enough food for its peoples in a century that has witnessed rainfall conditions similar to or, according to one expert (Nicholson 1984), quite possibly worse than those experienced in precolonial times. Political economy theorists who tend to emphasize the deleterious influence of colonialism—not a difficult thing to do given the facts of the case—generally describe the suffering and deprivations of those years. One writer (Watts 1983) argues that rainfall was similar in the nineteenth and the twentieth centuries. Famines when they occur should therefore be directly traceable to colonial policy and administration. By contrast, precolonial food shortages were cushioned, he notes (Watts 1983:141), by a benign and rather utopian form of "moral economy" which helped the ordinary peasants and the urban poor through periods of want. Those in authority, the ruling groups, shared their surplus extractions with the poor when the crops failed in successive years threatening widespread famine. This originates in a traditional political culture of redistribution buttressed by Islamic codes (in northern Nigeria) of charity and public responsibility. On the other hand, colonial rule, it is argued, replaced this integrated and adaptive system with an exotic (European) authority that initiated and then enforced the cultivation of cash export crops, making peasants more vulnerable and dependent upon factors outside the control of their traditional political and economic systems. If a zero sum outcome of cash versus food crops is added, then colonialism took peasant labor out of food production and into cash exports with a correlated drop in per capita food available for home consumption. The argument is logical, but significantly there are no reports of consistent trends in accelerating per capita food deficits from the colonial period. Indeed quite the reverse is true for almost the entire period, with the exception of the one large and the several smaller droughts already mentioned. But the fact of the matter is that at no time during the colonial period are there records of such a consistent downward trend in per capita food production as there has been since the country achieved its independence.

The precolonial political systems of northern Nigeria were a far cry from the felicitous structural-functional models of equilibrium and moral economy described by some writers (e.g., Watts 1983). Certainly an ideal of noblesse oblige redistribution is deeply imbedded into the political culture and has been for centuries. Generosity by those who have, or wish to be regarded as having, more than their neighbors is one of the most essential features of social stratification in the region as a whole (Cohen 1970). However, anyone familiar with the detailed observations of the nineteenth century travelers to the area can cite many examples of leaders plundering, and enslaving, their subjects, while destroying entire villages and the surrounding food crops at the same time (see Richardson 1853; Barth 1857). Villages close to the central rulers' capital town were generally safe and even well looked after in terms resembling the classic redistributive model. Settlements farther away, or in the border areas between emirates, often found it impossible to be as loyal and obedient as expected. These recalcitrant peripherals had to be constantly disciplined and coerced into delivering tributes. If not, they tended to seek autonomy or the protection of a ruling power elsewhere (Cohen 1971). Rulers with debts to pay often chose to punish rebellious villages on the peripheries thereby plundering and quelling at the same time. If debts were severe, as Richardson (1853:228-297) so graphically points out, then grievances against a subject group or locality could be trumped up and expeditionary forces dispatched to garner in the booty. This meant taking everything they could lay hands on, including local women and children as slaves, horses, cattle, sheep, goats, and stored foods (Richardson 1853:228-297; Cohen and Brenner 1987). Certainly, the emirates and chieftaincies of northern Nigeria collected taxes and tributes in kind from those under their sway and redistributed them during hard times to loyal followers and subjects. Generosity and charity are important norms of public and private life in precolonial societies, especially Islamic ones. But the safety and security of one's household, family, property, and crops was as much a matter of political relations as a rainfall or economic conditions.[1]

Placing the blame for African food shortages on colonialism is a popular and partially valid theory. Colonial rule did introduce and enforce taxation, first in kind and soon after in cash, creating the requirement for a cash economy that was much more widespread than before. The colonialists quite avowedly did this by introducing new products—iodized salt, cloth, and other imported goods—and by pressing for cash export crops. All of which they took to be the beginnings of "development," that would as well contribute to the economic well-being of the colonial power and pay for colonial rule itself. Conquest had a price and colonial rulers extracted it from the conquered. On the other hand, whether or not colonial policy constrained indigenous food production with the introduction of these new forms of economic activity, or whether these new demands stimulated new land cultivation, or both, varies enormously across Africa, and even within the same region.

Colonial complacency about food supplies carried over into the independence period. Expert evaluations by the Food and Agriculture Organization (FAO) and the World Bank (1974:127-128) predicted that using present (1970s) technology the country would have food surpluses for export well into the 1980s. This contrasted with rising food imports and warnings by in-country researchers (Oliyade 1972; Norman 1972) who by the end of the 1960s and early 1970s called attention to the growing dependence on imported wheat, rice, and maize. Indeed, by the end of the 1970s food grain imports topped the billion naira mark annually, and per capita food production was on an accelerated decline. The World Bank eventually (1981) reversed its earlier predictions and declared a negative per capita growth rate in food production for Nigeria and for most of the continent as well.

What Happened?

The main factors involved and their relevant interrelations are summarized in Figure 9.1. The flowchart reverses the pessimism expressed in the literature, which concentrates on the decline in Nigerian self-sufficiency and blames the trend on a combination of structural factors in the economy, the failure of government policy to combat the growing dependency on imported wheat, and the influence of foreign, especially U.S.-based, wheat interests (Watts 1983; Andrae and Beckman 1985). In contrast, the chart depicts a progression from what was clearly a deepening crisis through to a government-led change towards agricultural transformation and self-sufficiency. It would be naive to declare that all the problems have been solved. Rural equity issues, and a serious lack of efficiency in many of the public-sector activities, remain or in some instances have been exacerbated. Nevertheless, the production issues, i.e., food supply shortfalls and rising food grain imports, have for the time being, and hopefully with some enduring capacity, been resolved.

Briefly, Figure 9.1 illustrates the observation that population growth and urbanization, acting on factor relations inherently incapable of meeting rising per capita demand, fired up the problem originally. The oil boom and the 1972-1974 drought interacted to accelerate an easy shift to imports. However, the increased revenues were also spent on policy experiments and projects aimed at increased food-crop production. Concomitantly the 1980s saw a sudden downturn in easy money from oil, massive debt-servicing requirements, and a foreign exchange crisis. This, plus dramatic government inefficiencies and venality, provoked a military takeover just after the elections of 1983 and a policy of severe belt-tightening, including the privatizing of many parastals and the retrenchment of government employment. An early-1980s drought heightened the sense of crisis (see Mabogunje, Chapter 8), and food prices rose quickly leading to enhanced food-crop commercialization by the larger farmers. This was followed by bumper crops in 1984 and 1985 with a similar outlook for 1986/87. All of these events and trends helped the government to go forward with its plan to stop rice, maize, and wheat imports during 1986 and 1987. To everyone's surprise this has not been accompanied by food riots in the cities, although it seems clear that the country is heading into a period—in the 1990s—of urban and environmental problems, given their neglect in the 1980s. Solutions always create problems.[2]

Let me go over the factors responsible for these developments, not to repeat what is already fairly well known, but to add less well-known features that modify those more widely referred to.

Demography

Nigeria's population growth is high—possibly as much as 3.5 percent per year (i.e., 1 percent over the official figure). The most serious issue is that of redistribution of the population. Urbanization runs at

FIGURE 9.1 The Framework For Agricultural Change in Northern Nigeria

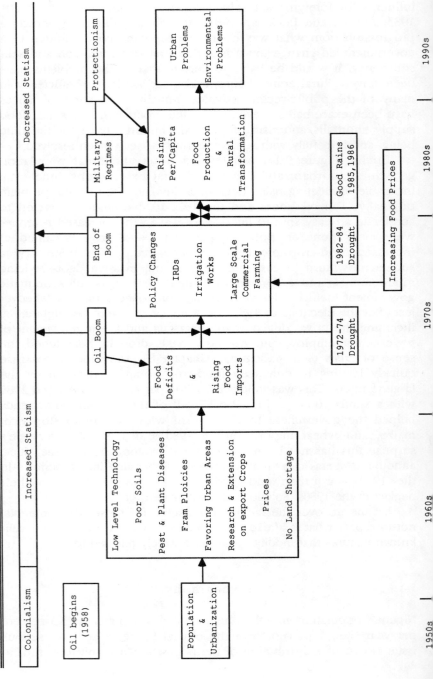

double the rate of population growth. And as one study (Grigg 1982) shows, agricultural transformation is more closely linked to urbanization than to overall population increases. In Europe, for example, agricultural production and productivity are correlated to antecedent urbanization and transportation improvements that set the stage for the consequent development in technology and productivity. Where these antecedent conditions were not present, even with overall population increases, improvements in farm technology and productive increases remained sluggish (Grigg 1982:128). In Nigeria what had been a growing tendency under colonialism—movement to the cities—became a flood after independence. The population of Maiduguri in Borno State, 35,000 in 1956, has grown to between 350,000 and 500,000, up over 1,000 percent in thirty years. Although many of these in-migrants retain ties to the land, many do not, or did not until very recently.

If we add other features to this growth, such as a vastly improved road system, many more rural schools, better urban health and better salaries, then it is no wonder that the nonfood producers are increasing at the expense of the rural population. Road access to the cities means the urban pull encompasses ever-larger numbers. More rural schools means many more "school leavers" who see their future as salaried workers in the cities. And better urban health facilities means a higher quality of life. In more general terms, higher levels of per capita income in the country as a whole are correlated with a lowered proportion of the work force in farming—as has been shown for the entire continent (Paulino 1987:28). Nigeria's economic successes have in this sense helped produce a proportionately smaller farm sector. Although the rural population is growing in absolute terms, the facts of demography mean that each farm family must feed an increasing number of nonfarm people every year if the country is to solve its food deficit problem. Nigerian agriculture has simply not kept pace with such demands.

A well-known concatenation of factors helped keep production behind its growth potential and the needs of the population. Colonial policies favoring research and extension on cash export crops were continued by the early independence governments (Rimmer 1981). By the end of the 1960s much was known about agronomic constraints. Research on soils, plant diseases, and pests, as well as successful inputs and new varieties of crop species that could increase productivity, were available (Norman et al. 1981). But little was done to implement such improvements, and food-crop prices remained low until the drought of the early 1970s. Cash-crop prices were also kept low by government monopoly-buying through marketing boards and licensed buying agents. The abundance of arable land fueled this nonchalance. If more food were needed it could easily be grown by the "underemployed" rural workers. And outside experts on economic development argued early in the 1960s that investing scarce resources on rural development was wasteful for this same reason. Rapid growth demanded an emphasis on urban industrial investment that could absorb excess farm labor and move these Third World countries to "takeoff" (Staatz and Eicher 1986).

The Policy Result

The now well-documented result was that in the early independence years food production and rural development in general had low priority on the national agenda (Rimmer 1981). The central concerns of government policies were national unity matters (in a plural society that had suffered a devastating civil war), access to education and elite jobs, and proportional distribution of resources. By the end of the 1960s and early 1970s, textile mills, urban housing projects, car assembly plants, roads to the main cities, and the proliferation of state capitals—and state bureaucracies—were the order of the day. Presumably the rural sector would continue to do its job as it always had. And though a few isolated voices (Oliyade et al. 1972; Norman 1972) were beginning to warn of food shortages, rapid urban industrialization was stressed in the country's development thrust.

In Nigeria, as in much of Africa, developments, especially those involving large investments, are considered to be the purview of government. And underlying this belief is the emotionally charged much-publicized issue of indigenization. To counter neocolonialism and dependency forces it was deemed essential that Nigerians, not foreigners, be in control of the destiny and planning of development. this led to indigenization policies and decrees and to an emphasis on the public sector as the only trustworthy means to control truly indigenous interests. Almost all large-scale industrial development entails dominant parastatal involvement. The textile mills, cement factories, and car assembly plants are primarily joint public and private (foreign) ventures. Large-scale private-sector developments are generally foreign owned.. The only counterweight with enough capital is the government. Fueled by the oil boom, Nigerian industrial growth is in effect a form of state capitalism linked to multinationals through an oil-rich bureaucracy that has been extraordinarily venal. As with most of the new states of Africa, statism—the use of the public sector to manage and direct development—has been the most widely accepted form of postcolonial political culture, whatever its outward form of ideological commitment, or whether it is under civilian or military control (Young 1982).

As Mabogunje points out in Chapter 8, there has been an important change at the government level in the 1980s. The fall in oil prices, and the elections of 1983 that were deeply mistrusted in many parts of the country, brought on a military coup, the first of two, that had to cope with falling revenues and massive foreign debts. Belt-tightening has become the order of the day. Import restrictions, bureaucratic cutbacks, and strict control (even suppression) of many urban developments were instituted under the military. Deregulation of the currency has been added recently, increasing inflation and the cost of living, especially in urban areas. At the same time, government has continued to encourage agriculture, expand programs of rural development, give priority to the importation of inputs and machinery, and force the banks to provide a strictly enforced percentage of their loan funds to farming.

Along with these developments, although still a minority view expressed primarily among intellectuals in southern universities, a belief and actual experiments in private sector initiatives are emerging. Well-known northern commentators like Bala Usman (1986) retain a more traditional (1960s) statist position and a dependency-theory posture towards development. Nevertheless, given the failure of the public sector to accomplish specific development goals, while serving instead as an arena for sectional conflict as well as being the chief source of immense waste and corruption, an indigenous interest is developing in privatization. Although this trend is too new to gauge accurately, its presence in the emerging political culture is unmistakable. The Awe rural development project near Oyo in which farmers, with outside private support, have organized themselves into a corporation is one of the models. Others involve the large indigenous holding companies that are creating diversified rural and urban enterprises whose survival depends on efficiency and market forces rather than on patronage and sectional interests. As Hyden (1983) has noted, private-sector development may be one of the only avenues by which African states can evolve national level, pan-ethnic loyalties, discipline, and the commitment to organizational rather than personal and sectional advancement. This does not mean that the state has no role to play in the development process. Infrastructure installations, such as roads, schools, and agricultural research and extension, as well as some protection against cheap food imports from surplus-producing nations, are essential. Nonetheless, those with knowledge and experience of national affairs in and out of government are beginning to think about a greater role for the private sector, where lack of success carries a greater cost to those making the decisions.

The Rise of Agricultural Priorities

The early theories of modernization that stressed rural underemployment and urban industrial growth soon fell victim to events. Although it was not seen to be of great significance at the time, except by a few locally based scholars, food imports began to accelerate by the end of the 1960s. In that period (1965/66-1969/70), the food import bill more than doubled—from N45.4 million to N95.1 million.

The first serious drought of the independence period focused the attention of government and the public on the food issue. Starvation, or its possibility in the Sahelian countries to the north, and the concomitant flow of refugees into northern Nigeria, along with serious drought conditions in the northern states, turned food into a topic of national concern. Throughout that entire dry period (1972-1974) crop failures, cattle deaths, food shortages, and sudden outbreaks of disorder were constant topics on the radio and TV and in the newspapers. The exceptionally wet period of the 1950s, followed by a moderately wet 1960s decade, misled outsiders and many Nigerian policymakers into overlooking the fact that rainfall fluctuations make droughts inevitable in the northern savanna region (Nicholson 1984). Although Nigerians suffered much less than Sahelian countries to the north, many areas lost from 10 percent to 70 percent of their average rainfall in the 1972-1974 period. Unfortunately, recovery was poor to fair throughout the rest of the 1970s, and serious droughts reappeared in 1982 and 1983. It is heartening to realize that during all of these bad times, national drought relief campaigns organized by religious groups, newspapers, and other organizations, as well as individual help offered by families, appeared spontaneously out of the Nigerian social fabric. It was difficult to avoid. Dead and dying cattle strewed the countryside. Refugees from neighboring countries were ubiquitous, their plight obvious and deeply troubling. But Nigerians helped, not by asking for foreign assistance, but by sharing.

None of this was particularly unique to Nigeria. The oil boom did, however, add a special quality (Watts and Lubeck 1984). Pumping oil began in 1958 at the end of the colonial era. Revenues, interrupted somewhat by the civil war, rose steadily, to about $1 billion U.S. in 1973. They then doubled the next year with the rise in world oil prices, and continued to rise to $10 billion by 1979. Altogether, Nigeria's oil earned the country over $41 billion from 1973 to 1979 (Watts and Lubeck 1984). This torrential infusion of capital fueled the major policies of the late 1970s and early 1980s, resulting in massive projects, programs, the planning and development of a new capital city, nearly two dozen universities and technical colleges, and dozens of partnerships with international corporations, many of which simply failed after a few years (see, for example, Agbonifo and Cohen 1976).

The drive for greater autarky and indigenization resonated with the oil money to create runaway growth of the public sector. For those of us who watched this spectacle at close range it was clear that interest-group competition among ethnic and regional sections of the population defined and determined public life. A national political culture soon developed in which politics and public service were devoted to both official and surreptitious distribution of revenues among contending parties through their representatives in government. At the beginning of Nigeria's independence, approximately 10 percent of GDP went to finance the public sector. By the end of the 1970s, the figure was over 50 percent. This includes only public services, defense, and administration, leaving out of the calculation most of the parastatals. Added to this is a political tradition of almost completely ineffectual accountability for public expenditures (Cohen 1981) and a correlated boundlessness in nepotism and corruption. No wonder then that the net result for the 1970s was one of history's biggest and most extended state-run bank robberies.

All of these factors, events, and trends form the political and economic background for a turnaround in agricultural policies. After the drought of the early 1970s, the rising food imports, the availability of oil boom money, and a commitment to statism, the Third National Development Plan proclaimed a change in the country's priorities. Although agriculture's share was to increase only a few percentage points in the new plan—from 8 percent to 10 percent—the actual funds deployed went from N30 million (1970) to N600 million (1979) annually. Along with increased funding came a package of new policies, programs, experiments, and enhanced awareness of the importance of food production in the affairs of the nation.

What finally emerged was characteristically Nigerian, a pluralistic approach that one Ibadan University publication called a "viable mix" of policies aimed both at increasing farm production and at import substitution (Eweka et al. 1979). This included a solid and strong effort at helping smallholders, expanding large-scale commercial farming, and investing in massive irrigation projects that could use advanced technology to grow wheat in the savanna during the dry season. Other schemes included smaller irrigation works and food processing (Agbonifo and Cohen 1976). Reasons for this catholicity involved the heterogeneity of the society and disagreement among both local and expatriate experts on the proper paths to follow—a situation that still exists, because

> [t]here is no consensus as to the appropriate types of organizations for different farms...large and small farms can co-exist. Each category possesses certain advantages and drawbacks...it is therefore not safe to be dogmatic about the superiority of any one particular [farming] system. (Ijere 1983:304).

Indeed, some ideas were instant failures. A quick-fix scheme (in the late 1970s) to use the National Youth Corps as one-year conscripts to work on farms in a project labeled Operation Feed the Nation was found to be impractical. The young people drew wages and did little or no work in areas of the country foreign to their upbringing. Local farm practices, and in many cases even the local language, were new to them. On the other hand, such examples indicate the bandwagon effect that was beginning at this time to grip the entire government establishment. By the later 1970s, increasing food production was moving into prominence on the national agenda, and Nigerians with their characteristic energy were trying to advance across a broad front of effort and projects.

Smallholder Program

Throughout all of the discussions, official conferences, and advice given by outside experts, the central importance of smallholder farmers is taken for granted. As Delgado (Chapter 2) and many others have noted, the bulk of the food supply is produced by these peasant households. Even a very modest increase in their farm-unit productivity will, it is claimed, automatically result in large increases and at the same time spread the benefits of growth more equitably among the population. Nigerian policymakers are clear in their support for this position. Thus Eweka et al. note that 95 percent of the country's food is produced by small farmers, and the food problem in Nigeria must be solved by "focussing attention on and mobilizing..." this segment of the population (Eweka et al. 1979:182). Both the Third and the Fourth National Development Plans (1975-1980 and 1980-1984) make special mention of this point, although they also refer to diversification and a viable mix of rural development efforts.

In northern Nigeria the smallholder Integrated Rural Development (IRD) program began, with World Bank support, as a series of pilot studies in the 1970s (see Balcet and Candler 1982). By the Fourth Plan (for 1980-1985) N2.3 billion were set aside to expand this program to cover the entire country. In the north the goal is to reach 3.8 million farm households by the mid-1980s. The plan is to include approximately 15-20 million people, or 50 to 60 percent of the entire rural farm population. this involves setting up and expanding farm service centers, new roads, vastly increased extension services, subsidized fertilizers and chemical inputs for pests and plant diseases, research on new high-yield and drought-resistant crops, along with demonstration and seed multiplication plots, farm credits, and tractor rentals.

Results

Reports vary about the accomplishments of the IRD program. The pilot project at Funtua was condemned at first on equity grounds because so-called "progressives" were given favored access to fertilizers and extension services (Forrest 1981). In Gombe, the eastern pilot site, Tiffen (1976) describes the project as successful in achieving its goals of increased production. And the more intensive evaluation of Balcet and Candler (1982) comes to much the same conclusion. On the other hand, others dispute this and speak of the program as a pathway to rural impoverishment (D'Silva et al. 1980; Watts and Lubeck 1984). Figure 9.2 summarizes the IRD impact in terms of the overall goal of rural transformation.

In Borno, where we examined the program in some detail, a number of points are worth making. First of all, the organization of the project is important. It is a semidifferentiated bureaucracy with its own budget and a crash-program ideology. Young men have been seconded to it from the State Ministry of Agriculture. They know their careers are on the line. They have greater degrees of freedom in this smaller unit (BOADAP-Borno Accelerated Development in Agriculture Program) and are keen to show successful results. By the end of their first two years of operation (1982-1984), working in only two zones (of four for the state as a whole),[3] they had hired and

FIGURE 9.2 The Impact of IRDS in North Nigeria

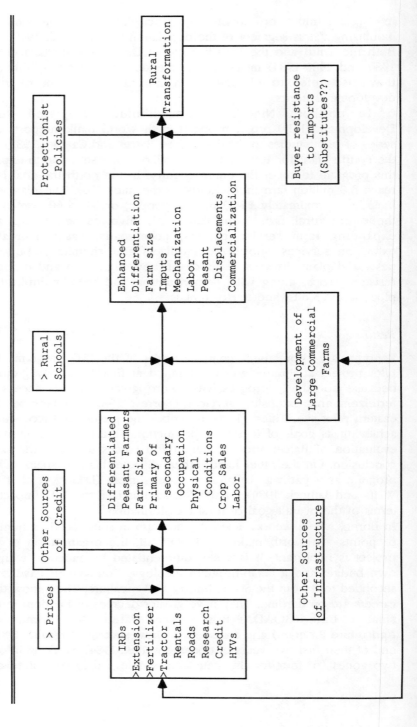

trained a complement of 165 extension workers, set up 132 selling points for fertilizer, incorporated nearly 1,000 villages in the two zones into the program, and contacted over 55,000 farmers. Funds expended came to an estimated N12 million (4 million the first year, 8 million the second) and were to be expanded in succeeding years when all four zones would be included. Farm service centers with tractor rental programs were in place, as were large storage facilities, demonstration plots, and seed multiplication units. The roads program was curtailed for lack of funds, and in the second year it was decided to take the subsidy off the price of fertilizer because of the black market that had developed. This was also linked to the expansion of selling points into the smaller villages in order to spread the availability and discourage resale (BOADPAP *Quarterly Reports* 1982-1984; interviews with BOADAP Officials).

The agency reports that the program is a success. Major food crops have, they say, increased by 10-20 percent among the 5,000 "high-contact" farmers. This includes approximately 9-10 percent of all farm units affected in some way by BOADAP's efforts in its first two years of operation (BOADAP *Quarterly Reports* 1982-1984). There are no figures on the distribution of these increases, but the high-contact farmers are almost all in the larger towns, living closer to farm service centers and roads. Our survey data indicate that they are generally those with larger farms who use more household as well as more hired labor. They are also more likely than the poorer farmers, to have off-farm occupations. In the pilot projects, yields increased over time for all those connected to the project, but for the larger farms (those with six hectares and over), maize production increased fifty kilograms per hectare for every extra hectare under cultivation (Balcet and Candler 1982:116).

It is important to look a little more closely at this differentiation. Borno peasant households vary a great deal in their productive capacities—and it is into this socioeconomic baseline that peasant-oriented programs are thrust. Initial analyses of our (1984) survey data indicate that over 75 percent of the variance in reported crop yields is accounted for by inputs from labor, 21 percent of which is hired. Almost all households have used hired labor at some time, but it is noteworthy that just over two thirds of all hired labor is employed by the largest 25 percent of the households. Those households with the largest supply of family labor are the ones that hired most of the nonhousehold labor as well. And this same group also has the highest number of farm plots (five or more) per household. Although most (74 percent) of the surveyed households have off-farm work, 23 percent claim that off-farm work is their primary occupation (Makumba 1982). In our 1984 survey, only 8 percent of those observed to have the highest material wealth indicators reported themselves to be full-time farmers with no off-farm occupation, while 34 percent in the lowest wealth category are full-time farmers. Better-off farmers are therefore most likely to have off-farm occupations and operate larger farm units. In other words, the program aimed at the rural smallholder is being utilized by a highly differentiated producer group.

And the results are not unexpected—farmers benefit differentially. Thus, 73 percent of all fertilizer users have three or more farm plots, and this same group accounts for three quarters of all tractor rentals.[4] Whereas almost everyone wants to use chemical fertilizers, 90 percent of those in the farm service center neighborhood actually purchase these inputs, while only 61 percent farther away report having used them in the previous two years (1983/84). After only two years of operation, a survey conducted by BOADAP (1984) showed that 286 small farm units, whose median size is 1.7 hectares for the area as a whole (Makumba 1982), now exceed 25 hectares of cultivated land. Much of this land was newly cleared, but a significant amount—just under 10 percent—was purchased, compared to under 1 percent in the 1950s when I carried out my first studies in the area. The project has increased rural differentiation, stimulated the development of larger, commercialized farms among the peasant producers, and increased the commoditization of land.

The sale of crops is related to a number of factors, the most important of which is recent experience of droughts. Almost all respondents mention recent droughts and rising food prices as reasons why they do not wish to sell their crops. Other sources of income, farm size, location near markets and main roads, household size, and the belief that life is better now than it used to be are all positively related to farm sales. Nevertheless, over 40 percent of the smallholders questioned claimed that they had not sold food grains in the last two years, and would not do so unless they harvest a surplus over household needs. On the other hand, beans, rice, and cotton are thought of as cash crops outside these calculations.[5]

The development of larger farms from a variety of sources has led to warnings of an impending landless and impoverished peasant "class" (Watts 1983). No evidence of this has turned up, nor is it discussed as a possibility in the official reports, by farmers themselves, by government officials speaking off the record, or by the large commercial farmers who have purchased peasant land and use local villagers as a source of labor. Instead, those who work on large farms report that they welcome the extra source of cash income. Lennihan (personal communication) reports the same for the Zaria area where she has made a special study of the topic. It is important in this regard to see farming ethnographically as well as economically. As an occupation it has very low status. Forty-seven percent of our respondents report that they do not wish to have their sons become farmers. Despite the rise in producer prices, the recent attempts to make farming a more important occupation, and the programs aimed at increasing the quality of rural life—despite all this, older assessments endure. Smallholder rainfed farming in northern Nigeria is hard, risky, often unrewarding work. Other occupations have higher prestige, and are believed to provide better incomes and greater hope for personal advancement.

Large-Scale Farms

Large-scale and modern farms have been expanding in Nigeria throughout the 1970s and 1980s. It is reported that the amount being produced on large modern farm units went from 2 percent of value added (=quantity times price) to 27 percent in the decade of the 1970s.[6] At the same time, agriculture is declining in relation to the other sectors of the economy—from 65 percent of GDP in the 1960s to 28 percent in the late 1970s (see Federal Office of Statistics n.d.).

The source of this group of farmers is mostly, albeit not exclusively, urban: bureaucrats, business people, professionals, and other formal sector workers. A few of these went into large-scale farming as early as the 1960s. By the 1980s the trend became a full-fledged fad. Today it is hard to find any household in northern cities with middle- to upper-level income whose head is not farming, planning to buy farm lands, or working as a manager-partner on someone else's farm. In a number of instances, wives have set up commercial poultry ventures. Reasons given are to earn extra income; to achieve market independence under conditions of scarcity and rising food prices; to invest in land, especially at the rim of expanding urban growth; to have a useful hobby; to engage in nonpolitical activity; to help one's home village area; to be patriotic; or simply to conform because everyone else is doing it. Indeed, farming is a constant topic of conversation at social gatherings where such conversation was unheard of five to ten years ago. The trend has been stimulated even more by the post-1983 military regimes that initiated a policy of constraining urban construction and foreign imports. At the same time, government encouraged investors to go into farming while forcing the banks to increase their loans to agriculture on a massive scale. Monthly reports to the Central Bank have to show a percentage (10 percent) of all loans going to the farm sector. The parastatal Agricultural Development Bank manager reported to us (in 1984) that almost all of his loan funds were to the larger farmers. His small-farm program was a revolving fund (under N100,000), whereas his large loans could come from his own working capital. Or in the case of very large loans, he arranged for the farmer to deal directly with his regional office in Kaduna.

But this is not the only source for the development of large-scale farms, although it is certainly the predominant one. Traditional processes of rural differentiation have been intensified by the IRD smallholder programs even though they are designed to, and undoubtedly do, help small farm units. Nevertheless, as we have seen, these same programs promote the development of large farms among the peasants. In addition multinational corporations have been encouraged to go into the clearing of new arable lands and to set up large commercial farms. Given the shortage of foreign exchange, many of these companies have, until recently (1986), had difficulty repatriating their allowable profits. This led firms like Shell Oil to open up large-scale commercial farms in order to use waiting funds languishing in banks for want of foreign exchange. As with the indigenous urban liquidity, government was stimulating investment in farming by directing foreign companies to use their repatriable profits in the farm sector; at the same time they promised a higher rate of repatriation for profits. So far, very little is known of this policy and its effects.

Commercial large farms vary in size and diversity. Most are under 200 hectares. A few, possibly a dozen to two dozen for the entire state of Borno, are over 1,000 hectares. With the exception of the very large ones, almost all of the farm owners were planning to expand their holdings. The medium-size enterprises grow the same crops as smallholdings. If they obtain better water supplies they may add vegetables for truck farming, and many of the largest raise poultry and cattle. They are sensitive to mechanization, modern inputs, soil testing, and new crop varieties. They try to obtain extension help or the services of people trained in agriculture. The largest are equipped with their own farm machinery, trucks, feed mills, electrification, and scientifically run poultry sheds. A few have bank loans in the six figures, and all of them provide a market for hired farm labor.

ADVERSITY AND TRANSFORMATION   229

Results

The results of this new form of large-scale farm enterprise are not difficult to see, nor are they particularly surprising. Given the encouragement of government loan programs, and the stringent constraints placed on urban investment, urban capital is flowing into the countryside. Local experts in Borno predicted to us that by the 1990s over half of all marketed crops in the state will come from large farms. They are clearly more receptive to modern innovations, they are expanding rapidly in number of owners and in size per farm unit, and, as we have seen, programs aimed at helping smallholders are adding to their number. It is also true, especially near the larger population centers, that commercial farmers are buying up smallholder units, consolidating them, and forcing some of the small farmers to move out to the more isolated bush areas, or continue their migration into the towns and cities.

The overall trend is neither difficult to see, nor unfamiliar. A rising proportion of Nigerian food production is being produced by a falling proportion of the overall population and by a falling proportion of the farm units.

Large-Scale Irrigation Works

As already noted, it was politically expedient, and seemed emminently rational to government planners who first reacted to the food deficits, to invest some of the country's massive oil revenues in large-scale irrigation works in the semi-arid northern areas of the country. This followed from the logic of the times, viz., that there must be a significant residue of fixed capital investments to replace oil once that source of funding was used up. Moreover, it must be spent according to national needs, with some equitable sharing in terms of regional and ethnic segmentation. Feasibility studies were carried out in the 1970s, and by the end of the decade a number of irrigation works were coming into operation in the west (Bakalori), central (Tiga), and east (Lake Chad) of the northern part of the country.

Most writers have been intensely critical of these projects, saying that they absorb the largest amount of rural development capital outlays and benefit only a small handful of farmers in the irrigated areas. Many of those farmers, it is said, are being replaced by larger urban-based farmers who rent the lands and displace the original owners. Flooding large areas behind dams means that many rural residents have been forcibly removed from their ancestral lands and deprived of economic and social supports they were used to before the projects began. The projects not only sop up large amounts of funding for start-up but continue to do so because maintenance cost are so high, yet technically poor, in terms of equipment and the clearing of silt from the water channels. And on top of all this, antagonism develops between the bureaucratic management and the farmers who must obey orders if the scheme is to work in the coordinated manner demanded by the technology. Finally, critics suggest that productivity increases from these projects have been disappointing (Wallace 1981; Watts and Lubeck 1984; Ogunbameru 1986).

Results

Closer examination of these criticisms in the field produces a more mixed evaluation. At Lake Chad where I examined the South Chad Irrigation Project (SCIP) the original plan for two crops a year (rice and wheat) was soon given up for lack of irrigation water in the wet season when the Lake is still low. Lake Chad rises in the late rains when the incoming rivers have swollen, especially the Logone, which accounts for 90 percent of the inflow. On the other hand, the farmers still put in traditional course grains (millet and sorghum) on nonirrigated fields, and the winter wheat has produced a significant crop each year of the project during the dry season. Project farmers have done well. Those participating in the scheme average over double the income of nonparticipants, and there is very high demand to be included among the 7,500 households now involved. Those chosen were the ones whose lands were appropriated for inclusion in the scheme. They cultivate land off the project as well and generally evince satisfaction with the project. There is no evidence that urban-based farmers have rented these enriched lands, as has occurred at Tiga, south of Kano (Wallace 1981). The peasant smallholders on the scheme have long lists of complaints against management for having to give up one-half their irrigated crops as payment for inputs of seeds, extension services, water resources, and mechanized harvesting. Plot allocations for farm households seem arbitrary to the farmers and may shift from year to year, depending on technical engineering criteria rather than on more traditional matters such as labor and distance from the home settlements. This latter problem is exacerbated by shortages of bridges over main canals, which can significantly increase the distance from household to farm plot. The SCIP locality has excellent schools, including post-primary and secondary levels for both sexes, electrification, paved roads, feeder roads to all villages, and cheap transport to nearby urban centers.

The project in the central area, SCIP, was planned originally for 67,000 hectares, but as of 1983/84, there were just under 22,000 hectares in the scheme. Whether it will ever reach its planned-for goal is debatable and depends heavily on who is asked. There are no plans, as far as I know, to increase the numbers in the project or even to raise the present three hectares per household to the ten originally envisaged. It is also difficult to see how production, even if it were to reach "full" capacity as planned for (187,000 tons of wheat, 175,000 tons of rice, 33,000 tons of cotton, plus sorghum, millet, maize, and vegetables), could ever come to more than a fraction of national food needs. (The figures are taken from the CBDA/SCIP Report, 1983.) Thus, the present harvest of winter wheat is said to produce 1 to 2 percent of the national consumption (as of 1984), a far cry from the 33.3 percent predicted when the project was on the drawing board.

In the meantime, the project and its parent parastatal, Chad Basin Development Corporation (CBDA), have become avid and complex interest groups at both the state and federal levels. Whenever agricultural matters are to be discussed, whenever foreign visitors arrive in the area, the CBDA leadership moves quickly to ensure that its personnel and its interests are represented. CBDA has a 25 percent share of the local flour mill, and its senior personnel sit on advisory boards at state and national levels. Its leader goes to international meetings and works constantly to advertise and advance high-tech water management in Nigerian government circles. Added to this is CBDA's ethnic support. The project personnel are almost exclusively Borno people, and top-level administrators are primarily Kanuri, the major ethnic group of the area. High-placed Borno civil servants at the federal level see CBDA and SCIP as tangible manifestations of their fair share of national development resources. Cutting back support would raise the cry that Borno's share has been curtailed. In a nation-state committed to pluralism, pork-barrel budgeting is normal; rational, strictly economic allocations are impossible given the realities of politics, regionalism, ethnicity, and bureaucratic competition. With this in mind SCIP officials are laying plans for more extensive water management in the state and for backup water if and when Lake Chad should ever become an unfeasible water supply.

Whether the project is a white elephant or the basis for an agroindustrial development, it cannot be ignored. It can be cut back, refocused, or whatever, but its claim on national resources is now part of the national planning and budgeting process. Possibly greater farmer participation in its governance will actually develop, although there is no sign of it at present. One can only hope that the benefits of the scheme can be extended by both state and federal agencies to those surrounding it who have fallen through the cracks of local development efforts. Whatever happens, the project has given the country a basis for understanding the nature, costs, complexities, and outcomes of high-tech water management for semi-arid agriculture. Ultimately Africa must solve its dependence on rainfed farming, and these projects serve to provide a forecast of what lies in store when that becomes feasible on a continent-wide basis.

Conclusion

The Nigeria case tells its own story. Accelerating food deficits have resulted from causes similar to those in many other African contexts—low-level technology, and very little attention paid to the problem during the colonial era. This nonchalance was associated with rapid population growth and an even more rapid expansion of urban centers, so that the market for foodstuffs increased by leaps and bounds. On the supply side, production did not rise and the new food needs were met instead by rising imports. The droughts of the 1970s and early 1980s focused attention on the problem, and the government used its new-found oil wealth to strike out in all directions for a solution.

As with many other newly independent countries it was believed that government initiative and control over projects was the most desirable means of protecting the national interest. Because the smallholders grow most of the food, they seem, logically, to hold the solution to the problem. At the same time, water management and high-tech irrigation were chosen as sensible modes by which the federal government could spend development funds directly in rural areas even when state governments were in the hands of opposition parties. Large-scale farming was also encouraged, quietly at first, but with ever-greater emphasis, until finally after the military coups of the 1980s it was very strongly fostered through credits and very active policies against urban investments, including the restriction of import licenses. This latter policy was forced on the country when the oil boom ended and the enormous debt had to be serviced while revenues shrunk. Such conditions called for a cutback in rapidly rising food-import costs, along with a general retrenchment of government expenditures and the privatization of many parastatal organizations.

These policies have not all paid off in equal amounts. The smallholder programs have succeeded in reaching the peasant farmers by spreading the acceptance of modern inputs: fertilizers (especially), tractor rentals (to a lesser extent), extension services, and new varieties of seeds. However, social and economic differences among the rural population have been exacerbated, and commercialization has been limited to the larger, more successful farmers. Some are becoming large-scale capitalist entrepreneurs. Others are using the rural development programs to expand their nonfarming occupations, which are their dominant interest. Peasants are not only not full-time farmers, but many also have a strong desire to see their sons leave the farm and go to the cities, or at least become successful at nonfarming occupations. In other words, programs aimed at the development of the rural smallhold farmer have accelerated the development of a small group of wealthy farmers, and at the same time the movement out of farming into other occupations has been speeded up.

The large-scale irrigation projects have absorbed vast amounts of capital with a disproportionately low amount of food production return on investment. Farmers on the project have benefited and some small increases in productivity and import substitution have been gained, especially for winter wheat. The main positive advantage is the experience and the expertise that are now part of the nation's social capital in the field of water management under semi-arid conditions. The irrigation sites themselves, with their high-tech installations, provide rural centers for industrial development, education, employment, service occupations, and some counter to the overcrowding of existing urban areas (c.f. the China case in Chapter 4).

Large-scale farming has become a widely accepted and practiced sideline for urban entrepreneurs and formal-sector workers who have enough money to buy land, and pay for inputs and the labor costs involved. In a few (significant) cases, urban entrepreneurs have gone into farming as a large-scale business enterprise. Although it is too early to tell, it seems as if commercial farming has come to Nigeria and is a permanent and rising portion of agriculture. There are no indications as yet that these large farmers are driving the peasants into landless impoverishment. But there is every indication that these new enterprises are an important nucleus for the transformation of food production both technologically and in terms of the social and economic organization of farm units. High prices, urban stringencies related to inflation and unemployment, government encouragement, and faddism have made this form of farm organization very widely popular. It remains to be seen to what degree a residue of permanence will remain once the fad is over and urban investment and opportunities rise again. Many of these large farms are, however, permanent parts of diversified private-sector corporations, or "holding companies," with both rural and urban operations in varying types of farming, construction, manufacturing, and transportation. And many of the urban farm owners have begun to sell off urban investments to become more involved in farming.

What the Nigerian case teaches in a more general way is that food production is and must be thought of in terms of national requirements. Rural social welfare, including the raising of living standards and productivity among smallholders, is an essential aspect of the development process. But the most important finding of this research is the generalization that smallholders alone may not hold the solution to per capita food deficits. By investing in a broad-scale mix of food-production development policies, including the banning of cheap imports, Nigeria has hit upon a formula that works: support for a wide variety of projects and programs designed to help rural peoples, and to develop commercial food production for the home market under protected conditions, while agriculture itself undergoes a transformation in both organizational and technological terms.

Notes

1. This is not meant to imply that precolonial droughts were not severe, and often beyond the capacity of the redistributive system. Indeed, many of the serious upheavals of precolonial social, economic, and political life are correlated with crop failures and the search for pasturelands by nomads. The resulting intensification of competition for resources forced greater numbers from stricken areas to move to new locations where local history was often drastically altered (Cohen 1981b).

2. In March 1987 Christian-Muslim conflict and violence broke out in the north-central area of the country. How closely related this was to higher costs of living and unemployment in urban areas is unknown. The correlation is a matter of fact.

3. These were in the middle zones along the main paved road into Borno from Kano, Jos, and other urban centers. The other areas are in the more arid northerly section and the wetter more fertile soils of the south. According to local officials, the World Bank argued to include or to begin the project in the southerly area at the outset. Borno State government refused this suggestion, arguing for the greater need in the main and middle areas, but compromised by leaving out the most arid zone in the far north. As of

of 1987 the project has been extended to include the entire state.
4. This refers to rentals from BOADAP. There are other sources spread across a number of state and federal programs as well as privately owned machines. Smallholders report using the BOADAP program aimed especially at them, while urban-based farmers use a wider variety of sources, depending upon their own network of relationships.
5. The price of beans to producers shot up as high as N300 to N400 per bag (200 kg.) in the 1983/84 period of droughts. Farmers who had not done so before, or who had done very little of it, put in as much bean crop as possible, often intercropped with subsistence foods (millet, sorghum, and maize) to take advantage of this extraordinary rise in price. Indeed, city-based salaried workers tried to find a plot of land anywhere they could to join in the profits, and urban middle-class residents who heretofore had not done so were encouraged to start up commercial farming as a secondary occupation.
6. Official statistics (NISH 1981) show large farms as 5 percent of all farm units in the country by the end of the 1970s. These observations have been discontinued in the 1980s so that the trend data on large farms are not available during what has been their most obvious increase. The increase (2 percent to 27 percent) of "modern" farming very likely includes some smallholder units that use modern technology. Nevertheless, I assume that the 1970's trend to increase the number of large farms has continued and accelerated in the 1980s. along with intensified and smaller specialized farms (e.g., poultry). Driving along the main roads in the 1970s I observed a few larger farms here and there close to the larger towns. In 1983 and 1984 there were dozens along any road leading out of the main towns, many with billboards announcing the owner's name and/or the incorporated company owning and operating the farm.

References

Agbonifo, P.O. and R. Cohen. 1976. The Peasant Connection: A Case Study of the Bureaucracy of Agri-Industry. *Human Organization* 35:367-379.
Andrae, G. and B. Beckman. 1985. *The Wheat Trap*. London: Zed Press.
Balcet, J.C. and W. Candler. 1982. *Farm Technology Adoption in Northern Nigeria*. Vol. 1. Ithaca, N.Y.: Cornell Department of Agricultural Economics.
Barth, H. 1857. *Travels and Discoveries in North and Central Africa 1849-1855*. London: Longman, Brown, Green, Longman, and Roberts.
BOADAP (Borno Accelerated Development in Agriculture Program). *Quarterly Reports 1982, 1983, 1984*. Maiduguri: Mimeo.
Cohen, R. 1970. Social Stratification in Borno. In *Class and Status Sub-Saharan Africa*. A. Tuden and L. Plotnicov, eds. New York: The Free Press.
Cohen, R. 1971. Incorporation in Borno. In *From Tribe to Nation in Africa*. R. Cohen and J. Middleton, eds. Scranton: In-Text (Chandler).
Cohen, R. 1981a. The Blessed Job in Nigeria. In *Hierarchy and Society*. G. Britan and R. Cohen, eds. Philadelphia: ISHI.
Cohen, R. 1981b. State Foundations: A Controlled Comparison. In *Origins of the State*. R. Cohen and E.R. Service, eds., Philadelphia: ISHI.

Cohen, R. 1987. The Multimodal Model of Development. Paper delivered at the annual meeting of the Society of Economic Anthropology, Riverside, California, March 1987.

Cohen, R. and L. Brenner. 1987. Borno in the Nineteenth Century. In *History of West Africa*. A.A. Ajayi and M. Crowder, eds. New York: Cambridge University Press.

D'Silva, B. and M. Raza. 1980. Integrated Rural Development in Nigeria—The Funtua Project. *Food Policy* 5:282-297.

Economist Intelligence Reports. 1985, 1986. London: The Economist.

Eweka, J.A. et al. 1979. *Village Development: Food Basket Management Strategy*. Ibadan: Center for Agricultural and Rural Development, University of Ibadan.

Federal Office of Statistics. 1980. *NISH (Nigerian Integrated Survey of Households*. Lagos: Federal Government of Nigeria.

————. h,d, *National Accounts of Nigeria 1960/61–1975/76*. Lagos: Federal Government of Nigeria.

Forrest, T. 1981. Agricultural Policies in Nigeria. In *Rural Development in Tropical Africa*. J. Heyer et al. eds. New York: St. Martin's Press.

Grigg, D. 1982. *The Dynamics of Agricultural Change*. New York: St. Martin's Press.

Hyden, G. 1983. *No Shortcuts to Progress: African Development Management in Perspective*. Berkeley: University of California Press.

Ijere, M.O. 1983. The Socio-Economic Aspects of Food and Nutrition Policy for Nigeria. In *Nutrition and Food Policy in Nigeria*. T. Atinmo and L. Akinyele, eds. Kuru, Jos: National Institute for Policy and Strategic Studies (Nigeria).

Johnston, B.F. 1985. Agricultural Development in Tropical Africa: The Search for Viable Strategies. Paper prepared for the Committee on African Development Strategies and The Council on Foreign Relations, and The Overseas Development Council. Unpublished MS.

Makumba, E.B. 1982. *Borno State Report on the Baseline Survey*. Kaduna: Agricultural Projects Monitoring, Evaluation, and Planning Unit. Mimeo.

Matlon, P. 1981. The Structure of Production and Rural Incomes in Northern Nigeria: Results of Three Village Case Studies. In *The Political Economy of Income Distribution in Nigeria*. H. Bienen and V.P. Diejomaoh, eds. New York: Homes and Meier.

Mellor, J.W. et al. 1987. *Accelerating Food Production in Sub-Saharan Africa*. Baltimore: The Johns Hopkins University Press.

Nicholson, S. 1984. Climate and Man in the Sahel During the Historical Period. In *Environmental Change in the West African Sahel*. Advisory Committee on the Sahel, Board on Science and Technology for International Development; National Research Council. Washington: National Academy Press.

Norman, D. 1972. Problems in Agricultural Development. University Lecture, Ahmadu Bello University, Mimeo.

Norman, D. et al., 1981. *Farming Systems in the Nigerian Savanna*. Boulder, Colo.: Westview Press.

Ogunbameru, B.O. 1986. Socio-economic Impact of the South Chad Irrigation Project. *Annals of Borno* 3:137-146.

Oliyade, S.O. et al. 1972. *A Quantitative Analysis of Food Requirements,, Supplies and Demands in Nigeria, 1968-1985*. Lagos: Federal Department of Agriculture.

Paulino, L.A. 1987. The Evolving Food Situation. In *Accelerating Food Production in Sub-Saharan Africa.* J. Mellor, C. Delgado, and M. Blackie, eds. Baltimore: The Johns Hopkins Press.

Richardson, J. 1853. *Mission to Central Africa.* London: Chapman.

Rimmer, D. 1981. Developments in Nigeria: An Overview. In *The Political Economy of Income Distribution in Nigeria.* H. Beinen and V.P. Diejomaoh, eds. New York: Holmes and Meier.

Staatz, J.M. and C. Eicher. 1986. Agricultural Development Ideas in Historical Perspective. *Food in Sub-Saharan Africa.* A. Hansen and D.E. McMillan, eds. Boulder, Colo.: Lynne Rienner.

Tiffen, M. 1976. *The Enterprising Peasant.* London: H.M. Stationery Office.

Usman, B.F. 1986. *Nigeria Against the I.M.F.* Zaria: Institute of Administration.

Wallace, T. 1981. The Kano River Project. In *Rural Development in Tropical Africa.* J. Heyer et al., eds. New York: St. Martin's Press.

Watts, M. 1983. *Silent Violence.* Berkeley: University of California Press.

Watts, M. and P. Lubeck. 1984. The Popular Classes and the Oil Boom: A Political Economy of Rural and Urban Poverty. In *The Political Economy of Nigeria.* I.W. Zartman, ed. New York: Praeger.

World Bank. 1974. *Nigeria: Options for Long-Term Development.* Baltimore: The Johns Hopkins Press.

————. 1981. *Accelerated Development in Sub-Saharan Africa.* Baltimore: The Johns Hopkins University Press.

Young, C. 1982. *Ideology and Development in Africa.* New Haven: Yale University Press.

Index